The Worst of Crimes

The Worst of Crimes

Homosexuality and the Law
in Eighteenth-Century London

NETTA MURRAY GOLDSMITH

Ashgate

Aldershot • Brookfield USA • Singapore • Sydney

Published by
Ashgate Publishing Limited
Gower House
Croft Road
Aldershot
Hants
GU11 3HR
England

Ashgate Publishing Company
Old Post Road
Brookfield
Vermont 05036–9704
USA

The author has asserted her moral right under the Copyright, Designs and Patents Act, 1988, to be identified as the author of this work.

British Library Cataloguing in Publication Data

Goldsmith, Netta Murray
  The Worst of Crimes: Homosexuality and the Law in
  Eighteenth-Century London.
  1. Homosexuality — Law and legislation — England — London —
  History — 18th century.
  I. Title.
  346.4'2'013

Library of Congress Cataloging-in-Publication Data

Goldsmith, Netta Murray.
  The worst of crimes: homosexuality and the law in eighteenth-
  century London/Netta Murray Goldsmith.
    Includes bibliographical references and index.
    ISBN 1–84014–631–1 (hardcover)
    1. Gay men — England — London — History — 18th century. 2. Sodomy —
  Great Britain — History — 18th century. 3. Gay men — Legal status, laws,
  etc. — Great Britain — History — 18th century. I. Title.
  HQ76.2.G7G65 1998
  306.76'62'094212—dc21

                                                   98–25007
                                                   CIP

ISBN 1 84014 631 1

This book is printed on acid free paper

Typeset in Sabon by Manton Typesetters, 5–7 Eastfield Road, Louth, Lincolnshire.
Printed and bound in Great Britain by MPG Books Ltd, Bodmin, Cornwall

Contents

CONTENTS

Part VI Last questions

List of figures

To Ernest,
my husband and friend

Preface

This book began in the Cambridge University Library where, browsing through the book catalogues, I came upon an entry for a virtually forgotten man, though his last name was a familiar one because he was the son of England's first prime minister, Robert Walpole, and a brother of Horace, who created Strawberry Hill. The entry I saw referred to a pamphlet describing the trial held on Friday 5 July 1751 in the court of King's Bench, in which several defendants had been accused of a 'Conspiracy against the Hon. Edward Walpole Esq.'.

Curiosity, along with the fact that I had an hour or so to spare, led me to ask for the pamphlet to see what it was about. When it arrived, a comprehensive title page, headed *The Tryal* ... , told me that the accused had been charged with trying to extort money from Edward Walpole by threatening to expose him for a supposed 'Assault, with an Intent to commit Buggery on the Body' of one of the defendants. As I read on I discovered that the story was a complicated one. The previous year Walpole had already succeeded in clearing his name in the same court of King's Bench, where he had been tried for attempted sodomy. The trial in July 1751 represented the culmination of a lengthy campaign, waged by the prosecutor, to track down and punish the so-called conspirators for trying to blackmail him and destroy his good name. He succeeded. The defendants were all convicted.

I found out, later on, that at least two anonymous pamphleteers had written up the case. The document of forty-four pages which I read that afternoon in Cambridge was a Dublin reprint of one that was on sale in London at the end of the summer in 1751. This version would later be reissued as *The Whole Proceedings* ... , with additional information about the heavy sentences which, after some delay, had been passed on the convicted men.

The other journalist had rushed into print ahead of his rival. His version of the day, which he called *A Genuine Narrative of the Conspiracy* ... , was on hand for the customers in Tom's Coffee House in Devereux Court, near the Strand, within a week of the trial in the King's Bench. In his hurry, however, the writer of this pamphlet, having misheard the names of important witnesses, had written them down in forms that were barely recognizable. He (or the printer) had also misinterpreted key terms so that, at one point 'Buggery' became 'Burglary'. Still, he later corrected the more egregious of the errors in a new edition of his account, entitled *A Full and genuine Narrative* ... , in which he included some interesting comments on the background of two of the defendants.

Both writers were clearly responding to public interest in the trial in the court of King's Bench and both expressed considerable satisfaction with the verdicts reached. In other respects they differed markedly. *The Tryal* was indeed different from most other works of its kind, written to satisfy a public appetite for details of sensational cases, the most obvious difference being that it was authorized, in so far as the writer of it had been given access to the King's Bench official papers. At the end of his narrative he reproduced these in a lengthy appendix 'for the Use of Gentlemen of the Law', who were told that they were 'well worthy of Perusal' because the case had been 'settled by the greatest Men of the Profession'.

There is every indication that the trial had been regarded as a triumph for the judicial system, as well as a victory of good over evil. Yet, even as I read *The Tryal* for the first time, I was unconvinced that justice had been done. Instead I was aware that a determination on the part of the judiciary to secure convictions had outweighed any wish to arrive at the truth. Even the defence lawyers did not have their hearts in the task they had undertaken.

Wondering why this should have been so led me to consider the effect on both homosexuals and heterosexuals of having a law on the statute books which decreed that sodomy was a capital charge, and of a good deal of official rhetoric which declared that it was a more heinous crime than killing a man. The following pages describe my findings after studying what happened to those who were arraigned for homosexual offences, or who sought redress from blackmailers in the London courts, particularly the Old Bailey and King's Bench. Some of these findings surprised me, as did the discoveries I made when I went to the Public Record Office to read for myself papers about the Edward Walpole case.

As is already apparent from these few pages, the terminology regarding homosexuality has changed since the eighteenth century. In that period 'buggery' and 'sodomy' were the words used in legal documents and formal English generally to describe sexual intercourse between men, while homosexuals were called 'sodomites'. As ever, there were also slang words, one of the most popular being 'molly', which referred at first to effeminate homosexuals, though as time went on it was used indiscriminately to describe ostensibly masculine ones as well, so spawning a verb 'to molly'. Throughout this book I have used the older words whenever the context made employment of the modern ones incongruous. I have also used 'transvestite' as well as the preferred modern alternative 'cross-dresser', as this enabled me to make more precise distinctions between those individuals who habitually dressed as a member of the opposite sex because of a particular predilection and those who did so occasionally, most probably when going to a masquerade, where it could be convenient to do so for a variety of reasons.

New words are added to the vocabulary of sex in every era and the reader will come across others in this book that are no longer current, though their meaning is clear enough from the context. He or she will also find that legal terminology has changed to a certain extent. So, for reasons that will be explained, the term 'blackmail' was more narrowly applied in the eighteenth century than nowadays. The common term for an attempt to get money by making threats of any kind was 'extortion'. Similarly, if the victim of what we now call 'blackmail' was anxious to buy off his persecutor, it was said that he was willing to 'compromise' the affair.

The notes to this book will show how deeply I am indebted to past and present scholars. I am also grateful to a variety of people who were patient and helpful when I approached them personally with my queries. These include the staff of the Public Record Office, the Greater London Record Office and members of the University Library and Squire Law Library in Cambridge, the Bodleian Law Library, various departments in the British Library, the London Library, Guildhall Library and Lincoln's Inn Library, as well as archivists at the Imperial Society of Knights Bachelor, the National Portrait Gallery, the Museum of London, the Royal Bethlehem Hospital and Finchcocks in Kent.

Many other people allowed me to read and quote from the manuscripts they guarded. In particular I would mention Peter M. Meadows in the Cambridge University Library and Peter Day, Keeper of Collections at Chatsworth. Furthermore in America I received this kind of assistance from Anna Malicka at the Lewis Walpole Library, Susan M. Swasta of the William L. Clements Library and Paula Y. Lee of the University of Chicago Library, as well as from the University of North Carolina Press who gave permission for me to requote from Lord Mansfield's trial notes which they published in 1992 in J. Oldham's *The Mansfield Manuscripts and the Growth of English Law in the Eighteenth Century*. I am also grateful to Dr David Brown, Consultant Histopathologist at the Whittington Hospital in London who read and interpreted the autopsy of Sir Edward Walpole for me.

Lastly, may I say thank you to my family and friends who all too often had to listen to me telling them about the vicissitudes endured by men in the eighteenth century who found themselves in the Old Bailey and court of King's Bench, accused of what the powers that be called the 'worst of crimes'.

Netta Murray Goldsmith

Abbreviations

Add. MSS Additional Manuscripts

BL British Library

*Full
and
genuine
Narrative* *A Full and genuine Narrative of the Confederacy carried on by Cather, Cane, Alexander, Nixon, Paterson, Falconer, and Smith, which last was executed at Tyburn with McLeane, against The Hon. Edward Walpole, Esq. Charging him with the detestable Crime of Sodomy, in Order to extort a large Sum of Money from him; together with an Account of their remarkable Trial and Conviction before the Rt. Hon. the Lord Chief Justice Lee, in the Court of King's-Bench, Westminster, July 5th, 1751. The Second Edition with Additions.* (London, 1751)

*Genuine
Narrative* *A Genuine Narrative of the Conspiracy by Kather, Kane, Alexander, Nickson, etc. against The Hon. Edward Walpole, Esq. With an Account of their Trial before the Right Hon. Lord Chief Justice Lee, in the Court of King's-Bench, Westminster-Hall, July 5th. 1751.* (London, 1751)

GLRO Greater London Record Office

*Horace
Walpole,
Corr.* *Horace Walpole's Correspondence*, ed. W. S. Lewis et al., 48 vols (New Haven, Connecticut, 1937–83)

PRO Public Record Office

*Sessions
Papers* *The Whole Proceedings upon the King's Commission of Oyer and Terminer and Gaol Delivery for the City of London, and also the Gaol Delivery for the County of Middlesex.*

*Whole
Proceedings* *The Whole Proceedings on the wicked Conspiracy carried on against the Hon. Edward Walpole, Esq. by John Cather, Adam Nixon, Daniel Alexander, Patrick Cane alias Kane, and others. In Order to extort a large Sum of Money, under Pretence of an Assault, with an Intent to commit Buggery on the Body of the said John Cather. In which are inserted, the Tryal at large of the said Cather, Nixon, Alexander and Cane; and a full Account of the Attempt of Smith (who was executed at Tyburn for*

Forgery) and Patterson, to charge Mr. Walpole with For-gery, etc. (London, 1751)

PART I
Affirmation and denial

CHAPTER ONE

Homosexuals in eighteenth-century London

Sexual explorers

Just before the beginning of the eighteenth century English people, especially those living in London, noticed that there were more homosexuals in their midst than they had supposed. This discovery took place in the context of a heightened interest in everything to do with sex that possessed Europe. The Age of Enlightenment was also the age of sexual exploration, when the Italian Casanova criss-crossed the Continent, pursuing and recording his amorous adventures wherever he found himself, and when the legendary Spaniard Don Juan, alias Don Giovanni, reached his apotheosis with the Prague performance of Mozart's opera in 1787. In Paris libertine ethics found expression in a libertine literature that became an art form, culminating in the fantasies of sexual perversion written in the Bastille by the Marquis de Sade. Meanwhile in Germany scholars presented dissertations and gave addresses in universities on what one commentator called 'very strange and scabrous subjects', that is in which 'sodomy, or simple masturbation, or connexion with animals was minutely regarded'.[1] Nor were these specialized investigations confined to pedants. Curiosity about unorthodox manifestations of the sex instinct was characteristic of the time.

In England people flocked to fairs to gaze at hermaphrodites, drawn by the notion that these beings could enjoy both male and female amorous delights. Some Londoners practised, and more of them read about, flagellation and semi-strangulation as a means of enhancing, or reviving, male potency.[2] Despite the obscene libel laws, pornography was readily available, sometimes translated from the French and published by the notorious Edmund Curll. One of the most popular books ever issued by Curll was *Venus in the Cloister, or the Nun in her Smock*, from the original by Jean Barrin, the Preceptor of Nantes.[3] This, as the title suggests, purported to make startling revelations about life in a convent.

Nor did the English lack their own sexual researchers at every literary and social level. From 1698 to 1709 the journalist Ned Ward wrote a monthly magazine, the *London-Spy*, in which he undertook to expose 'Vice and Villainy' as well as the 'Follies of Mankind'.[4] This he did with

gusto and an eye to his readership figures, regaling his public in one
paper with a lively account of a brothel wherein the proprietor ensures
her girls have an adequate supply of rods with which to whip elderly
clients who come to her establishment for that pleasure.[5] In 1715
Alexander Pope composed a comic letter about a visit to a hermaphrodite, who assures 'the Ladies he has the inclination of a Gentleman',
while telling the 'Gentlemen she has the *Tendre* of a Lady'.[6] We might
be inclined to excuse this exercise (painful to modern sensibilities) on
the grounds of the poet's youth – he was only twenty-two – except that
he was not alone. At about the same time he was joined by others from
the literary association called the Scriblerus Club (whose members included the first minister and Queen Anne's physician) in writing a
bawdy spoof about their hero Martin's elopement with Siamese twins.[7]

Then there was the genteel son of one of Pope's lifelong friends,
William Cleland. John Cleland produced three studies of philology and
served as a consul in Smyrna, as well as writing his way out of a
debtors' prison in 1748 with that work of enduring appeal, *Memoirs of
a Woman of Pleasure*. *Fanny Hill*, as Cleland's story is more often
called, was enhanced by Charles Eisen's engravings. Indeed, much written pornography was lavishly illustrated, sometimes by well-known
artists who also produced erotica independently. On the other side of
the Channel François Boucher and P. A. Baudouin were among these,
while Thomas Rowlandson in England frequently augmented his income in this way.

As well as reading about and poring over pictures of the erotic
activities of others, the English were given an unprecedented opportunity to engage in their own amorous experiments once the Swiss
impresario John James Heidegger began organizing masquerades for
Londoners in 1717. These fancy-dress balls were immediately popular
with all classes of society. Anyone could go to them who could find the
money for a ticket and a costume, and up to eight hundred people at a
time did so. Thereafter from nine or ten in the evening until the small
hours all ceremony was laid aside since, as the *Weekly Journal* reported
in 1724, 'the Peer and the Apprentice, the Punk and the Duchess are,
for so long a time, upon an equal Foot'.[8] Masquerades were denounced
by moralists and depicted over and over again by novelists and dramatists. One play which Theophilus Cibber wrote in 1730 gives a fair idea
of both the attractions and mishaps which were a feature of these
crowded events. In *The Lover, a Comedy*, Captain Smart recounts his
success at a masquerade the previous night with an unknown beauty
when, as he said, 'in one Quarter of an Hour, being mask'd, I made
farther Progress towards gaining her Heart, than I'm satisfied I cou'd
have accomplished barefac'd in a Twelvemonth'. Meanwhile the Captain's

friend from the country, Squire Timberdown, had become involved in a fracas. He tripped up a nun in the crush who thundered out 'a bloody Oath', which surprised him until he saw 'she' was wearing jackboots.[9] Many a man or woman who went to these entertainments did so as a character as far removed from their everyday self as possible. Early in 1742 Horace Walpole went to two masquerades, the first time exotically and gorgeously attired as the Indian Emperor Aurengzebe.[10] The second time he donned stays and a petticoat and went as an old woman.[11] In this latter disguise he had a most enjoyable evening because it gave him the freedom to tease everyone in sight, including the Duke of Cumberland.

A primary attraction of the masquerade was the sense of liberation it bestowed on the participants, not least the sense of sexual liberation. As Terry Castle has put it, 'The appeal of the mask ... was that it permitted an escape from self; internalised moral and psychological constraints disappeared – for how could one be held responsible when one was not oneself?'[12] Cross-dressing was commonplace at masquerades and produced a fair amount of sexual confusion. Writers of the day, including John Cleland, described occasions when men picked up boys supposing they were girls, or vice versa.[13] At least one case that came up at the Old Bailey referred to an episode in which an old gentleman was outraged to find the transvestite he had taken to bed after a masquerade at Ranelagh was actually male, though the fact that the youth involved had let the affair go so far suggests that he was hopeful his client would make the best of the situation when he discovered his mistake.[14]

It was only to be expected that in an age of sexual exploration homosexuals would become more confident about their way of life. When this was noticed, the phenomenon met with varying degrees of resistance. Some of the fiercest opposition was found in England, for although throughout Europe the laws which stated that any man convicted of sodomy be burned at the stake remained in place, it was possible there for individuals such as Montesquieu to say that this was excessive and no better than the already discredited practice of burning witches.[15] In England, however, no public criticism was possible of the 1533 Buggery Act which decreed that sodomites be hanged.[16]

Sodomites and mollies

Homosexuals had always existed in England, though the word 'homosexual' was not current until the nineteenth century. They were called sodomites, a term which emphasized the biblical injunction against them because it reminded everyone of God's destruction of Sodom and

Gomorrah. Until the end of the seventeenth century such men were mythologized as monsters, akin to werewolves and basilisks, outside a divinely appointed, natural order of things, believed by some to be literally the offspring of Satan.[17] However, it is difficult for anyone to see himself as a non-human, so it has been persuasively argued that many males who engaged in casual sex with their own kind never thought of themselves as being sodomites at all.[18] Instead, by a process of doublethink, they created a more acceptable picture of themselves as men in whom an active libido led them to make love to both sexes equally, as the occasion arose. Hence we have the well-known image of the Tudor and Stuart rake with a girl on one arm and a pretty boy on the other. The openly bisexual Lord Rochester was in this tradition. Respectable members of the community recoiled from him but he did not fill them with alarm. They tended to explain his sodomitical tastes as extraordinary evidence of a jaded palate, only to be expected in an individual who was a dedicated debauchee. Nor was Rochester despised. His 'unnatural' vice in no way compromised his masculinity. The fact that he made love to Sylvia, Phyllis and Olinda, as well as link boys, exempted him from the contempt with which those who were exclusively homosexual were regarded. As for the rest of the country beyond the court, although it was realized that occasional sodomy took place at every social level, and even that London had its male brothels, it was not felt to be a major problem and very few prosecutions took place.[19]

By the beginning of the eighteenth century the picture had changed, especially in the capital. In 1700 London had a heterogeneous population of nearly 700 000.[20] There were therefore enough homosexuals to form coteries. They found one another in up to twenty cruising grounds scattered across the town from Wapping to Westminster, making themselves known to each other by signs, such as using handkerchiefs and patting the back of the other's hand.[21] The convenient assumption disappeared that confirmed sodomites were solitary beings, maybe spawned by the Devil, hardly ever encountered by the majority of the population. In a climate of heightened interest in everything to do with sex, English heterosexuals looked around them and discovered the mollies. The word 'molly' described an effeminate homosexual, who liked dressing up in women's clothes and was possibly known by a girl's name, 'Kitty' or 'Mary', or fancifully grand ones such as the 'Countess of Camomile' and the 'Queen of Bohemia'.[22] There were also molly houses, which were not brothels but clubs, some of them with several dozen members who met, in various venues all over town, to hold parties and make love.[23]

In the last twenty years or so the rise of the molly subculture in the capital has been perceptively discussed and analysed by social historians on both sides of the Atlantic, including Randolph Trumbach, Alan Bray, G. S. Rousseau and Rictor Norton, to name but a few.[24] Much of the following account of what was happening to homosexuals in London at the beginning of the eighteenth century summarizes the findings of these writers.

Quite early on Ned Ward helped to publicize the molly houses. In 1709 he enlightened his readers with a description of homosexuals who met regularly in one of the taverns in the City. These men had 'so far degenerated from all Masculine Deportment' that they fancy themselves female, 'affecting to speak, walk, tattle, curtsy, cry, scold & mimick all Manner of Effeminancy'. Ward recreated a scene that he knew would interest a public avid for details about the odder aspects of sexual life. 'Not long since,' he told his readers, on one of their festival nights, the mollies 'had cushion'd up the Belly of one of their Sodomitical Brethren, or rather sisters, as they commonly call themselves, dignifying him in a Woman's Night-Gown, Sarsner-Hood and Nightrale, who, when the Company were met, was to mimick the wry Face of a groaning Woman, to be delivered of a joynted Baby they had provided for that purpose, and to undergo all the Formalities of a Lying-in.' Other club members played the parts of a country midwife, in a 'high-crown'd Hat and Pinner', the happy father-to-be and a parson who, after the leading molly 'was disburthened of her little jointed bastard', performed a christening.[25] These specialized amateur theatricals were not held in every molly house but they were an enduring feature in some of them. Nearly twenty years after Ward wrote his account, James Dalton, a footpad, tried to curry favour with the magistrates after his arrest by claiming he had had various mollies apprehended. Among other things he mentioned the weddings and mock childbirths he had witnessed.[26]

Many mollies enjoyed dressing up elaborately as female characters from the world of pastoral and high fashion, not only because this was fun, but also perhaps because acting out specific feminine roles helped to fix them in their new identity. Jonathan Wild once described how a number of homosexuals, so attired, were arrested as they were leaving 'a House near the end of Old Bayly'. Next morning they were carried before the Lord Mayor in the same clothes they were taken in. 'Some were dressed like Shepherdesses, others like Milk-maids with fine green Hatts, Waistcoats and Petticoats, and other had their Faces patched and painted, and wore very extensive Hoop-petticoats, which were then very lately introduced.'[27] The house near the Old Bailey mentioned by Wild may have been Mother Clap's in Field Lane. Mother Clap (that really was her name) ran one of the most popular of the molly houses. It had a large room for drinking and dancing, lit by a good fire, as well as several other rooms, all of which had beds. There up to forty or fifty homosexuals met any of seven nights a week and could confidently be themselves in comfortable, cheerful surroundings, putting to the back of their minds the people who regarded them as outcasts.[28] The existence of Mother Clap's notorious establishment with its large clientele confirmed that London now had a molly subculture.

A flood of information from various quarters about the mollies helped to establish a stereotyped picture of homosexuals, to the extent that the general public supposed that they were all effeminate, and the term 'molly' became the popular word to describe any man who preferred making love to his own sex. Descriptions of them were invariably couched in homophobic language. The one by Ned Ward quoted earlier is a relatively mild example because, although he shared every current prejudice, he was not a moral crusader. His racy journalism was not designed to instigate a pogrom. This task was undertaken by the zealous members of the Societies for the Reformation of Manners, the first of which was founded in 1690, with the aim of eradicating vice of every description in a land it considered sunk in immorality. In the first three decades of the eighteenth century these organizations multiplied rapidly and homosexuals became one of their chief targets.

The pogroms

Around the turn of the century there was a marked increase in arrests for sodomy throughout the country. In 1702 four men found guilty of this offence at the Maidstone Assizes were sent to the gallows.[29] Figures are hard to come by as comprehensive statistics were not kept, but a study of what was happening in Somerset in the eighteenth century suggests that punishments meted out to practising homosexuals were even harsher in the provinces than in the capital.[30]

In London the Reforming Societies were particularly energetic, sending out their own people as undercover agents to entice homosexuals with spurious propositions. By threats and bribes they also persuaded some mollies to become informers.[31] Their efforts appeared to be spectacularly successful when almost a hundred sodomites were arrested in 1707 and nine more were taken in a single foray to a brandy shop in Jermyn Street two years later.[32] Their achievement was somewhat marred in that most of those arrested were released for lack of conclusive evidence but this did not unduly discourage the Societies. For even if they could not bring a case that would stand up in court, they spread fear and distrust in the homosexual community. The campaign reached a peak in 1726 when Mother Clap's was raided in February and forty mollies arrested there, as well as many more at similar houses in the town.[33] Arrests on this scale were possible because males who frequented molly houses were ordinary working folk, labourers and tradesmen, who lacked influential friends. Aristocrats who became the subject of a homosexual scandal might find themselves in court but more often they were dealt with by their peers in a less ostentatious fashion.

In April and July trials were held at the Old Bailey of several of the arrested mollies who had been charged with sodomy and attempted sodomy, with the result that by August three of them had been hanged on the same day at Tyburn. Another man died in prison. Two more were given prison sentences, made to stand in the pillory and fined. Only one was acquitted and another subsequently reprieved though, as had happened previously, the majority of the mollies arrested had not been brought to trial at all.[34] The career of Mother Clap was cut short, however. Convicted of keeping a disorderly house, she was made to stand in the pillory, serve two years in prison and fined twenty marks, that is a little over £13.30.[35]

After the hangings in August 1726, this particular moral crusade lost momentum, mainly because the authorities and the general public reacted against the Societies. The special constables they recruited to stamp out vice were found to be both officious and corrupt. Ned Ward reflected popular opinion when he waged a vigorous attack on the 'reforming Constables'.[36] By 1738 the Societies had decided to disband, but well before that date the mass arrests of mollies had ceased and when new molly houses opened, as they soon did, these were for the most part left alone. Of course men, singly or in pairs, were still charged with sodomitical offences. In the twenty years from 1731 twenty-two suspected sodomites appeared in the Old Bailey but none of those convicted was hanged. This pattern continued for the rest of the century, with executions of sodomites averaging fewer than one per decade.[37]

Homophobic misconceptions

If, for a while, homosexuals were hunted down less vigorously than they had been, this was not because the official attitude towards them had changed. The all-important religious prohibition, based on an interpretation of the story of Sodom and Gomorrah, stayed in place. There were also non-religious objections. Fear of depopulation played a prominent part among these. Voltaire wrote that if homosexuality were encouraged it could lead to the demise of the human race.[38] It was also believed that intercourse between males, along with masturbation, damaged the health. In the opinion of Montesquieu, the passive partner in a homosexual relationship was particularly in danger of becoming physically debilitated.[39] Homosexual desire was not understood by those who wrote about it. So some writers doubted whether it was a natural instinct, among them Jonathan Swift, who created his primitive Yahoos exempt from 'these politer pleasures', which he said were 'entirely the productions of art and reason'.[40]

In England misconceptions about homosexuals were adhered to passionately, making it perilous for anyone to publish a reasoned discussion of homoerotic love, let alone a defence of it. When Thomas Cannon (doing what German academics did) produced *Ancient and Modern Pederasty Investigated and Exemplified* in 1749, he and his printer were prosecuted.[41] On the other hand homophobic pamphlets were published throughout the century. *Satan's Harvest Home*, containing a diatribe against the 'abominable Practice' of sodomy, went on sale throughout London in the same year that Cannon fled abroad to avoid trial. Earlier, in 1707, a gruesomely illustrated broadsheet, *The Women-Hater's Lamentation*, promulgated the notion that all mollies were misogynists.[42] And later, in 1763, the woodcut for a popular ballad, *This is not the Thing: or, Molly Exalted*, showed a convicted homosexual in the pillory, surrounded by a jeering crowd, in which one woman was calling for the prisoner to be flogged and another demanding that he be castrated.[43] Women were popularly supposed to be resentful of mollies because they saw them as rivals, though there was little evidence that this was other than an invention of the male writers of homophobic propaganda.[44]

How many homosexuals?

In 1700 there were about five million people living in England. No one knows how many of them were homosexuals, though if Randolph Trumbach is correct in suggesting that the percentage has remained constant throughout the history of the country, there could have been a quarter of a million of them, that is, 5 per cent of the population – a fairly conservative estimate.[45] Dennis Rubini, on the other hand, believes that throughout England there were only a few thousand who thought of themselves as mollies and only a few hundred who adopted that lifestyle permanently.[46] To these statements one might add that some psychologists agree that bisexuality 'can be discerned in most human beings'.[47] This conclusion that sexual predilection is not immutable is worth bearing in mind as we look at England three hundred years ago when certain economic and cultural factors encouraged homosexual behaviour because, as a result of these, there were possibly a fair number of men who, at least at some period in their lives, might have been charged with sodomy if they had been unlucky enough to be exposed.

Institutional life

In the first place, the way society was structured encouraged homosexuality, in that men and boys were often herded together in larger or smaller groups. As well as an army and navy, as in most countries, there were other predominantly masculine worlds, some of them very English in character. Among those who worked for a living there were all the domestic servants, apprentices and journeymen. Men in this class did not usually marry until they could support a wife, which might not be until they were in their early thirties. Meanwhile they lived in close proximity to one another in the house of their master. Justices of the Peace and other authorities monitored irregular heterosexual unions strictly because they did not want the financial responsibility of caring for bastards. In such circumstances, as Alan Bray has noted, a young man might well be tempted to indulge in casual homosexual activity which at least had the advantage of not producing a burden on the parish.[48] Furthermore, life below as well as above stairs was hierarchical, so that a young apprentice or stable boy might be afraid to complain if an adult, with whom he worked and probably shared a bed, selected him as a target.

Higher up the social scale many of the sons of gentlemen spent their formative years in the major boarding schools, and then Oxford or Cambridge. In these exclusively male institutions they formed some of their earliest and most intense attachments. Later on the spirit of camaraderie established at school was continued among those men who joined the fashionable London clubs. This is not to suggest that establishments such as White's were homosexual in character. They were not, though some of the Hell Fire clubs may have been.[49] It is just that from boyhood on, the well-bred English male was accustomed to being with his own kind whom he understood, in a way he rarely learned to understand women, even when he was attracted to them.

The cult of friendship

Moreover, gentlemen in the eighteenth century lived at a time when there was a cult of friendship. They looked to their male friends for companionship rather than to their wives, if they married at all. Actually a fair number of them remained bachelors – far more than is the case nowadays – unless marriage was necessary in order to carry on the family name and produce an heir for an estate, in which case a gentleman might well choose a partner for her connections and money as much as for love. English aristocrats had always been aware of the advantages of marrying an heiress, of course, but as Lawrence Stone has pointed out, seeking a wife from purely mercenary motives was more common than ever before in the early eighteenth century.[50]

The sons of the first minister, Robert Walpole, were not untypical in their relationships with women. Only the eldest acquired a wife, Margaret Rolle, who brought him (or rather his father) the control of two parliamentary boroughs, as well as great estates, after which the pair lived unhappily together until she left him and the boy she had given birth to.[51] Edward, Sir Robert's second son, was unable to find a bride who would satisfy his father's ambitions for him. Instead he lived with a seamstress and had four children by her. After she died, though, in her early twenties, he did not take another mistress. In so far as he sought society at all, this was almost exclusively male. Nevertheless, most people believed he was heterosexual and, as we shall see further on in these pages, an opportunistic attempt to convict him of attempted sodomy ended in failure. The sexual status of his younger brother Horace was, and still is, regarded as ambiguous. Certainly he remained a bachelor; we cannot be sure he ever slept with a woman. Instead he cultivated a vast number of friends, mostly male, until he was old, when he acquired female ones as well. Timothy Mowl has gone further than anyone else so far in arguing that Horace Walpole was a covert homosexual who was, in his youth, totally obsessed by Lord Lincoln, 'the handsomest man in England', whom he had first met at Eton.[52] The case Mowl makes for this contention is all the more plausible because the reasonably good-looking first minister's son would not have been an unlikely lover for the Earl, who was reputedly bisexual.[53]

Whether or not ardent friendships between men developed into love affairs depended on external circumstances, including physical appearance, as much as on the emotions of the people involved. So there has been virtually no speculation about homoerotic tendencies in Alexander Pope who, being crippled and sickly, could not physically attract either men or women. Nevertheless, his fervent devotion to Henry St John, Lord Bolingbroke, could hardly have been exceeded by a medieval troubador's adoration of his lady. To Bolingbroke this did not seem strange. His toast after dinner was usually *Amicitiae et Libertati* (friendship and liberty) – in that order.[54] And Pope, in addition to paying what one contemporary called 'idolatrous homage' to Bolingbroke, also loved

Martha Blount for well over thirty years from the time he first met her as a boy.[55]

In Pope we encounter the eighteenth-century cult of friendship at its zenith. The number of friends he wooed throughout his life was even greater than the number of enemies he provoked, and with very few (if notable) exceptions, he kept them all until they died, whereupon he felt diminished. For as he told Swift, with the death of every friend 'we lose a part of ourselves, the best part'.[56] As he lay on his own deathbed, after receiving the last rites, he declared, 'There is nothing that is meritorious but Virtue and Friendship, and indeed Friendship is only a part of Virtue.'[57]

Pope found his ideas on the value of friendship reinforced in an essay on the subject by his favourite writer, Montaigne, who had written that the bond between true male friends was finer than any other, filial, fraternal or marital, because it was the only one in which the partners were free and equal. True love between men also ranked more highly than love between men and women which, while it was 'more active, more eager and more sharp', was 'more precipitant, fickle, moving and inconstant'. When Montaigne adopted, as he did, Cicero's definition that 'Those are only to be reputed friendships, that are fortified by judgment and length of time', it enabled him to exclude the homosexual relationships that existed in the ancient world because, as he claimed, these were temporary and, as they were between older men and boys, judgement played very little part in them.[58] Most of Montaigne's successors followed him in condemning homosexuality at the same time as they exalted male friendship, though Cicero himself would have been surprised to learn of such a viewpoint as, according to Pliny, he was unapologetic about his love affairs with young men.[59]

To sum up, the cult of male friendship provided an emotional climate and opportunities for homosexual relationships, even though many of those who made it their ideal insisted on its platonic nature.

A classical education

There was always a certain amount of sophistry involved in the arguments devised by the moderns, anxious to marginalize evidence of homosexuality in the ancient world even as they embraced the Greek and Roman exaltation of male friendship. Jeremy Bentham poured scorn on his contemporaries' efforts to deny what he saw as the plain facts of the case about homosexuality among the ancients. 'Everybody practised it; nobody was ashamed of it', he wrote in the 1780s and, speaking of the sexual nature of many of the relationships between

men, he went on, 'the Greeks knew the difference between love and
friendship as well as we – they had distinct terms to signify them by; it
seems reasonable therefore to suppose that when they say love they
mean love, and that when they say friendship only they mean friendship
only'. Finally he drove the point home with the following observation:
'With regard to Xenophon and his master Socrates, and his fellow-
scholar Plato, it seems more reasonable to believe them to have been
addicted to this taste when they or any of them tell us so in express
terms than to trust to the interpretations, however ingenious and however well-intended, of any men who write at this time of day, when they
tell us it was no such thing.'[60] Wisely Bentham never published these
reflections. They would have provoked a furore. Nevertheless one cannot help wondering if his views were not shared by others who were
equally discreet.

The classical education which all gentlemen received had to be a
factor which encouraged homosexuality, if only because it revealed that
highly civilized people had once held a view of the matter which was
different from the Judaeo-Christian one. Furthermore, knowledge that
homoerotic love had previously been accepted filtered down the social
scale, with references to Ganymede and Hephaestion in plays attended
by footmen and their masters. Meanwhile the mollies took comfort
from their classical predecessors, as the following verse from one of
their songs shows:

> Achilles that Hero great
> Had Patroclus for a Mate,
> Nay, Jove he would have a Lad,
> The beautiful Ganymede.[61]

The example of their betters

Nor was it necessary for homosexuals in search of precedents and
models to go as far afield as the ancient world for them. They had only
to look at their own rulers. Information about the fondness of James I
for pretty young men had been available since 1651,[62] while rumours
about William III began soon after he landed at Torbay in 1688, bringing with him the young page Van Keppel whom he later made Earl of
Albemarle.[63] Furthermore, it was impossible for aristocratic homosexuals who had male lovers to keep that fact a secret. For one thing they
had servants who gossiped and sometimes they had enemies who ensured that the gossip was published. This happened to the Earl of
Sunderland, who in 1721 was blamed for the South Sea Bubble disaster.
Among his attackers was a journalist named Thomas Gordon who,

primed with information about the statesman's private life, wrote in a pamphlet that the Earl 'had a most unnatural Taste in his Gallantries: And in those Hours when he gave Loose to Love, the Women were wholly excluded from his Embraces'.[64]

Ten years later Lord Hervey fought a duel with a fellow Member of Parliament, William Pulteney, who had labelled him 'a delicate Hermaphrodite' in a popular Opposition journal, *The Craftsman*.[65] Hervey's honour was satisfied by this action, but gossip was not silenced because over the next few weeks the London bookshops sold various prints depicting the encounter between the two gentlemen in Green Park. Of course the aim of those who wrote about the unconventional sexual tastes of some members of the ruling classes was to make the general public think the worst of them. At the same time they gave comfort to ordinary people who were homosexually inclined, in assuring them that they had illustrious models. In 1730 Williamson Goodman, an uneducated Londoner, tried to seduce an unresponsive Henry Thompson by telling him of 'great Persons that us'd that way'.[66]

The effect of travel

Travel was another source of inspiration and encouragement for anyone who was unsure of his sexual orientation. Successive generations of young English gentlemen made the Grand Tour, taking with them their servants, or they went to the Continent to study. There, despite the European laws prohibiting sodomy, they were likely to encounter practising homosexuals, taking advantage of a relatively relaxed atmosphere which encouraged experimentation even among men who were predominantly heterosexual. Voltaire, for example, while writer in residence at the homoerotic court of Frederick the Great, decided to try what he called the *péché philosophique* (philosophical sin) and slept with a young Englishman on one occasion, although, as he did not enjoy the experience, once was enough.[67] Voltaire does not give us the name of his partner but he does mention that the youth told him he had gone on to make a second experiment of the same kind a few nights later.

Being abroad was one of those situations, like going to a masquerade, that freed a man from customary restraints and, although the experience of being in a foreign country was more prolonged, afterwards the traveller could put behind him any unconventional behaviour he had indulged in. It is doubtful whether the young Englishman whom Voltaire met told many people about the encounter once he returned home, any more than the young John Wilkes broadcast the fact that two philosophers, the Scot Andrew Baxter and the German Baron d'Holbach, had been in love with him when they were all part of a homosexual coterie in Holland, though he was never to be reticent about his later heterosexual adventures. This coterie, which has been described by G. S. Rousseau, existed at the universities of Utrecht and Leiden, and included more than a dozen tutors and students from the United Kingdom among its members.[68]

Homosexuality in literature

For obvious reasons men in real life were reluctant to write about socially unacceptable encounters they might have had. However, creative writers, free to invent characters, were less inhibited, so we can learn something about the homosexual scene, particularly the one abroad, from the plays and novels of the period. In literature we can also trace an evolution in the way the subject was approached from about the turn of the century. In *The Relapse* (1696) Vanbrugh expressed no sense of moral outrage as he presented his audience with Coupler, the homosexual who earns money matchmaking for heterosexuals. The lively young Fashion, while not responding to Coupler's advances, accepts him as part of the social scene. 'Stand off, old Sodom' is how the hero greets this character, who takes the rebuff in good part with the following ironical rejoinder: 'Hast thou been a year in Italy and brought home a fool at last?' And thereafter the two cheerfully plot to outmatch Fashion's insufferable brother.[69] This degree of tolerance continued for a few more years. At the beginning of *Love Makes a Man, or The Fop's Fortune* (1701), Colley Cibber's not unsympathetic coxcomb Clodio returns from France and lightheartedly tells his father, 'I love to kiss a Man, in Paris we kiss nothing else.'[70] However, as time went on, the tone of all creative writers became more self-consciously moralistic until by the 1780s a curtain of silence fell, so that the treatment of homosexuality, even in works of the imagination, became taboo, as if not mentioning it at all would make it go away.

Tobias Smollett, in the novels he wrote in the middle of the century, enjoyed a fair degree of freedom in depicting homosexuals because he had no difficulty in observing the homophobic conventions as he did so. In *Peregrine Pickle* (1751) there is a comic scene involving the discomfiture of an Italian marquis and German baron who are discovered making love to one another in a boarding house in Paris. As in similar episodes in Smollett's novels the hero is a non-participant and we are assured he 'entertained a just detestation for all such abominable practices'.[71] In *Roderick Random*, published three years earlier, the hero is an innocent who does not at first understand why Earl Strutwell clasps him 'to his breast with surprising emotion'. Even when his supposed patron eloquently defends sodomy, he thinks this is a test, imposed upon him because the Earl fears he has 'been infected with this spurious and sordid desire abroad'. In making Roderick somewhat obtuse, Smollett can allow him to dispense with the courtesy he would usually show a host and launch into an impassioned attack on an 'appetite unnatural, absurd, and of pernicious consequence'. He rounds off this expression of conventional morality by heaping 'eternal infamy' on the wretch 'who first planted that vice on British ground', so echoing a widespread belief among Britons that sodomy would never have existed among them if it had not been imported. Nevertheless, before this point is reached Earl Strutwell has been allowed to make an even longer speech in which he marshals half a dozen arguments in support of a practice not only avowed 'by the most celebrated poets' in the ancient world and permitted by Plato in his Commonwealth, but which, at the time of speaking, prevails throughout the East and in most parts of Europe. What is more, he goes on, 'it prevents the debauchery of many a young maiden' and is 'unattended with that curse and burden upon society which proceeds from a race of miserable and deserted bastards'. But the Earl saves till last the mention of a motive 'more powerful than all of these, that induces people to cultivate this inclination, namely the exquisite pleasure attending its success'.[72]

Earl Strutwell is a villain who, among other crimes, cons the hero out of his watch. Inveterate heterosexuals who read the novel in which he appeared could dismiss his defence of homoerotic love as evidence of his perfidy, though for those open to homosexual suggestion, the arguments listed were ones they had heard before, even if they had not seen them in print.

Polemical writers

Throughout the century it was a different matter if a philosopher or scholar offered for sympathetic consideration even an oblique defence of the vice the general public called sodomy. Those writers who had the courage to try suffered accordingly. Yet excoriated though they were, what they had to say remained there on the printed page to influence the intellectually curious. When the lifelong dissident thinker Alberto Radicati, Count of Passerano, fled from persecution to England in 1726 he wrote *A Philosophical Dissertation upon Death*, in which he gave a comprehensive account of Christian and pagan customs, his intention being to prove that morality was relative, so that there was nothing inherently wrong in many acts which were regarded as criminal in modern Europe, including suicide and homoerotic love. His book was translated and published in England in 1732, whereupon he, his translator and printer were all taken into custody.[73] Nevertheless, once written, his book lived on and was read, unlike Thomas Cannon's, no known copy of which has survived. Radicati was eventually forced to leave England but before that happened he was invited to discuss his ideas with Queen Caroline and General Wade.[74]

Later in the century the Judaeo-Christian view of sexual relations was questioned again by Richard Payne Knight in his *Discourse on the Worship of Priapus, and its Connexion with the Mystic Theology of the Ancients* (1786–87). This work was a study in comparative religion, designed to show that pagan and Christian rituals 'have the same meaning and only differ in the modes of conveying it'.[75] Knight showed that Priapus, far from being a peripheral figure in Greek religion, was central to it and that the ancient religious rituals were phallic in origin. In a fascinating study G. S. Rousseau argues that 'Christian morality is the pre-eminent target of this work, enlightened paganism, especially its toleration for homosocial desire, its primary endorsement'.[76]

The *Discourse on the Worship of Priapus* was meant to be a private publication but copies of it escaped into the public domain, where it was denounced, not so much for its anti-clerical subtext, as for obscenity. Its twenty-four sexually explicit illustrations provided extra ammunition for the moralists in condemning the book. Furthermore, by the time it was published in 1786–87 prudery about sex had won the battle with libertinism. Pagan phallicism was not a subject to be discussed or written about openly. Nevertheless the *Discourse*, written by a wealthy man known to the fashionable world and sponsored by the reputable Society of Dillettanti, was sent to a number of celebrities, including Horace Walpole, Edward Gibbon, James Boswell, John Wilkes, the Duke of Portland and the Prince of Wales. Of these, only Walpole is known to have been disgusted by Knight.[77] If this reaction appears surprising it may be that, despite his youthful passion for Lord Lincoln, he was reluctant to consider any line of argument that forced him to face his own sexual nature. So he preferred to align himself with the majority of the public for whom Knight became an anathema.

Yet, notwithstanding a steadfast refusal by most people to countenance anyone who attempted openly to defend sodomy, the fact that Radicati and Knight wrote and were read suggests that there was a tacit admission on the part of some that the orthodox view of sex and its place in life was not writ in stone. As Rousseau concludes at the end of his essay, the significance of Knight's 'phallic campaigns' is that they 'reveal the presence of another eighteenth-century Enlightenment'.[78]

Jeremy Bentham's essay on 'Paederasty'

In 1785, at about the same time that Richard Payne Knight was putting the finishing touches to his *Discourse on the Worship of Priapus*, Jeremy Bentham was penning a polemic about homosexuality. Writing in his capacity as a law reformer, he called for its decriminalization. His ideas on this subject did not appear in print until 1978 when Louis Crompton, having deciphered the manuscript of three hundred pages, ensured that the essay on 'Paederasty' was published.[79]

In the process of arguing that homosexuality should not be treated as a crime, Bentham produced a matter-of-fact and comprehensive defence of homoerotic love that was all the more effective because he wrote as a heterosexual who admitted that he found any man's wish to have sexual relations with his own kind a 'preposterous propensity'.[80] Having admitted his own aversion to a taste he did not share, he went on to say that this was no excuse for condemning it, though such an attitude helped to explain virulent homophobia because 'in persons of weak minds, anything which is unusual and at the same time physically disgustful is apt to excite the passion of hate'.[81] Delving further into the causes of homophobia, Bentham decided it was exacerbated by the realization that homosexuals enjoyed themselves. It was a constant source of sorrow to him that many people of a religious turn of mind regarded pleasure as sinful in itself. For 'It may be asked indeed, if pleasure is not a good, what is life good for, and what is the purpose of preserving it?'[82]

As we might expect of the classical exponent of utilitarianism, Bentham begins his plea for changing the law on sodomy by asking what useful purpose is served by inflicting legal penalties on homosexuals. 'I have been tormenting myself for years', he writes, 'to find if possible a sufficient ground for treating them with the severity with which they are treated at this time of day by all European nations: but upon the principle of utility I can find none.'[83]

That being said, Bentham proceeds to demolish one by one all the objections that have ever been raised about tolerating homosexuality in society. He points out that if both partners are willing, it produces no pain to anyone. To state, as William Blackstone had done, that it endangered someone's security, without specifying whose, is 'just as if a man were to make no distinction between concubinage and rape'.[84] Nor can he find any evidence to support Montesquieu's contention that homosexual activity is debilitating of either the agent or the patient. In an extended discussion about the prevalence of homoerotic love in the acient world, Bentham points out that it did not prevent the Greeks and Romans fighting with valour.[85]

Nor was there any danger, as Voltaire had claimed, of the world becoming depopulated if homosexuals were to be encouraged because they are in the minority and likely to remain so. For the majority of men to prefer making physical love to their own kind exclusively would require a total change in human nature. In any case, 'if merely out of regard to population it were right that paederasts should be burnt alive monks ought to be roasted alive by slow fire'.[86]

Bentham believed that a large number of so-called homosexuals were actually bisexual and that, contrary to popular opinion, they were not enemies of women. Many of them married for the usual reasons such as the desire for children and the need for family alliances, as well as the wish for a lifelong companion. This last reason he mentioned because he believed most homosexual relationships were temporary, involving an adult falling in love with a youth. Yet, as he also realized, when a homosexual is persecuted he is more likely to become resentful of women because it is natural for all oppressed people to hate those they regard as responsible for their wretched state. He compared latter-day homosexuals to negroes who, 'we may suppose, have not any violent affection for Negro drivers'.[87]

As Bentham knew, the overriding reason why sodomy was condemned in Christian society rested on the biblical injunction against it. The term arose because God destroyed Sodom and Gomorrah, whose male citizens were homosexuals. Bentham deals with this point by taking another look at chapters 18 and 19 in Genesis where the story is told. He concludes that the biblical narrative is more ambiguous than is usually supposed. To begin with, the offences imputed to the inhabitants of the two towns 'are in the English translation termed by the general names of "wickedness" and "iniquity" and their conduct opposed to "righteousness"'.[88] It is true that the only offence which is mentioned as having been committed by them on any individual occasion involved homosexuals. This is when we are told of a mob, the members of which arrive at the house of Lot and try to take by force his two male guests, refusing the patriarch's offer to give them his virgin daughters instead. However, as Bentham sees it, these men are condemned, not for sharing the sexual tastes of the ancient Greeks, but because they are guilty of attempted rape and a grave abuse of the laws of hospitality.[89]

In any case, Bentham adds, it is not advisable for us to use the particular acts of God described in the Bible as a sanction for our own behaviour. For 'if a man without a special commission from God is to be justified in doing any violent act that has ever been done by a special commission from God, a man might as well kill his son because God commissioned Abraham to kill Isaac'.[90]

If Bentham had published his essay he would never have been able to live in England again. It was way ahead of its time. Even now to come upon its plain common sense after all the passion, misapprehension and obfuscation that characterizes the writings of most of his contemporaries on the subject of sodomites and mollies is like leaving the darkness and confusion of a Hogarthian Bedlam to walk out into the light of common day.

The consequences of homophobia

There was no possibility of homosexuality being officially condoned in the eighteenth century. Nor could it be eliminated. As we have seen, attempts to suppress it faltered around 1726. However, the homophobic campaign waged at the beginning of the eighteenth century had important consequences.

An immediate result of the publicity given to what is now termed the molly subculture was that blackmailers flourished as never before. It became a regular ploy of footpads to threaten to accuse their victims of attempted sodomy unless they handed over their valuables quietly. Sophisticated extortioners concocted elaborate schemes to get money out of anyone who valued his good name. Those approached in this way usually paid up because the opprobrium and scorn heaped upon anyone openly proclaimed a sodomite was hard to bear. Innocence was no safeguard. Only a very steadfast or desperate man took his persecutor to court because, even if he won his case, he had to endure unpleasant publicity and the possibility that doubts would linger in the minds of the uncharitable.

The problem with blackmailers could be solved by a change in the law, as happened eventually. However, the anti-molly crusade had another long-term consequence that has proved more difficult to eradicate. The attention focused on mollies and the homophobic reaction to them affected all Englishmen, whatever their sexual orientation. As well as consolidating a clearly identifiable homosexual underground, it changed the way heterosexual men came to regard themselves in that they learned to suppress the feminine side of their nature.

When some eighteenth-century commentators, convinced that sodomy was on the increase, wondered why the mollies, especially transvestite ones, had become so prominent, they decided it was because many Englishmen had become effete. This was felt to be the case at all levels in urban society. In *The Female Tatler* in 1709, the gossip columnist Mrs Crackenthorpe described a visit to a fashionable shop in Ludgate Hill where the three male assistants were the 'sweetest, fairest, nicest dished out Creatures', adding, with a sexual innuendo that would not be lost on her readers, 'by their Elegant Address and Soft Speeches, you would guess them to be Italians'. They swarmed over her and her companions as they plied their wares with, '"This, Madam, is wonderful Charming. This, Madam, is so diverting a Silk. This, Madam – My Stars! How *Cool* it looks! But *this*, Madam – Ye Gods! Would I had 10,000 Yards of it!" Then gathers up a Sleeve, and places it on our Shoulders. "It suits your Ladyship's Face wonderfully well."'[91] The shop assistants Mrs Crackenthorpe described took their cue from men of means who led the fashion. Like them they had 'their Toilets and their Fine Night-Gowns; their Chocolate in the Morning, their Green Tea two Hours after; Turkey Polts for Dinner; and their Perfumes, Washes and Clean Linen to equip 'em for the Parade'.[92]

The anonymous author of *Satan's Harvest Home* (1749) restricted his criticisms to those members of the upper classes whose behaviour was being imitated by aspiring shop assistants. He blamed education in the first place for what he saw as decadence.[93] He lamented that only a few schools maintained a traditionally Spartan regime which encouraged the manly virtues in their pupils. The kind of school he admired was Westminster, where, although he did not mention the fact, the boys had once been given a general pardon for murdering a bailiff.[94] However, as he saw it, a son of genteel parents not sent to Westminster or Eton often had far too easy a time of it. He was kept by his mother in the nursery at home until he was five or six years old, after which he was first taught by women in a girls' school where he was encouraged to become girlish himself, often learning 'his Minuet before his Letters'.[95] He got no exercise and only went out to pay visits with his Mama in a coach. If this early cosseting was not counteracted at some stage in his boyhood, his 'whole Animal Fabrick' became enervated and he grew up markedly effeminate in dress and manners.[96] That is, he became a fop. This pamphleteer was particularly severe about fops. Barely distinguishing them from mollies, he declared they were 'the Shame of their Age and Country'.[97]

The fop was a feature of the eighteenth-century fashionable world, though one suspects he was the product not so much of changes in the education system, as the author of *Satan's Harvest Home* claimed, as of a burgeoning consumer society, in which the increasing availability of luxurious materials and items of adornment encouraged the male instinct for display. The fop, beau or 'pretty fellow' spent an inordinate amount of time with his tailor, shoemaker, perrukier and hosier. His extravagant concern with setting the fashion and his affected manners made him seem effeminate though, notwithstanding the suspicions of the pamphleteer, he was not usually homosexual.[98] He devoted at least some of his time to courting rich and preferably beautiful women, though this would be for financial and social reasons because, in truth, the only person he was in love with, male or female, was himself. His vanity and exhibitionism made him the butt of his more sober-minded brethren and he was a gift to the dramatists, becoming a stock figure in the comedies of the day.

Colley Cibber made his name as an actor playing Sir Novelty Fashion in a work he wrote himself, *Love's Last Shift* (1696), wherein this anti-hero, impervious to mockery, says proudly, 'I was the first person in England that was complimented with the name of Beau,' listing his achievements as follows: 'the cravat-string, the garter, the sword-knot, the centurine, bardash, the steinkirk, the large button, the long sleeve, the plume, the full peruque, were all created, cry'd down or reviv'd by me'.[99] In *The Relapse*, John Vanbrugh's sequel to Cibber's play, Sir Novelty has bought a peerage and has become Lord Foppington, an even more fantastic prince of coxcombs in a perriwig down to his knees. This character was such a success with the audience that Cibber never escaped from it. He adopted a modified Foppington persona when he was out and about in society, including the hours he spent in that masculine establishment, White's Club. However, such a strategy became perilous once fops and mollies were confused in the public mind.

Kristina Straub has shown how, by the time David Garrick came to dominate the London stage, he was well aware of the need not to seem effeminate. He was fortunate in having his first major success in 1741 as Shakespeare's Richard III, and when he took on the part of a fop, as he did in *Miss in Her Teens* in 1747 and *The Male Coquette* ten years later, he was careful to keep a certain distance. Therefore the audience admired his versatility but did not suppose he was playing himself, seeing him rather as 'the satirist who mocked a peverted masculinity that was other to his "real" identity'.[100] Even so, as there was a tradition which associated the theatre with sodomy, he did not escape at least one malicious attack. In 1772 William Kendrick published *Love in the Suds*, in which he suggested that Garrick had had an affair with the dramatist Isaac Bickerstaff, who fled abroad after he was caught propositioning a guardsman. Kendrick's verses were disregarded as the actor was popular and no one believed the accusations. Nevertheless Garrick was anxious, and toyed with the idea of taking legal proceedings against Kendrick.[101] The fact that this attack was made at all showed that the actor's caution in how he presented an image of himself was not misplaced.

The adverse public reaction to transvestite mollies meant that it was not just the fop's sartorial fantasies which became suspect and ultimately unacceptable. For fear of being thought homosexual, men learned to suppress any form of behaviour which might be thought womanish – weeping for instance, and ostentatious displays of affection towards male friends, especially kissing. The Duke of Newcastle, born in the last decade of the seventeenth century, would burst into tears on any emotional occasion. This did not hinder him in his long career as a statesman. Once, when for no very clear reason he was sobbing in the presence of George II, a sympathetic Lord Coventry called on the standers-by to retire with – 'For God's sake gentlemen, don't look at a great man in distress.'[102] However, by the time the King died in 1760, Newcastle's tears at the royal funeral had come to be seen as ridiculous.[103] Yet in both the ancient and earlier modern world men had cried freely.

At the turn of the century kissing between men had become fashionable. In Colley Cibber's *The Lady's Last Stake* (1707) two of the young men about town are energetically pursuing heterosexual adventures. One of them, Lord Wronglove, irritated by a jealous wife who resents his pursuit of other women, catches sight of the other, his friend Sir George Brilliant, and greets him, 'Ah, my Georgy! Kiss,' to which Sir George responds with, 'And kiss, and kiss again, my Dear – By Ganymede there's Nectar on thy Lips. O the pleasure of a Friend to tell the Joy! O Wronglove! Such hopes!'[104] The reason for this euphoria is that Sir George thinks he is making headway with Lady Gentle, a virtuous married woman on whom he has designs, even though he is engaged to yet another girl he says he loves. However, such an unabashed interchange between two incorrigible rakes as the one depicted by Cibber was not possible for very long in the eighteenth century. The author of *Satan's Harvest Home* wrote that of all the customs produced by effeminacy, none was more pernicious than that of men kissing, 'For it is the first Inlet to the detestable Sin of Sodomy.'[105] Many of his readers agreed.

The resulting social pressure exerted on the male sex not to appear effeminate produced an unnatural situation in which the traditionally masculine virtues of energy, courage and fortitude were thought incompatible with the expression of tender feelings. It was left to women to cry easily and demonstrate their affection for one another with hugs and kisses. Such behaviour was considered appropriate in the weaker sex. Meanwhile, males became emotionally inhibited. The phenomenon that two centuries later E. M. Forster was to describe as the 'undeveloped hearts' of Englishmen had its origin in this fear of being thought homosexual.[106]

Notes

1. Pisanus Fraxi (Henry Spencer Ashbee), *Catena Librorum Tacendorum*, in the *Encyclopaedia of Erotic Literature* (New York, 1962). Dissertation 'De Mitigatione Poenae in Crimine Sodomiae' presented by Friedrich August Braun to the Law Faculty of Frankfurt University in 1739, published Frankfurt, 1750.

2. *The Effects of Strangulation*, illustration from *The Bon Ton Magazine* (1739).

3. When Curll published a translation in 1724, *Venus in the Cloister* had already appeared in English, following a sixth French edition.

4. Edward Ward, *The London-Spy Compleat in Eighteen Parts* (1701), Part II, 'To the Reader'.

5. 'The Widow's Coffee-House' in *The London-Spy*, Part II: 5–9.

6. *The Correspondence of Alexander Pope*, ed. George Sherburn, 5 vols (Oxford: Clarendon Press, 1956), I: 277.

7. *The Memoirs of the Extraordinary Life, Works and Discoveries of Martinus Scriblerus*, ed. Charles Kirby-Miller (Oxford University Press, 1950), pp. 146–65.

8. January 25, 1724, quoted by Terry Castle, 'The Culture of Travesty: Sexuality and Masquerade in Eighteenth-Century England', in *Sexual Underworlds of the Enlightenment*, eds G. S. Rousseau and Roy Porter (Manchester University Press, 1987), pp. 156–80, esp. pp. 172–3.

9. *The Lover: a Comedy* (1730), Act I, sc. 1.

10. Horace Walpole, *Corr.*, 17: 339. Letter to Horace Mann, 18 February 1742.

11. Ibid., 17: 359. Letter to Horace Mann, 3 March 1742.

12. *Sexual Underworlds of the Enlightenment*, p. 172.

13. John Cleland, *Memoirs of a Woman of Pleasure*, ed. Peter Sabor (Oxford University Press, 1985), pp. 154–6.

14. *Sessions Papers*, July 1732, case no. 37, pp. 166–70.

15. *L'esprit des lois* (1748), trans. Thomas Nugent, revised J. V. Prichard (University of Chicago Press, 1952), Book 12, ch. 6.

16. 25 Henry 8, c. 6.

17. Alan Bray, *Homosexuality in Renaissance England* (London: Gay Men's Press, 1982), p. 19.

18. Bray, pp. 66ff.

19. *The Calendar of the Home Counties Assizes*, ed. J. S. Cockburn for the period 1559–1625 shows only four indictments for sodomy. For a summary of this and other researches see Bray, p. 71.

20. Roy Porter, *English Society in the Eighteenth Century* (Harmondsworth, Penguin Books Ltd, 1982), p. 54.

21. Randolph Trumbach, 'London's Sodomites: Homosexual Behaviour and Western Culture in the Eighteenth Century', *Journal of Social History*, 2 (1977), 1–33.

22. Rictor Norton, *Mother Clap's Molly House: The Gay Subculture in England 1700–1830* (London: Gay Men's Press, 1992), pp. 92ff.

23. Ned Ward, *A Compleat and Humorous Account of all the Remarkable Clubs and Societies in the Cities of London and Westminster* (London: 1709), 7th edition, 1756, 'The Mollies Club', pp. 265–9.

24. *The Pursuit of Sodomy: Male Homosexuality in Renaissance and*

Enlightenment Europe, eds Kent Gerard and Gert Hekma (New York and London: Harrington Park Press, 1989). As well as essays in this volume, see other works already cited here.

25. 'The Mollies Club', op. cit., p. 266.
26. *A Genuine Narrative of all the Street Robberies of James Dalton* (1728), p. 36.
27. *An Answer to a Late Insolent Libel* ... Anon. but probably written by Jonathan Wild (May 1718?). Quoted Gerald Howson, *It Takes a Thief: The Life and Times of Jonathan Wild* (London: Hutchinson, 1987), p. 63.
28. Norton, p. 55.
29. Ibid., p. 49.
30. Polly Morris, 'Sodomy and Male Honour: the Case of Somerset, 1740–1850', in *The Pursuit of Sodomy*, pp. 383–406.
31. Norton, p. 49.
32. Ibid., p. 51.
33. Ibid., p. 55.
34. Ibid., p. 66.
35. Ibid.
36. *The London-Spy*, December 1698, February 1699 and January 1700.
37. A. D. Harvey, 'Prosecutions for Sodomy in England at the Beginning of the Nineteenth Century', *Historical Journal*, 21.4 (1978), 939–48.
38. 'Socratic Love' in *The Philosophical Dictionary* (1764), ed. and trans. Theodore Besterman (Harmondsworth: Penguin Books Inc., 1971), pp. 31–4.
39. *L'esprit des lois*, Book 12, ch. 6.
40. *Gulliver's Travels and Other Writings*, ed. Louis A. Landa (Boston: The Riverside Press, 1960), 'Gulliver's Travels', Part 4, ch. 7.
41. David Foxon, *Libertine Literature in England 1660–1745* (New York: New Hyde Park, 1965), p. 54.
42. The first verse runs: 'Ye injur'd Females see / Justice without the Laws / Seeing the Injury / Has thus aveng'd your Cause.' The illustrations include two of mollies, one cutting his own throat, the other being taken down by a woman after hanging himself. Copies in the British Museum Print Room and Guildhall Library.
43. Reproduced in Peter Wagner, *Eros Revived: Erotica of the Enlightenment in England and America* (London: Secker and Warburg, 1988), p. 38.
44. Dennis Rubini, 'Sexuality and Augustan England: Sodomy, Politics, Elite Circles and Society', in *The Pursuit of Sodomy*, pp. 349–81.
45. Trumbach, 'London's Sodomites', op. cit., p. 33.
46. Rubini, op. cit., p. 350.
47. Anthony Storr, *The Dynamics of Creation* (London: Secker and Warburg, 1972), p. 137. See also Alfred C. Kinsey, Wordell P. Pomeroy and Clyde Martin, *Sexual Behaviour in the Human Male* (Philadelphia: University of Pennsylvania Press, 1948), p. 638.
48. Bray, pp. 46ff.
49. G. S. Rousseau, 'In the House of Madam Vander Tasse on the Long Bridge: a Homosexual University Club in Early Modern Europe', in *The Pursuit of Sodomy*, pp. 311–47.

50. *Broken Lives: Separation and Divorce in England 1660–1857* (Oxford University Press, 1993), p. 28.

51. J. H. Plumb, *Sir Robert Walpole: The King's Minister* (London: Cresset Press, 1960), p. 91.

52. Timothy Mowl, *Horace Walpole: The Great Outsider* (London: John Murray, 1996), p. 87. Mowl is quoting George II on Lincoln's good looks.

53. Mowl, p. 53 and *passim*.

54. Joseph Spence, *Observations, Anecdotes and Characters of Books and Men*, ed. James M. Osborn, 2 vols (Oxford: Clarendon Press, 1996), no. 279.

55. Spence, no. 274n.

56. *Correspondence of Alexander Pope*, 5 December 1732, III: 335.

57. Spence, no. 656.

58. *Essays of Michel de Montaigne*, trans. Charles Cotton, 3 vols (London: 1685–86), 1: 191–206.

59. Pliny the Younger, *Letters*, trans. William Melmoth (1746), VII.

60. 'Jeremy Bentham's Essay on "Paederasty"', edited and introduced by Louis Crompton, Part I in *Journal of Homosexuality*, 3 (1978), 383–405 and Part II, 4 (1978), 91–107; I: 392–3.

61. Norton, p. 118.

62. Anthony Weldon, *The Court of King James* (1651). Reprinted 1817. The original edition of this work was on sale at the King's Head, in the Old Bailey.

63. Nesca A. Robb, *William Orange: A Personal Portrait* (London, 1962–66), vol. 2, ch. 25 and *passim*.

64. Britannicus (Thomas Gordon), *The Conspirators, Or, The Case of Catiline* (1721).

65. Letter signed 'Caleb D'Anvers', 20 January 1731.

66. *Sessions Papers*, 16–20 January 1730, p. 16.

67. Quoted by Norton, p. 119.

68. Rousseau, op. cit., in *The Pursuit of Sodomy*, pp. 311–47.

69. Act I, sc. 1, ll. 83ff.

70. Act I, sc. 1.

71. Ch. 49 (Oxford University Press, 1969), p. 242.

72. Ibid., ch. 51.

73. *Gentleman's Magazine*, 23 November 1732, vol. 2, p. 1081.

74. *Diary of Viscount Percival, afterwards First Earl of Egmont*, ed. R. A. Roberts, 3 vols (London: Historical Manuscripts Commission, 1920–23), 1: 299.

75. *Discourse on the Worship of Priapus*, reprinted in Ashley Montagu, *Sexual Symbolism: A History of Phallic Worship* (New York: Julian Press, 1957), p. 26.

76. 'The Sorrows of Priapus: anticlericalism, homosocial desire and Richard Payne Knight', in *Sexual Underworlds of the Enlightenment*, p. 102.

77. Horace Walpole, *Corr.*, 29: 339. To the Rev. William Mason, 22 March 1796.

78. *Sexual Underworlds of the Enlightenment*, p. 142.

79. Bentham, op. cit.

80. Bentham, I: 402.

81. Bentham, I: 106.

82. Bentham, II: 96.
83. Bentham, I: 389.
84. Bentham, I: 391.
85. Bentham, I: 394–5.
86. Bentham, I: 397.
87. Bentham, I: 403.
88. Bentham, II: 105.
89. Bentham, II: 106.
90. Bentham, II: 105.
91. Quoted by Gerald Howson, op. cit., p. 64. from J. P. Malcolm, *Anecdotes of London in the Eighteenth Century* (London, 1820).
92. Howson, op cit., p. 64.
93. *Satan's Harvest Home* (London, 1749), ch. 1.
94. John Lawson and Harold Silver, *A Social History of Education in England* (London: Methuen, 1973), ch. 6. The incident took place (within living memory of some of the Westminster School alumni) in 1679.
95. *Satan's Harvest Home*, p. 45.
96. Ibid., p. 48.
97. Ibid., p. 49. See also Chapter 3.
98. Ned Ward, *A Compleat and Humorous Account* ... pp. 90–95. In a description of 'The Beaus Club' we are told the members 'compare Dresses, invent new Fashions, talk lucious Bawdy and drink Healths to their Mistresses'. See also Susan Staves, 'A Few Kind Words for the Fop', *Studies in English Literature*, 22 (1982), 413–28.
99. Act 2, sc. 1.
100. Kristina Straub, *Sexual Suspects: Eighteenth-Century Players and Sexual Ideology* (Princeton University Press, 1992), p. 61.
101. See George W. Stone and George M. Kahrl, *David Garrick: A Critical Biography* (Carbondale: Southern Illinois University Press, 1979).
102. Horace Walpole, *Corr.*, 35: 169–70. Letter to Richard Bentley, 17 March 1754.
103. Horace Walpole, *Corr.*, 9: 323. Letter to George Montagu, 13 November 1760.
104. Act 1, sc. 1.
105. *Satan's Harvest Home*, p. 52.
106. 'Notes on the English Character', in *Abinger Harvest* (London: Edward Arnold, 1920).

PART II

Rhetoric and practice

CHAPTER TWO

Homosexuals and the law

When a homosexual in eighteenth-century London woke up in the morning he knew less than most people what was likely to happen to him that day. He lived dangerously and might at any time have an unlucky encounter which could lead to his prosecution and trial. If that happened he could not predict whether he would next find himself on the gallows, in prison, in the pillory at the mercy of a volatile mob, or free to walk the streets again. How severely he was treated varied from court to court and from decade to decade, if not from year to year. His fate was all the more unpredictable because, although a law on sodomy was in place, there were a number of practical and psychological reasons why this law was difficult to implement.

Legislation

The law itself was uncompromising. When a legal scribe penned an indictment of a suspected sodomite he used William Blackstone's definition and wrote that the man was accused of a crime 'not to be named amongst Christians', though for the sake of clarity he added the phrase 'commonly called Buggery'.[1] Buggery was a portmanteau term. As well as encompassing homosexuality and sexual congress with animals, it was employed where we now use the word 'paedophilia', since no distinction was made between normal homosexuals and paederasts who preyed on very young boys.

Jeremy Bentham quoted an ancient treatise, the *Miroir des Justices*, which showed that sodomites were being hanged in England as early as the reign of Edward I.[2] However, in the eighteenth century the judiciary went by laws passed by the Tudor monarchs. In the first of these, a temporary measure passed in 1533, buggery with man or beast became a capital offence. This ruling was made permanent in 1540. It was then refined during the reign of Edward VI, only to be repealed by Mary Tudor, along with other new legislation that had been passed by Henry VIII. Under Elizabeth I it was placed on the statute books again in 1562 where it stayed until 1861 when it was decided to replace the death penalty for convicted offenders with imprisonment for at least ten years, and possibly for life.[3]

Bringing a prosecution

Before a suspected homosexual could be tried, he had to be arrested and formally charged. Many Europeans who came to England from the seventeenth century onwards observed that the criminal procedure contained various safeguards for anyone accused of committing an offence. One visitor, Abbé Prévost, noted in 1727 that in England 'people are not arrested on vague suspicions and mere probabilities'.[4] The natives took this for granted, as they did the Habeas Corpus Act which prevented a person being arrested illegally or being kept in prison indefinitely without trial.

Nevertheless, Londoners were worried by the realization that, as the capital expanded, a growing number of law breakers were able to go on for years without being arrested at all. This was partly because there was no central police force, yet nobody wanted to see one established because it was feared that, as well as apprehending criminals, such a body would interfere with the liberty of ordinary law-abiding citizens. The Frenchman Le Blanc, writing in 1747, found it incomprehensible that Englishmen 'had rather be robb'd upon the highways' than have a professional law enforcement agency.[5] But then Le Blanc had probably never fallen into the hands of the average bumbling, often officious constable, who was the only kind of law enforcement officer many an Englishman had any experience of and who understandably he did not wish to see multiplied and empowered any further.

In the absence of a central, trained police force, Dogberry and Verges lived on.[6] In the eighteenth century the task of maintaining law and order was in the hands of parish constables whom Shakespeare's audience would have recognized immediately. They were ordinary householders, or their poorly paid deputies, some of them old and physically decrepit and not a few of them corrupt, augmenting their meagre wages with bribes from those they managed to apprehend.[7] In London there was also the Watch who, supplied with lanterns and cudgels, patrolled the streets at night but they, like the constables, were totally inadequate for similar reasons. Added to which they went off duty before daybreak so that the sensible burglar, for instance, waited until they were off the streets before he went about his business.[8]

Except during the first part of the eighteenth century when the Societies for the Reformation of Manners saw to it that 'reforming constables' were recruited at the rate of 12s. a week, there were too few law officers to go out of their way to look for homosexuals.[9] In the 1750s it is unlikely that London's constables and watchmen numbered more than 2000, the majority of whom patrolled the City, although the City had but 12 per cent of the capital's population.[10] For the most part a homosexual

was arrested only if someone to whom he had made unwelcome overtures decided that he ought to be charged, or if some especially zealous
citizen, witnessing what he considered were sodomitical practices, went
in search of a constable. In some cases, perhaps many, the accused would
plead that this was his first offence and/or that he was drunk and had
given in to sudden temptation. Whereupon the would-be prosecutor, or
even the constable, might well let the man go with a few rough words.[11]

Most of the prosecutions of homosexuals were brought by private
individuals. There were two ways in which charges could be brought. In
the first of these the citizen paid a shilling for a warrant to have the
supposed offender arrested. He, having been apprehended, was taken
before one of the local Justices of the Peace. This magistrate listened to
what the prosecutor had to say, examined the offender and, as the
offence he was accused of was serious, did not deal with him personally
but placed him in custody to await trial in court.[12]

Alternatively the prosecutor could go to any London court and frame
an indictment. The cost of an indictment for felony was 3s. 4d., payable
to the Clerk of the Peace or Clerk of the Assize who drew it up.[13] The
completed document was then considered by a Grand Jury, consisting
of 'grave and substantial Gentlemen, or some of the better sort of
Yeomen' who met regularly for this purpose and had the power to
dismiss the charge if it appeared unfounded.[14] The members met *in
camera*, hearing only the prosecution side of the case. If the Grand Jury
passed an indictment as a 'True Bill' in a matter touching life and death,
including sodomy, the accused was arrested, to remain in custody until
his trial. However, if he had money and reputable men to take out
recognizances for him, he was almost certain to be granted bail.

Costs

All the costs of a prosecution were met by the person bringing the case.
As we have seen, these began with paying for an arrest warrant and an
indictment. Thereafter the prosecutor might have to find money for
subpoenas to summon witnesses and for recognizances binding them
over to appear at the proper time. Furthermore, nearly all court em-
ployees, from doorkeepers to bailiffs and criers, as well as clerks, relied
mainly on fees for their income. So the prosecutor had to pay out more
money on the day of the trial, in addition to possibly losing wages if he
had to take time off from work. Finally he might have to meet his travel
expenses and those of witnesses, if the court was not nearby.[15]

It is hard to put an exact figure on the total cost of a prosecution as
there were so many variables, but it has been estimated that at its

lowest it amounted to 10s., which was the average weekly wage of a labourer in London, while it could come to £5 for a straightforward case.[16] Obviously this deterred many who were not well off or very determined from seeking redress in the courts. As a result homosexuals, like other law breakers, lived in hopes of escaping prosecution even if they were detected.

Trials for sodomy

If it was by no means certain that a man caught engaging in homo-sexual practices would be arrested, it was equally uncertain what would happen to him in a court of law, should he be so unfortunate as to find himself in one. In that event, ironically enough, his best chance of regaining his freedom was if he was put on trial for the capital offence of sodomy. The immediate reason for this was that there were strict rules of evidence that must be met before a defendant could be con-victed, whereby it must be shown that both penetration and emission had taken place. Such proof was difficult to provide, especially as hardly any of the participants in a homosexual act had been examined by a doctor. This rule evolved from the words *'rem habuit veneream et carnaliter cognovit'* (knowing sexually and bodily) in indictments for buggery when these were written in Latin, as they were before 1731.[17] In a previous century a looser interpretation had been given to the general idea of carnal knowledge contained in that phrase. In 1631 when Mervin Touchet, the Earl of Castlehaven, was tried for sodomy, a jury of his peers asked 'whether it were accounted Buggery within the Statute without Penetration' and the judges resolved that it was. Ac-cordingly the Earl was executed.[18]

After the more stringent definition of sodomy was adopted, few prosecutions involving the capital charge could be brought successfully. In some trials defendants were acquitted even when the testimony of an eye witness, who had caught them *in flagrante*, seemed to have estab-lished their guilt beyond reasonable doubt.[19] This happened not only in the civil courts but also in the Navy, after a new law in 1749 decreed that any person in His Majesty's fleet who committed sodomy, as well as his aiders and abettors, was to be tried by court martial and sen-tenced to death.[20]

Nor need the relatively few convicted sodomites lose all hope. At the Old Bailey from the middle of the eighteenth century some of those who had been condemned to hang received surprising pardons. In 1751 Michael Levi, a street trader declared guilty of raping a schoolboy, was set free for unknown reasons.[21] Ten years later Thomas Andrews, an

2.1   The courtroom of the Old Bailey, 1753

innkeeper, convicted of sodomizing an unemployed servant, was pardoned, 'to the astonishment of nine persons in ten who knew anything of the case'.[22] In 1772 Captain Jones, found guilty of forcing a thirteen-year-old boy to have sex with him on several occasions, was let off on condition he went to live abroad, this being after 'the utmost interest was exerted in his favour'.[23]

The strict interpretation of the Buggery Act had come into being to ensure as far as possible that a malicious prosecution would not succeed, but it was embraced fervently by those who had to administer the law for a more profound reason. For while no judge or juror in the eighteenth century would have consciously defended homosexuals, many of them were reluctant to send such men to their death. Therefore they welcomed the stringent laws of evidence required for a conviction as a way of escaping this onerous responsibility. Furthermore, bearing in mind what Alan Bray and other social historians have said about the prevalence of casual sodomy, it could also have been that some judges and jurors, in assessing the guilt of men arraigned, thought 'There but for the grace of God goes ... '.[24]

Be that as it may, those who actually had to conduct trials showed themselves unwilling to send to the gallows men and women found guilty of a number of non-violent crimes even though, in displaying this reluctance, they were flying in the face of laws they themselves had helped to pass. For legislators, who included the senior members of the judiciary, had been driven into thinking that the only way of dealing with crime was to hang ever-growing numbers of men, women and even children, for trivial misdeeds. Henry Fielding expressed the theory that determined this attitude. For while he admitted that 'no man of common humanity nor common sense can think the life of a man and a few shillings to be of equal consideration', he vigorously defended capital punishment for anyone who stole a yard or two of lace from a shopkeeper or a snuff box from a gentleman because he said 'the terror of the example' acts as a deterrent 'and one man is sacrificed to the preservation of thousands'.[25]

It was a policy of desperation which did not work. Not only were criminals incurably optimistic, believing that they would not be caught, but those who bore personal responsibility for sending them to their death drew back when it came to the point. Foreign observers, from B. L. de Muralt at the end of the seventeenth century to the Duc de Lévis at the beginning of the nineteenth, regularly expressed astonishment at the number of people who could, in theory, be hanged in England, pointing out that it was inevitable that ways would be sought to save the lives of those convicted of crimes where the statutory punishment was so disproportionate. For as de Muralt observed, when he compared the French and English criminal procedures, where the laws of the country 'happen to be more severe than ordinary, they are but faintly executed'.[26] And more than a hundred years later the Duc de Lévis noted that because of laws that punished a man who had stolen a guinea as drastically as the one who had killed a brother in cold blood, advantage was taken of every trivial circumstance to acquit the accused.[27] This last conclusion is also one a modern observer comes to when reading accounts of sodomy trials at the Old Bailey in the decades immediately following 1730.

Yet it proved impossible in eighteenth-century England to reduce the number of capital charges on the statute books. Indeed that number rose relentlessly. When de Muralt wrote in 1694, there were about 50 offences that carried the death penalty. During the reign of George II another 33 were added and 63 more under George III.[28] A House of Commons committee, set up in 1750, had recommended that alternatives to capital punishment should be adopted for some crimes but the recommendation failed to get through the House of Lords.[29] Twenty-five years later Jeremy Bentham proposed that the death penalty be retained only for murder and predicted that the time would come when even for that crime it would be replaced by life imprisonment.[30] However, as with his views on the decriminalization of homosexuality, Bentham was ahead of his time.

Nevertheless, as the century wore on, more and more people had their misgivings about seeing the capital statutes enforced in all their full rigour for any save the more serious offences. By 1771 the judges in London were recommending that the King pardon half those whom they were forced to sentence to death.[31] And well before that homosexuals were among those who benefited from a discrepancy between theory and practice. By 1730 a sodomite was less likely to be hanged than a highwayman or a forger.[32]

Because of obstacles placed in the way of securing a conviction for sodomy, the majority of men who found themselves in court for homosexual offences were indicted for attempting a sodomitical assault. On this lesser charge it was more unusual to be acquitted, though here again the outcome of a trial was rarely decided on purely objective grounds. The emotion generated by a case was just as important, while fluctuating public opinion, social prejudice and the personality of the judge all played their part.

Public opinion

The most obvious example of the way public opinion influenced the judicial process came in the first part of the century when the campaign waged by the Reforming Societies against the mollies, together with the sensational coverage of the activities of effeminate homosexuals by journalists and pamphleteers, convinced the populace that the molly subculture was a danger to society that must be eradicated. The public mood was carried over into the courts so that more homosexuals were put to death in the first three decades than in the whole of the rest of the century put together.

Yet even at that time there were counter-influences at work, so that when the pogrom was at its height not every convicted sodomite served his sentence. At the end of 1698 Edward Rigby, Captain of a man-of-war called *The Dragon*, was entrapped by Thomas Bray, a member of the Society for the Reformation of Manners who set him up with a nineteen-year-old servant and had him arrested. This was the second time Captain Rigby had been arraigned for a homosexual offence. Earlier in the year he had been tried for sodomy at a court martial but on that occasion had been acquitted. Now at the Old Bailey, Rigby was found guilty of making a sodomitical assault on the boy who, at Bray's behest, had tempted him in a tavern in Pall Mall. He was sentenced to stand in the pillory thrice, to serve a year in prison and fined £1000. However, he was helped to escape to France soon after this sentence was pronounced. There he became a highly regarded commander in the French navy, living to fight again – against the British![33]

Prejudice

All the usual prejudices to which human beings are prone could influence the verdict in trials for sodomitical offences. The Protestant peers who condemned Lord Castlehaven in 1631 may well have been swayed in their judgement by the fact that he was a Catholic. In the next century it did not help a prosecutor or a defendant in the London courts if he was Irish. On the whole, though, religious and national prejudice was spasmodic.

Social prejudice, on the other hand, was endemic. This did not mean that if you were a gentleman you would automatically be acquitted when charged with attempted sodomy. Prejudice of this kind worked in a more subtle fashion so that the middle-class jurors were hardly aware of how far they were influenced by an initial and superficial impression created by defendants and prosecutors. Yet anyone now reading the accounts of trials for sodomitical assault in any of the London courts notices how a confident witness, who came from the same background as the jurors, was more likely to receive a sympathetic hearing than an ill-educated, ill-kempt errand boy, even if the evidence produced by the latter was cogent enough.[34]

The judge

The personality of a judge was important, not least because his role in eighteenth-century trials was strenuous, in that he did more than adjudicate. Few prosecutors or defendants took counsel, so the judge acted as lawyer for both sides, cross-examining the witnesses, sometimes going through their testimony line by line. For the most part he did this dispassionately, though if he chose to browbeat any of those who gave evidence there was no one else to whom they could turn. Some men who sat on the bench were by temperament more brutal than others. Mercifully, there were no 'infamous Jeffreys';[35] nevertheless, few prisoners, including homosexuals, relished the thought of appearing before Sir Francis Page, who went out of his way to cultivate his reputation for 'insolence and severity'.[36]

In private life the vices of a judge might be writ large. Some, such as Sir John Willes, were disreputable rakes. Still more, like Robert Henley, Lord Northington, were alcoholics and numerous others were mercenary and grasping. Yet in their professional capacity most of them were competent in the law and conscientious, while quite a few of them were humane.[37] When they saw that the accused had no one to speak for him, they became what one journalist, writing in the *Whitehall Evening Post*, said every judge should be, 'the advocate for the prisoner in every way where justice would permit it'.[38] In trials for men accused of sodomitical offences they were usually careful to establish that the story told by the prosecutor was convincingly corroborated because they were aware that, short of being put to death, a man could suffer no worse fate than to be publicly branded a sodomite.

The case load of an English judge was heavy. Fifty trials or more might be held in a Sessions at the Old Bailey of three or four days.[39] Yet some of the hearings were extensive, including the ones involving sodomy. On the Continent a judge was given a dossier beforehand, summarizing the pre-trial investigations of the prisoner he was to see.[40] His English counterpart came to court unprepared for any of the trials he was to preside over that day and had to pick up the stories as he went along. So as well as working hard, he had to keep his wits about him. He usually took notes during the proceedings, using these when he summed up the evidence for the jurors before he told them what verdict he thought they should reach. When a man was on trial for sodomy it was up to the judge to remind the jury that the standard of evidence required to confirm the prisoner's guilt was high, going beyond the usual legal stipulation that this must be established beyond reasonable doubt. On several occasions the *Sessions Papers* for such trials show that a judge said this standard had not been reached.[41]

In the event of prisoners being convicted on any capital charge, it was usually the judge who made recommendations for pardons when he felt these were deserved. He kept a list and at the end of the Sessions forwarded this to the King for approval.[42] If the convicted man was a sodomite, however, it was more likely he, the prisoner, who, supported by his friends, applied via a secretary of state for royal mercy. When this happened the advice of the trial judge was always sought before any decision was reached. In the case of Captain Jones, who was respited on the day set for his execution, an express had been despatched to York requesting Sir John Willes to return to London so that he could be consulted before the man he had condemned to death was granted his reprieve.[43]

When a prisoner was convicted of a misdemeanour, including the charge of attempted sodomy, the judge had wide discretionary powers in deciding the punishment and his decision was final because the question of a pardon did not arise. Lord Mansfield once told a newly appointed colonial governor who was anxious because he had little knowledge of the law, 'Consider what you think justice requires, and decide accordingly, but never give your reasons.'[44] Most of his colleagues would have gone along with this advice. They were despots on the bench, benevolent or otherwise. They were supremely confident because, appointed by the Crown, they could only be removed by an address to both Houses of Parliament. Nor did the Constitution allow politicians to influence their judgement for any reason of state.[45] That being said, there was little conflict between the judiciary and the government in the eighteenth century. Members of both came from the same class and shared many of the same beliefs and attitudes, including an unspoken ambivalence about homosexuality.

The jury

Jurors were supposedly chosen at random by a sheriff from the list of householders in his area. In London these were often tradesmen. Not all those eligible wished to serve on a jury, however, and it was not unknown for those called to bribe the empanelling officers so as to be excused.[46] As a result men known to be willing to undertake this duty were called on a regular basis.[47] There is also evidence that some jurors were selected because they had experience of trials for certain types of crime, including sodomitical offences.[48] In theory prisoners were allowed to reject up to twenty-four possible jurors, but the system for doing so was complicated and few exercised this right. In practice a jury sworn in when the Sessions at the Old Bailey opened remained in place throughout successive trials held at that time.[49] Sometimes jurors played an active part in the proceedings, asking the witnesses, as well as the judge, questions.[50]

The system of trial by jury was praised by foreign observers and regarded with considerable satisfaction by the English themselves. As one contributor to the *Gentleman's Magazine* wrote, 'of all the boasted privileges of our constitution, there is none which shines more eminently conspicuous than trial by jury. This invaluable prerogative is the birthright of every Englishman and sets us apart from the arbitrary decisions in other countries.'[51] Jurors could ignore the direction of a judge when they brought in a verdict, and occasionally they did so, whereupon the judge usually accepted their decision, though he could send them back to reconsider, or even order a new trial if their verdict was against the weight of evidence.[52] For the most part, however, jurors felt a moral obligation to follow the judge's direction. Furthermore, they were likely to share his moral values. This seems to have been so in trials for sodomitical offences where there is no clear instance of disagreement between the jury and the Bench.[53] In any case most juries arrived at a verdict within fifteen minutes, without leaving the courtroom. If for any reason they did retire, they were deprived of food, water and light until they came to a decison – a state of affairs which no doubt discouraged argument.

Taking counsel

The practice of either a prosecutor or a defendant employing counsel to argue his case in court was in its infancy in the eighteenth century. It began with prosecutors hiring lawyers in the 1720s, followed by some defendants doing so in the 1730s.[54] After this it soon became apparent that anyone who could afford to take counsel found the expense worthwhile, especially if he wished to prove that a charge of sodomy was the result of a malicious prosecution.[55] One study of 171 cases heard at the Old Bailey in the 1750s has shown that lawyers appeared for clients in twelve trials, and that where they appeared for the defence the rate of acquittal was well above average.[56] This is hardly surprising. A defence counsel, unlike a judge, had time to prepare himself before coming to court. He took over the task of cross-examining witnesses and as a result of his prior investigations he was able to throw doubt on the reliability and motivation of those who spoke for the prosecution, pointing out if any of these bore a grudge against the prisoner, or stood to gain financially by giving evidence against him. As the defence counsel spoke for the client he was also able to prevent him from making damaging admissions.

In the majority of trials, however, a prisoner did not have the money to hire a lawyer, so he defended himself in court. To enable him to do so he was allowed to cross-examine the prosecution witnesses, with whose evidence every trial began. He could also call his own witnesses. Finally, he could give his own version of events. Few people at the time thought this was anything but fair because there was a long-established belief that an honest man could best show his own innocence.[57] Obviously, though, such a system favoured the more intelligent and articulate.

A prisoner without counsel also laboured under another disadvantage. The first time he heard the indictment of him read out was when he was arraigned, whereupon if he pleaded 'Not Guilty' his trial followed soon after, probably within days. Having heard the indictment he was still kept in ignorance of the names of witnesses and evidence against him until he appeared in court again. In these circumstances it was hardly possible for him to prepare his own best defence beforehand, particularly if he spent the interim in prison, as he was likely to do if he was poor and had not obtained bail. From prison it would also be difficult for him to find and summon witnesses on his behalf, let alone pay for subpoenas and recognizances that would bind them over to appear with him in court. Quite often in trials for attempted sodomy we find that whereas the prosecutor has been able to marshal several witnesses to support his story, the prisoner without means has no one to speak for him, even though he might name a person who could have done so.[58]

The law of evidence

In many kinds of trials jurors were influenced in the prisoner's favour if character witnesses came forward to speak for the prisoner, though in sodomy cases in particular there was no way of predicting what the outcome of such evidence would be. Sometimes the testimony of a single individual who swore that he did not believe the defendant was homosexual was enough to save him, while at other times similar affirmations by half a dozen citizens of probity and some standing in society were of no avail.[59]

On the other hand the testimony of a single prosecution witness was sufficient to ensure a conviction for many kinds of crime in the eighteenth century unless, as Baron Gilbert wrote in 1760, 'there be some probability to the contrary'.[60] Once again, however, the situation in trials for sodomitical offences was somewhat different. In these, because the courts were acutely aware of the danger of malicious prosecutions for sodomy, corroboration was usually demanded. So a young boy who claimed he had been raped might well lose his case if his testimony was unsupported.[61]

Above all, any suggestion that a victim of a supposed homosexual attack had hoped to gain financially by his accusation might well result in the prisoner going free. This was why the innkeeper Thomas Andrews received his surprising pardon after being convicted of sodomizing John Finnimore in 1761. The weight of evidence for the prosecution, which included stained bed linen and a surgeon's report, was finally discounted. Apparently, Andrews had been willing to pay Finnimore if he would sign a paper agreeing not to press charges – something even a blameless man might do when threatened with prosecution for sodomy. He was released unconditionally in the end because it emerged that Finnimore had been willing to do as Andrews suggested, but that one of his friends stopped him with the words, 'You shall sign nothing, we will have some smart money.'[62]

The same wish not to be duped by a malicious prosecutor also meant that the courts were usually strict about not accepting hearsay evidence in trials involving sodomy. For that matter the use of hearsay evidence in all trials was under suspicion before the eighteenth century began because the reported comments were made by persons not speaking under oath. However, in 1760 Gilbert wrote that 'though hearsay be not allowed as direct evidence, yet it may be in corroboration of a witness's testimony'.[63]

The law of evidence was still in a state of flux in the eighteenth century, so whether hearsay was allowed in corroboration of sworn testimony varied from court to court and judge to judge, though, as has been shown, the standard of proof required was so high that hearsay was unlikely to be accepted when a man was being tried for the so-called 'worst of crimes'.[64]

The sentence

More than one judge told a prisoner convicted of a homosexual offence that his was the worst crime he could have committed.[65] This was the official rhetoric which could not be gainsaid. Yet the sentences pronounced on men convicted of attempted sodomy were less severe than those for men and women found guilty of property crimes. When meting out punishment for a sodomitical misdemeanour, the judge usually imposed any or all of the following penalties: the pillory, prison, a fine.

Convicted homosexuals were often made to stand in the pillory at least once, usually near the scene of the offence. There were occasions when the mob threw stones and bricks, seriously injuring or killing the wretch at their mercy, but this was unusual. It came about when the prisoner was notorious and the crowd had been organized before-hand.[66] In the majority of cases a man exposed in public as a sodomite was pelted with rotting vegetables and the odd dead cat, emerging physically intact, if humiliated. On the other hand anyone convicted of grand larceny, that is of theft of goods worth more than a shilling, was liable to be branded for life by being burned on the hand, should he or she succeed in having the statutory death sentence commuted.

There was also considerable variety in the other sentences pronounced on men found guilty of attempted sodomy. Prison sentences might be as short as one month and were rarely longer than two years, whereas thieves were regularly transported for at least seven. Fines imposed on a convicted sodomite ranged from one thousand pounds to one shilling because they were supposed to reflect his financial circumstances. Nevertheless there were trials in which heavy fines were inflicted on poor men who, as they had to stay in prison until the fine was paid, might remain there interminably.[67] The size of the fine a judge imposed is a way of telling whether he was one of the harsher men who sat on the bench. A large one might well indicate that he thought it best if the prisoner were kept off the streets for as long as possible.

As was suggested at the beginning of this account of how the law on sodomy was applied in the eighteenth century, no homosexual could be sure from one day to the next what was likely to happen to him. The law and the official rhetoric declared that he deserved to be hanged. Yet, fortunately for those they condemned, English heterosexuals did not always practise what they preached. Their treatment of homosexuals was varied and complex.

The best place to study the diversity of response of eighteenth-century Englishmen to those they called sodomites or mollies is London, with its large, heterogeneous population. Anyone there whose way of life brought him into regular contact with other people was likely to encounter homosexuals from time to time. How he behaved when he did so can be studied by reading the testimony given in trials of defendants indicted for sodomitical practices. Of course most of the participants in these trials were male, including all the judiciary and jurors, but women did come forward as witnesses and their reactions were as varied as those of the men.

The next part of this book describes a series of cases involving sodomy that were heard in the Old Bailey between 1730 and 1751. These twenty-one years have been chosen, first of all, because the trials held then were no longer distorted by the fevered zeal of the Reforming Societies that affected the atmosphere in the courts earlier in the century. Second, there is an unbroken sequence of *Sessions Papers* available for the 1730s and 1740s, whereas after 1750 the extant records are spasmodic and do not always include the trials of those accused of sodomitical practices. Last, but by no means least, the presentation of seventeen case histories enables the reader to see for himself or herself how homosexuals fared at the main criminal court in London and decide whether or not the comments made in this general survey hold true.

The reporters who wrote up the trials of suspected sodomites during most of the period in question did so in considerable detail, using some form of speed writing, even before Thomas Gurney, who devised and popularized his own shorthand system, became the Old Bailey reporter in 1748. They tell us what was said by the assorted tradesmen, tailors, shoemakers, innkeepers and their wives, watermen and washerwomen who were called as witnesses. Some of those who gave evidence had an enviable command of the telling phrase, bringing such contrasting homosexuals as John Cooper and Richard Manning to life again on the page as we read.

This candour did not last very long. Already in 1742 we find one particular Old Bailey reporter who showed a new reticence in writing down the physical details of sodomy related by witnesses in the trials he attended because, he said, 'they were not fit to be committed to paper'.[68] By 1771 William Eden, in a pioneering work on penal reform, was questioning whether it was wise to have public prosecutions at all in cases of sodomy, 'which some have thought unsafe, and rather to solicit attention, than deter from crime'.[69] Predictably, the idea of abandoning public trials of this nature was too extreme to gain general support. If anything, the determination to prosecute and punish homosexuals increased in the decades after Eden wrote, so that by the 1830s the number of men executed for sodomy was ten times the average figure in the eighteenth century.[70] Many people, however, shared the belief that giving homosexuality publicity served more to encourage than 'deter from crime'. Soon hardly any reports of sodomy trials were printed and sold. Therefore the Old Bailey *Sessions Papers* for the couple of decades or so beginning in 1730 provide us with an unusual opportunity to discover what people from various walks of life said and did about a particular aspect of sexual life before it became the 'Love that dare not speak its name'.[71]

Notes

1. William Blackstone, *Commentaries on the Laws of England*, 4 vols, 9th edn (1783), 4: 215.
2. *Miroir des Justices*, ch. 4: 14, quoted in 'Jeremy Bentham's Essay on "Paederasty"', *Journal of Homosexuality*, 4 (1978), Part II: 94.
3. The laws referred to are: 25 Hen. 8, c. 6; 32 Hen. 8, c. 3; 2/3 Edw. 6, c. 29; 1 Mar. St. 1, c. 1, cl. 3; 5 Eliz. c. 17 and 24/25 Vict. c. 100, cl. 61.
4. *Mémoires d'un homme de qualité* (1728–31), trans. and ed. M. E. I. Robertson (London, 1930).
5. J. B. le Blanc, *Letters on the English and French Nations*, 2 vols. Written *c.* 1737, trans. from French 1747.
6. *Much Ado about Nothing* (1598–99).
7. Edward Ward, *The London-Spy Compleat in Eighteen Parts* (1701), December 1698 and January 1700.
8. Leon Radzinowicz, *A History of Criminal Law and its Administration*, 5 vols (London: Stevens, 1948–86), 2: 195.
9. *The London-Spy*, January 1700.
10. Donald Rumbelow, *I Spy Blue: The Police and Crime in the City of London from Elizabeth I to Victoria* (London: Macmillan, 1971), p. 79.
11. *Sessions Papers*, July 1749, case no. 472, trial of Richard Spencer.
12. J. M. Beattie, *Crime and the Courts in England 1600–1800* (Oxford: Clarendon Press, 1986), pp. 267ff.
13. Ibid.
14. Dr Cowell, *A Law Dictionary, or the Interpreter of Words and Terms* (London, 1727).
15. Beattie, pp. 41ff.
16. Beattie, p. 41 and note. See also Douglas Hay and Francis Snyder, eds, *Policing and Prosecution in Britain, 1750–1850* (Oxford: Clarendon Press, 1989), Introduction.
17. Giles Jacob, *Law Dictionary* (London, 1729). In his entry for 'Buggery' Jacob states 'some Kind of Penetration and Emission must be proved, but any the least Kind is sufficient'.
18. *A Complete Collection of State Trials*, ed. T. B. Howell (London, 1809–26), 3: 402–18.
19. *Sessions Papers*, December 1730, p. 8, trial of William Holiwell and William Huggins.
20. 22 Geo. 2, c. 33, s. 2, 29. See Arthur N. Gilbert, 'Buggery and the British Navy 1700–1861', *Journal of Social History*, 10.1 (1976), 72–98, especially the court martial of Martin Billin and James Bryan in 1762.
21. *Gentleman's Magazine* (1751), 'Historical Chronicle', 17 June, p. 281.
22. *The Newgate Calendar*, eds Andrew Knapp and William Baldwin, 6 vols (London, 1825), 2: 288.
23. *New and Complete Newgate Calendar*, ed. William Jackson, 8 vols (London, 1818), 5: 104.

24. John Bradford (1510?–1555), his comment on seeing men taken off to be hanged.
25. Radzinowicz, 1: 410.
26. B. L. de Muralt, *Letters describing the Character and Customs of the English and French Nations* (London, 1726), written *c.* 1694.
27. P. M. G. Lévis, Duc de, *L'Angleterre au commencement du dix-neuvième siècle* (Paris, 1814).
28. Radzinowicz, 1: 3–4, and Douglas Hay, *Albion's Fatal Tree* (London: Peregrine Books, 1975). Hay states that the latest evidence shows that 'the number of capital statutes grew from about 50 to over 500 between 1688 and 1820' (p. 18).
29. Radzinowicz, 1: 419 and 422.
30. *Rationale of Punishment* (London, 1775), quoted Radzinowicz, 1: 390.
31. Radzinowicz, 1: ch. 5, note 26.
32. A. D. Harvey, 'Prosecutions for Sodomy in England at the Beginning of the Nineteenth Century', *Historical Journal*, 21.4 (1978), 939–48.
33. *An Account of the Proceedings Against Capt. Edward Rigby* (London, 1698) and John Charnock, *Biographia Navalis* (1795), 3: 50–51.
34. *Sessions Papers*, May 1735, case no. 50, trial of Henry Wolf, and April/ May 1742, case no. 21, trial of William Nichols.
35. Baron George Jeffreys (1648–89) earned that appellation when he presided over the 'Bloody Assize' after the Monmouth Rebellion in 1685.
36. Samuel Johnson, 'Life of Savage' in *The Lives of the English Poets*, ed. G. B. Hill, 3 vols (Oxford: Clarendon Press, 1905).
37. According to Horace Walpole, Lord Henley realized eventually that drink had destroyed his abilities: Horace Walpole, *Corr.*, letter to the Earl of Hertford, 29 December 1763. Sir John Willes was commonly supposed to have modelled for the seducer in Hogarth's indoor *Before* and *After* in 1730. Hogarth, who obviously did not like him, also satirized him in *The Bench* in 1757 when Willes was Lord Chief Justice. See Jenny Uglow, *Hogarth: A Life and a World* (London: Faber, 1997), p. 607.
38. *Whitehall Evening Post*, 16 January 1783.
39. John H. Langbein, 'Shaping the Eighteenth-Century Trial: A View of the Ryder Sources', *University of Chicago Law Review*, 50.1 (Winter, 1983), 1–136, sections 1 and 7. In the Old Bailey Sessions 86 cases were heard in four days in September 1730 and in the next Sessions in December that year 83 cases were heard.
40. Ibid., section 8.
41. *Sessions Papers*, April/May 1742, case no. 21, trial of William Nichols.
42. Beattie, pp. 430ff.
43. *Annual Register*, 11 August 1772, p. 121.
44. John Campbell, *Lives of the Chief Justices of England*, 3 vols, 2nd edn (London, 1858).
45. Basil Williams, *The Whig Supremacy 1714–1760* (Oxford: Clarendon Press, 1962), p. 57. See also John Campbell, 2: 184 for Robert Walpole's abortive attempt to persuade Chief Justice Pratt to change his judgment on Richard Bentley.
46. James Oldham, *The Mansfield Manuscripts and the Growth of the English Law in the Eighteenth Century*, 2 vols (Chapel Hill: University of North Carolina Press, 1992), p. 91.
47. Langbein, p. 115.

48. Ibid.
49. Cèsar de Saussure, *A Foreign View of England in the Reigns of George I and George II* (1725–35), trans. Mdme van Muyden (London: John Murray, 1902), p. 118.
50. Beattie, p. 344.
51. *Gentleman's Magazine* (1777), p. 214.
52. Oldham, p. 90.
53. See, however, discussion of the trial of Michael Levi, Chapter 7 in this volume.
54. Beattie, p. 352ff.
55. See Chapter 6 in this volume.
56. Langbein, section 8.
57. Beattie, p. 341.
58. *Sessions Papers*, January 1745, case nos 142/3 and January 1746, case no. 87, trials of Richard Manning.
59. *Sessions Papers*, December 1742, case nos 27, trial of Thomas Pryor, and May 1751, case no. 389, trial of Michael Levi.
60. G. Gilbert, *The Law of Evidence, with Notes and Additional References to Contemporary Writers by James Sedgwick* (London, 1801), written 1760, p. 133.
61. *Sessions Papers*, May 1735, case no. 50, trial of Henry Wolf.
62. *Tyburn Chronicle*, 4 vols (London, *c.* 1769), 4: 137.
63. Gilbert, pp. 135–6.
64. *Sessions Papers*, May 1751, case no. 389, trial of Michael Levi.
65. *Sessions Papers*, January 1746, case no. 87, trial of Richard Manning and Judge Ashhurst, R. *v.* Hickman, 1784.
66. *Evening Post*, 2 May 1727 and *Parker's Penny Post*, 3 May 1727 have reports of the savage treatment by an incensed mob of the notorious Under City Marshal Charles Hitchen, who had been convicted of attempted sodomy.
67. Beattie, p. 459. See also *The London-Spy*, April 1699, p. 10 for Ned Ward's encounter with a 'ghastly skeleton' of a man in the Bridewell who had served his sentence but was kept there because he could not pay the fees extracted from all prisoners prior to release.
68. *Sessions Papers*, April/May 1742, case no. 21, trial of William Nichols, and December 1742, case no. 27, trial of Thomas Pryor.
69. William Eden, *Principles of Penal Law* (London, 1771), p. 269.
70. A. D. Harvey, p. 948.
71. Lord Alfred Douglas, 'Two Loves', first printed in the Oxford undergraduate magazine, *Chameleon*, December 1894.

PART III

Sodomy and the Old Bailey, 1730–51

CHAPTER THREE

Judge Page and others, 1730

In 1730 seven men came to the Old Bailey indicted in cases which, in one way or another, involved sodomy. All of them were convicted. Five of them were tried by Sir Francis Page who, in a long career on the Bench, had shown himself, in Alexander Pope's words, 'always ready to hang any man'.[1] However, it was not this notorious judge who despatched any of the men found guilty to the gallows, but James Reynolds, who is best known for the prayer he uttered every day before he began work, in which he asked God 'for that measure of understanding and discernment, that spirit of justice, and that portion of courage' as would enable and dispose him to judge and determine those weighty affairs that might that day fall unto his consideration, 'without error or perplexity, without fear or affection, without prejudice or passion, without vanity or ostentation'.[2]

Reynolds presided over the trial of Williamson Goodman who, in the January Sessions, was charged with making a sodomitical assault on Henry Thompson and with 'putting him in fear and taking from him 9/ 6d. in money'. Thompson as prosecutor told the court how he had stopped the defendant in Chancery Lane to ask him the way. Goodman had then invited him back to his lodgings in Mary Le Strand. Once there he had begun talking about sodomy and of 'great Persons that us'd that way'. The discomfited Thompson sat listening until Goodman offered him sexual favours, whereupon he jumped up to leave. At this the defendant changed tack and threatened to have Thompson himself taken up for sodomy unless he gave him money. When Thompson refused, Goodman 'seized him by the collar' and took 9s. 6d. from his pocket 'by force'. This was not the end of the matter because Goodman had found out where the prosecutor lived and shortly afterwards appeared at his house, this time accompanied by another man, who claimed to be a constable. He again threatened to 'swear Sodomy' against Thompson unless he paid him not to. Again Thompson refused, whereupon the supposed constable ran off and the prosecutor had the defendant arrested. The jury found Goodman guilty of both charges in the indictment and Judge Reynolds sentenced him to death.[3]

This is the most unusual result in any of the seventeen cases considered here. First of all, it is the only one in which we can be sure that the convicted man actually hanged. Second, it is not immediately clear why Reynolds arrived at the judgement he did. Goodman could not be sent

The Hon.ble Sr FRANCIS PAGE Kt.
one of the BARONS of his Majty Court of EXCHEQUER 1720.

3.1 Sir Francis Page. (1661?–1741). He served as a judge at the Old Bailey
until the year of his death, still 'hanging on, hanging on' as he had told a
colleague who, meeting him on the courtroom steps, asked how he was.

to the gallows for attempted sodomy as this was not a capital charge. Extortion was, under the Waltham Black Act of 1723, though the relevant section in that Act was designed to deal with threats made in letters, signed or unsigned.[4] Even so, it was by no means axiomatic that a person making a written demand for money in this way would receive a death sentence. Goodman was probably condemned under the Robbery Act of 1692.[5] This law covered theft from persons but was another of those pieces of legislation that was liberally interpreted. Much depended on the construction put upon the alleged crime by the courts, 'especially on the elements of violence and fear'.[6] Goodman had used force when he took the 9s. 6d. from Thompson. He was innately violent, breaking out of the Round House after his arrest, though he was soon recaptured. Above all, he had inspired fear in a respectable citizen by threatening to accuse him of the worst of crimes. So in all probability it was this which made the decent and conscientious Judge Reynolds decide that the world would be better off without him.

In May 1730 Judge Page presided over the first of the sodomy trials that came his way in the Old Bailey that year. Strictly speaking, Isaac Broderick, the defendant, was a paedophile rather than a homosexual. He was the Master at the Free School of the Coopers Company in Stepney and there were two indictments lodged against him. In the first he was accused of sexually assaulting Edward Caley, aged ten years, and in the second of committing a similar offence against William Ham, who was eleven years old. Both were pupils at the school and both testified. Their stories, which they told clearly and simply, were similar. Broderick had invented various pretexts to get them alone, and after making them take down their breeches, had stroked them 'all over'. In Caley's case he had gone somewhat further, stopping just short of buggery. According to William Ham, he and Caley were not the only objects of Broderick's attentions. He named five other boys, all between the ages of ten and eleven, who had also been molested. The case had been brought to the attention of the authorities by the children's parents when they found out what was happening.

When Broderick had first appeared before an examining magistrate he had said little, except that he had behaved as he had done with one of the boys 'to improve him in his Studies'. By the time he appeared in the Old Bailey, however, he was able to offer a more credible defence. He claimed that he was the victim of a malicious prosecution, concocted by his enemies who had wanted a Mr Vere appointed Master of the school in his place. He was also able to produce respectable character witnesses, including one from his days at Cambridge, who said 'I believe all Trinity College would give him a good Character.' None of this convinced Judge Page, who directed the jury to find the defendant

guilty of assaulting both William Ham and Edward Caley and, following instructions, the jury did so. Nor was the verdict surprising. The
evidence given by the two boys had been detailed, and of a kind that
indicated experience of the episodes described, rather than sounding
made up. Broderick was sentenced to stand in the pillory twice, spend
three months in gaol and pay a fine of fifty nobles, that is, £16.67.[7]

This punishment was comprehensive. Judge Page, as he usually did,
made full use of the varied penalties that he could exact in the case of a
man convicted of attempted sodomy. It was not an unduly harsh sentence, however. In deciding on it, Page had kept well within the possible
limits for an offence of this kind.

In December 1730 Judge Page heard two more cases which involved
sodomy. In the first one William Holiwell (or Hollywell) appeared at the
Old Bailey accused of making an assault on William Huggins with the
intention of committing sodomy. William Huggins was accused of consenting and submitting to the same. John Rowden, a guide in St Paul's
Cathedral, was the chief witness for the prosecution. He testified that one
day in November he was just going home to dinner at one o'clock when
he heard a noise. Looking through the light of the Newel Stairs, he saw
the defendants in 'a very indecent posture'. From the account that Rowden
then gave of what the men were doing, the court was left in little doubt
that Holiwell was engaged in buggering Huggins. Very soon the men
realized they were being watched and tried to run off, with Huggins
pulling up his breeches as he went. After a brief chase Rowden succeeded
in locking them both in a side aisle and went off to tell the Clerk of the
Works, who in turn told the Dean. The three men then went back into the
cathedral. By this time Holiwell had got out of the side aisle but was
found again in a gallery next to the organ loft. After that the defendants
were taken before a magistrate, who charged them and sent them for
trial. Huggins, a waterman, called several witnesses to testify that he was
'a loving husband and a tender father', but Holiwell made no attempt to
defend himself. Both men were convicted. They were saved from being
condemned to death on a capital charge because it was decided that
semen marks on Huggins's shirt could mean that penetration had not
taken place. Judge Page sentenced both men to stand in the pillory near
the cathedral for one hour. In addition, Huggins was given eight months
in gaol. Holiwell only got six months but, unlike his co-defendant, he was
fined £40.[8] As he might well have difficulty in finding such a large sum
and would have to stay in prison until he did so, the shorter sentence
meted out to him was a purely theoretical advantage.

This case is an example of the way in which a judge and jury made
use of the stringent legal requirements necessary before convicting defendants of sodomy, to avoid sending them to their death, even though

it was obvious from the tenor of Rowden's testimony that he thought he was saying enough to get them hanged. Nevertheless it is also clear, from the length of the prison sentences passed, as well as the sizeable fine imposed on Holiwell, that Judge Page took a sterner view of a homosexual act between two consenting adults than he did of paedophilia. In this he was very much a man of his time.

Judge Page was also a man of his time in his reaction to blackmailers. Later in the Old Bailey Sessions of December 1730 he tried John Lewis and John Jones. They were charged with conspiracy, in that they had threatened to accuse a reasonably prosperous master workman, John Battle, of sodomy unless he paid them hush money. Throughout, Jones had done the talking. Lewis, a sickly boy who had been in the Bridewell, played his part as a supposed victim. The scheme they concocted was more elaborate than the *ad hoc* one which had despatched Williamson Goodman to Tyburn earlier in the year. The story began when Jones called to see Battle at his workshop where an apprentice told him he would find the master at the Castle Inn in Mark Street. There Jones confronted Battle with Lewis, who stood, apparently in pain, leaning on a broomstick. Jones explained that the boy had a fistula and that a surgeon who had treated him said 'it came by Buggery'. Jones then demanded ten guineas to pay the surgeon's fee because Lewis declared that Battle was responsible for his plight. The alternative was exposure as a sodomite.

At the Old Bailey Battle admitted that he gave Jones half a guinea and promised more, 'being in great Confusion at having such a Crime charged upon [him], fearing that [his] Reputation would be blasted if it should come to the Ears of [his] Neighbours'. The following day, Saturday, 7 November, Battle paid the pair another nine guineas, for which he secured a receipt and the promise that Lewis would set sail for Holland forthwith. However, on Monday Jones was back, with a story that Lewis had lost all the money over the weekend in a gaming house. He demanded twenty guineas more, otherwise Lewis's mother would come to the house and 'make a riot'.

At this point Battle decided to consult a lawyer, who earned his fee by helping him to get a warrant for the arrest of his persecutors. Jones and Lewis had not expected such an outcome to their campaign and, when brought before a magistrate, went to pieces and made a confession in which they admitted that 'they had never seen John Battle before in their lives' prior to extorting money from him. The following month, in the Old Bailey, they were both convicted. Judge Page sentenced them to stand in the pillory twice, and spend a year in prison. Furthermore, before they could be released they had to provide security, ensuring their good behaviour for three years more.[9]

This sentence was a standard one for convicted blackmailers. The security they were asked to provide would have been financial, though the precise sum demanded is not quoted in the *Sessions Papers*. It is likely, however, that they would have been expected to provide the money themselves and find one or more guarantors willing to put up a similar sum. This would not have been easy in view of the fact that at least one of them had a prison record already. It is noteworthy, too, that Judge Page sent them to gaol for longer than either of the convicted sodomites he tried in the same month.

Sir Francis Page was rightly known to be severe. He was not merciful, but neither was he vindictive. He acted on fixed principles and he was consistent. Still, the contrast between his judgements and those of some his contemporaries is all the more marked when we consider what happened to Peter Vivian, who appeared in the fifth trial involving sodomy conducted in the Old Bailey in 1730. The judge on that occasion, during the September Sessions, was the Recorder of London, Baron Thompson. He was criticized for personal avarice and the way he sought and hung on to any remunerative office but, unlike Page, he was not especially feared by prisoners who came before him when he sat on the Bench.[10]

Peter Vivian was a young Dutchman who had been in London for a month, working as a journeyman to a peruke maker, when he was charged with attempted sodomy. John Brailsford, his prosecutor, told the court he had stopped in Popes-head Alley near the Royal Exchange, 'to make water' when Vivian came up to him, whereupon, he said, he 'caught hold of my Privities, and clap'd my Hand to his'. Brailsford seized him, intending to have him arrested, but he got away, helped by a friend who suddenly appeared. Brailsford chased the two of them into the Post Office courtyard where Vivian tripped up. Bystanders helped Brailsford capture both men and take them to a tavern to await a constable. Here Vivian's friend jumped out of a window and escaped. Vivian meanwhile pleaded with his captor to let him go, crying often 'My Dear, my Dear, first time, first time, and offered several times to kiss his prosecutor.' At the Old Bailey the prisoner offered no defence and was convicted. Baron Thompson sentenced him to stand an hour in the pillory, spend one month in gaol and pay a fine of five marks, that is, £3.33.[11]

This was the lightest sentence passed on any man convicted of attempted sodomy in all the cases under review here, though it has to be borne in mind that Vivian had already been punished before he reached court. The London mob regarded it as sport to manhandle sodomites, as well as pickpockets and footpads, if they got the chance. On this occasion they had torn the shirt and ruffles of which the young Dutchman was rather proud.

Isaac Broderick, who also received a comparatively light sentence, suffered far more grievously. Whether or not the mob ill-treated him when he was in the pillory, he had lost his good name when he was exposed as a sodomite, and this for a schoolmaster was the most enduring punishment of all, even if deserved.

Notes

1. *Dunciad* IV, l. 30 and note, volume V of *The Twickenham Edition of the Poems of Alexander Pope*, ed. John Butt and others, 11 vols (London: Methuen, 1938–68). There are numerous anecdotes about Judge Page's unrelenting approach to malefactors, and he made several unfavourable appearances in literary works, e.g. Johnson's *Life of Savage* and Fielding's *Tom Jones*, Bk 8, ch. 11.
2. Edward Foss, *A Biographical Dictionary of the Judges of England, 1066–1870* (London, 1870).
3. *Sessions Papers*, January 1730, pp. 15–16.
4. Leon Radzinowicz, *A History of Criminal Law and its Administration from 1750*, 5 vols (London, 1948–86), 1: 73ff.
5. Radzinowicz, 1: 637.
6. Ibid.
7. *Sessions Papers*, May 1730, pp. 10–13.
8. *Sessions Papers*, December 1730, p. 8.
9. Ibid.
10. Foss, op. cit.
11. *Sessions Papers*, September 1730, p. 20.

CHAPTER FOUR

The Princess Seraphina

After the five trials of 1730 in which all the defendants were convicted, there was a sharp reduction in the number of sodomy cases which reached the Old Bailey. Over the next couple of decades or so never more than one or two cases of this kind were heard in the central criminal court in any twelve-month period, while five years could go by without any being heard at all. Apparently the public had become less anxious about sodomy or, at least, less inclined to do anything about it. Furthermore, in the twelve trials which were held of men accused of sodomitical practices during the 1730s and 1740s, there were as many acquittals as convictions.

In July 1732 Tom Gordon was brought to the Old Bailey, accused of assaulting John Cooper and stealing all his clothes. Cooper had only fourpence halfpenny in his pocket at the time but the clothes had been especially fine. With a small windfall he had clad himself anew in a black coat and breeches, white waistcoat, shoes with silver buckles, his pristine shirt set off by a silver stock pin.

Asked by the court what business he followed, he replied that he was a gentleman's servant, though he was out of a place at present. He had last been employed by a Captain Breholt at Greenwich.

Cooper's manner was good and his diction genteel, whereas Tom Gordon was a rough fellow, frank and forthright. He had been a sailor until the Treaty of Seville beached him in 1729, since when he had been living with his parents in Colston's Court, Drury Lane, earning his living as a leather-breeches maker.

The judge at Tom Gordon's trial was James Reynolds, who had advanced in his profession since we last met him sentencing Williamson Goodman to death. He was now a Baron of the Exchequer. Probably when Judge Reynolds arrived on a July morning in 1732, and was confronted by Gordon and Cooper, he supposed he was about to hear yet another of the routine cases of robbery that came his way. In the event he, and the rest of the court, had a rather more interesting time than they expected.

Neither the victim nor his assailant were represented by counsel, so John Cooper, the prosecutor, was called upon first to give his side of the story. He told the court that on 29 May, Whit Monday, he had been out enjoying himself and returned late to his lodgings in Eagle Court, the

Strand, where, he said, 'I knocked once, but finding no Body answer'd, I went to a Night Cellar hard by'. Soon afterwards

> the Prisoner came and sat by me. He ask'd me if I did not know Mr. Price and some other Persons, and so we fell into Discourse. We drank three hot Pints together. I paid the Reckoning, Ninepence Halfpenny, and went up. I got about fifteen or twenty Yards off when the Prisoner came up to me, said it was a fine Morning, and ask'd me to take a Walk. I agreed and we went into Chelsea Fields, and turning up into a private Place among the Trees, he clap'd his left Hand to the right Side of my Coat, and trip'd up my Heels, and holding a Knife to me, 'God damn ye', says he, 'if ye offer to speak or stir, I'll kill ye. Give me your Ring'. I gave it him and he put it on his own Finger. Then he made to pull off my Coat and Waistcoat and Breeches. I begged he would not kill me, or leave me naked. 'No', says he, 'I'll only change wi'ye. Come pull off your Shirt and put on mine'. So he stript, and drest himself in my Cloathes, and I put on his. There was Fourpence Halfpenny in my Breeches and I found three Halfpence in his. He ask'd me where I lived and I told him. 'I suppose', says he 'you intend to charge me with a Robbery, but if you do, I'll swear you're a Sodomite, and gave me the Cloathes to let you B———r me'.

Cooper told the court that while Gordon was threatening him he saw another man in Chelsea Fields, 'at a little Distance'. He nearly called out to him for help but did not, as the passer-by was alone and he was afraid.

On leaving Chelsea Fields Cooper followed Gordon into Little Windmill Street, where he called on two men to help apprehend him. All four of them went into an alehouse, where both the protagonists gave their contrasting accounts of how Cooper came to give up his clothes. Cooper's assistants told him they would expect a share of the reward he got for turning Gordon in.

A preliminary attempt to have Gordon remanded by a magistrate failed because Cooper had not had his prisoner charged by a constable. While he went off to find one, Gordon wrote a letter to his mother. Meanwhile Cooper's assistants declined to help him further because they believed Gordon's story that he was a sodomite. Cooper told the court that he stopped another passer-by. 'I desired his Assistance, but they telling him I was a Molly, he said I ought to be hanged, and he'd have nothing to do with me.' The prisoner then ran off. Cooper chased after him but one of his earstwhile helpers tripped him up. Cooper 'spit Blood' as he hit the ground, while the three men jumped over a ditch and escaped.

Cooper said that when he got back to his lodgings in Eagle Court the neighbours were surprised to see him return 'in such shabby Dress'. They told him that his assailant was named Thomas Gordon, whereupon Cooper got Justice Giffard's warrant. Gordon was arrested in a brandy shop in Drury Lane and carried a few doors further down to Brogden Poplet's tavern, the Two Sugar Loaves, from where he was taken to the Round House. The following day he came before a magistrate and, as Cooper testified in the Old Bailey, 'told the Justice that I put my Yard into his Hand twice, and says the Justice, "You had a long Knife, it seems, why did you not cut it off?" to which the Prisoner replied "He was not willing to expose me so much."'

Cooper called one witness in support of his story. Christopher Sandford Taylor, known as Kit Sandford, said he had met Cooper in the King's Arms, Leicester Fields, on 29 May when he had been wearing his new apparel. The next day he had seen Cooper again 'in a dirty, ragged Suit of Cloathes and a speckled Shirt', adding that he had 'never set Eyes on a Man so metamorphosed'. A little later, having learned that Cooper had been robbed and by whom, he had met Gordon and told him, 'Hark ye Tom, as you have a Soul to be sav'd, I fancy you'll come to be hang'd, for [Cooper] has sworn a Robbery against you.'

Earlier Cooper, on looking round the courthouse, had noted the presence of 'certain Ladies that belong to Brogden Poplet', who he supposed would have 'an abundance to say for the Prisoner'. As indeed they did, but first it was the turn of the prisoner to speak in his own defence.

According to Gordon, Cooper spoke to him first in the night cellar where, like the prosecutor, he had gone late on Whit Monday night because he knew that if he went home he would find he was locked out. Gordon also said that he, not the prosecutor, had left first. Cooper followed him and suggested they walk together. Once they were among the trees in Chelsea Fields Gordon told the court, 'He kissed me and put his privy Parts into my Hand. I ask'd him what he meant by that, and told him I would expose him. He begged me not to do it, and said he would make Amends. I ask'd him what Amends? He said he would give me all his Cloathes, if I would accept them, and so we agreed and chang'd Cloathes.'

They walked on as far as Knaves Acre, where Cooper charged Gordon with robbery and Gordon in turn charged him with sodomy. Later, while the prosecutor was obeying the magistrate's instructions to get a constable, he 'raised a Mob' and, Gordon went on, 'squalled as if I had been murd'ring him, so that I was glad to get away. He afterwards met me again as I was talking to my Master in Drury Lane, and carried me to Mr. Poplet's.'

After Gordon had finished speaking, more than a dozen men and women came forward to plead his cause. This was extraordinary. It was usually difficult to persuade anyone not directly concerned to appear as a witness in a trial. For working people it meant a loss of time and money. Gordon's supporters came on this occasion, not because they felt any particular animosity towards the prosecutor, but because they wanted to save Gordon from the gallows. All of them had good memories. In the course of giving their evidence they built up a graphic picture of the personality and daily life of John Cooper, who earned a living supplying the special needs of certain Londoners.

The first to be called was Margaret Holder, keeper of the night cellar where the two men met. She testified that Gordon had come into her place at about 10 p.m. on 29 May and that at 2 a.m. Cooper had entered. She confirmed Gordon's story that the prosecutor had begun the conversation with him. He had gone up to the prisoner, saying, 'Your Servant Sir. Have you any Company belonging to you, for I do not love much Company?' After that the two sat drinking gin and ale made hot till 4 a.m. Gordon then said he would go home because his mother would be up and she could let him into the house without his father knowing. Cooper had said, 'If you go, I'll go too.' Mrs Holder concluded her testimony by affirming, 'I believe the Prisoner is an honest Man, but the Prosecutor and Kit Sandford too, used to come to my Cellar with such Sort of People.' Judge Reynolds wanted this last statement clarified, so the following interchange took place:

Court:	What Sort of People?
Holder:	Why to tell you the Truth, he's one of the Runners that carries Messages between Gentlemen in that Way.
Court:	In what Way?
Holder:	Why he's one of them as you call Molly Culls. He gets his Bread that Way. To my certain Knowledge he has got many a Crown under some Gentlemen, for going of sodomiting Errands.

Robert Shaw, landlord of the White Hart in Knaves Acre, testified that Cooper and Gordon arrived at his tavern about 6 a.m. on Tuesday, 30 May. Gordon told him, '"Cooper gave me his Cloathes to let him commit Sodomy with me, and now wants them again." They called for Drink and after the second Pot disputed who should pay. Says the Prosecutor, "You know when I gave you my Breeches there was Fourpence Halfpenny in 'em, and when I took yours, I found three Halfpence in the Pocket."' Asked by Judge Reynolds, 'Did the Prosecutor contradict what the Prisoner said about changing Cloathes?' Shaw replied 'Not in my Hearing.' The dispute about the reckoning ended when Cooper, accompanied by another customer named John Thorp, went out to borrow a shilling from his cousin, a distiller who lived nearby.

The next witness to come forward was Edward Pocock. He was the passer-by in Chelsea Fields, whom Cooper mentioned he saw and nearly summoned for assistance. Later that morning Pocock happened to go into Mrs Holder's night cellar where everybody was talking about the robbery. Saying 'I'll be hanged if these were not the two Men I thought were going to fight', he went to Newgate where Gordon then was and, recognizing him, agreed to come to court. After testifying that he saw two men 'stripping among some Trees in Chelsea Fields at 5 a.m. on Tuesday, 30 May', Pocock went on, 'I thought they were going to fight but I soon found there was no Quarrel, for when they put their Cloathes on, they went away lovingly and the Prisoner smil'd. They look'd as if they had not been a-bed all Night. No more I had, for you must know, being Holiday Time I got drunk, and fell asleep with my Cloathes on.' Asked by the Judge how far off from the two men he was when he saw them, Pocock said 'about twenty or thirty Yards'.

John Thorp, a stocking-maker, spoke next. He met Cooper and Gordon in Windmill Street. While they were vainly try to rouse the landlord of the Two Brewers, Cooper said to him '"This Man has my Cloathes on his Back", and says the Prisoner, "He gave them to me to commit Sodomy"'. On hearing this, Thorp, supported by a gathering crowd, told the men, 'It was a scandalous Business, and advised them to make it up between Themselves, and change Cloathes again, but the Prisoner would not consent.' Thorp had then tagged along after the pair and when Cooper went ahead with trying to get Gordon arrested, he delivered the letter the prisoner wrote to his parents. Asked in court whether he had also gone with Cooper to borrow money from the prosecutor's cousin, Thorp replied, 'Yes. He told his Cousin he was pawned for a Shilling. Says his cousin, "As you are in the Neighbourhood I don't care to be scandalized by you. There's a Shilling, but go about your Business, and let me hear no more of you, for you are a vile Fellow, and I am afraid you'll come to an ill End."'

Jane Jones, a washerwoman in Drury Lane, began her story *in medias res*, by describing how she was in Mr Poplet's for a pint of beer and said, 'There's the Princess Seraphina. And the Prisoner was in the same Box and says he to the Princess, "What a vile Villain was you to ———."' Judge Reynolds understandably lost the thread of the narrative at this point and interrupted, 'What Princess?' 'The Prosecutor,' replied Jane Jones, 'he goes by that Name.' And she continued, '"What a villain was you" says the Prisoner, "to offer so vile a Thing. Did you not do so and so?"' The Judge interrupted again. 'So and so? Explain yourself.' To which the answer came, 'Why in the Way of Sodomity, whatever that is. "So", says the Princess "If you don't give me my Cloathes again I'll swear a Robbery against you."' The next day, Wednesday, Jane Jones was in Mr Stringer's, the pawnbroker in Vinegar Yard, Drury Lane. There, she told the court, 'I saw the Princess pawning her Shirt. "O

Princess" says I "are you there? You will have no Occasion to pawn your Linen when you get the Reward hanging Tom Gordon. But how can you be so cruel to swear his Life away when you owned you chang'd Cloathes with him?"'

It was the turn of Mary Poplet, keeper of the Two Sugar Loaves, to give evidence next. She testified that she had watched Gordon and Cooper quarrelling in her tavern. Then she improved on the sketch of the Princess Seraphina begun by Jane Jones, as she went on, 'I have known her Highness a pretty while. She us'd to come to my House from Mr. Tull to enquire after some Gentlemen of no very good Character. I have seen her several Times in Women's Cloathes. She commonly us'd to wear a white Gown, and a scarlet Cloak, with her Hair frizzled and curl'd all around her Forehead; and then she would flutter her Fan, and make such fine Curtsies, that you would not have known her from a Woman.' Mrs Poplet added that the Princess 'takes a great Delight in Balls and Masquerades, and always chuses to appear at them in female Dress, that she may have the Satisfaction of dancing with fine Gentlemen'.

Mary Poplet also knew something of Cooper's domestic arrangements. 'Her Highness lives with Mr. Tull in Eagle Court, The Strand and calls him her Master because she was a Nurse to him and his Wife when they were both in a Salivation. But,' she added, 'I believe the Princess is rather Mr. Tull's Friend than his domestick Servant.'

The serving girl at the Two Sugar Loaves came to the Old Bailey, though she had little new to offer. Mary Riley testified that she had met Gordon in Drury Lane where he told her that Cooper gave him the clothes and now wanted to charge him with robbery. She also knew the Princess well and was able to reinforce Mrs Poplet's account, saying, 'She goes nursing sometimes and lives with Mr. Tull.' Referring to Cooper's habit of going to masquerades in women's clothes, she said a recent occasion had been the *al fresco* ridotto at Vauxhall.

Mary Robinson, who gave evidence next, had greater pretensions to gentility than any of the other witnesses who had come forward so far. She kept a servant and dressed well. It is hard to place her socially. She may have been a widow of independent means, or possibly she was one of the more prosperous 'nymphs' of Drury Lane, or even a 'Madam'. Whatever her status, she was free to choose her own company. She was one of several women who lent Cooper her clothes when he wanted to look particularly fine as the Princess. Once he had asked to borrow her red damask because 'it looked mighty pretty'. Another time he had hoped to wear her laced pinners which he had seen at the mantua makers they shared in the Strand. This was when he was going to the ridotto at Vauxhall. On that occasion she had refused, but he took this in good part and went instead in a calico dress and mob cap of Mrs Nuttall's. The next time they met she had asked 'Did you make a good Hand of it Princess?' '"No Madam" says he, "I picked up two Men who had no Money, but they proved to be my old Acquaintances, and very good Gentlewomen they were."' Whereupon he launched into an account of an evening that had gone from mediocre to disastrous. One of the old acquaintances was arrested and had since been transported. 'T'other, who had gone to the Masquerade in a velvet Domino, picked up an old Gentleman and went to Bed with him, but as soon as the old Fellow found out he had got a Man by his Side he cry'd out "Murder".'

Mrs Robinson told the court that Cooper 'us'd to be very meanly dressed as to Men's Cloathes until he suddenly appeared in a handsome black suit, acquired he said because 'his Mother had lately sold the Reversion of a House'. On Whit Monday he had announced his intention of going in his new apparel to stroll in the park. The next morning Mrs Robinson's servant told her 'that her Highness was robbed by a Man in a Sailor's Habit who had chang'd Cloathes with him'. So Mrs Robinson had sent for Cooper. On seeing him, she exclaimed, 'Lord Princess, you are vastly chang'd', and he told her about being robbed. 'But', he said, 'I shall get the Reward for hanging the Rogue.'

A ninth witness, Elizabeth Jones, made it clear that Cooper had felt obliged to go ahead with his prosecution of Gordon, even though most of his acquaintances disapproved of this course of action. She testified that she saw the Princess Seraphina standing outside Brogden Poplet's. '"What have you been robbed?" says I. "Has Tom Gordon stript your Highness naked?"' Mrs Jones then advised him to make the matter up, rather than expose Gordon. To this Cooper had replied, 'I must prosecute, for those that were concerned in taking him up, expect their Share of the Reward, and won't let me drop the Prosecution.'

Following Elizabeth Jones, several of Tom Gordon's neighbours gave him a good character as an honest working man. Finally, Judge Reynolds directed the jury to acquit the defendant, and this popular verdict was brought in.[1]

The witnesses who had described the life of the Princess Seraphina did so not because they wanted to get John Cooper into trouble, but because they wanted to get Tom Gordon out of it. Cooper, who had mistaken his man when he propositioned Gordon, offered up his clothes in a moment of panic, a sacrifice he quickly regretted. Gordon was determined to keep him to his bargain but was not outraged for long to find that his companion was a molly. According to Edward Pocock, the two of them left Chelsea Fields 'lovingly'. They then had yet another drink together at the White Hart.

This case illustrates the full range of eighteenth-century reactions to sodomites. At one end of the scale there is Cooper's cousin who called him a 'vile Fellow' and the passer-by who refused to help him because he was a molly who ought to be hanged. Nor can we forget the magistrate who jovially suggested castration as a way of dealing with buggers. At the other extreme there were the ladies who viewed the Princess with tolerance and amusement, helping her in her way of life by lending her dresses, scarves and bits of jewellery. Mary Robinson found Cooper entertaining company and encouraged him to tell her of his adventures. Her attitude supports the theory that female loathing of homosexuals, expressed in verses such as *The Women-Hater's Lamentation* or *The Women's Complaint to Venus* was by no means universal, even though the men who wrote these broadsides liked to think so.[2]

Cooper's relationship with Mr and Mrs Tull is also intriguing. They could hardly have been unaware of his other life as the Princess, as this was common knowledge. Apparently they did not mind, and allowed him to share their home after he nursed them back to health. When Mrs Poplet made a point of saying that Mr Tull was Cooper's friend rather than his master, she may merely have meant that the Tulls were grateful, unless she was suggesting that the three of them were living in a *ménage à trois*.

Drury Lane was a raffish district with more than its fair share of prostitutes, thieves and cut-throats. But law-abiding, hard-working folk who earned an honest living also had their homes there. Several of these came to the Old Bailey to save Tom Gordon. Most of them had known John Cooper for some time and knew that he was a molly and a pimp for other mollies. They did not understand him or approve. Nor did they treat him like a pariah. He had his place in a community that was used to all sorts. Without this acceptance he would have been turned in to the authorities long ago. It would have been comparatively easy for one of these honest citizens to lay a trap for Cooper and then claim the reward once he was convicted. None of them did, nor was any attempt made to prosecute him after he lost his case, and his beautiful new clothes. The Princess Seraphina survived, for the time being at least.[3]

The men who had hoped to share the money from a successful prosecution of Tom Gordon were probably professional thief-takers who made a living out of the reward system. If so, they would have been dangerous people to cross for someone as vulnerable as the Princess.[4] However, Cooper was not the only person to bring an ill-advised prosecution in 1732. For rather different reasons the one brought by William Curtis was also surprising.

Notes

1. *Sessions Papers*, July 1732, case no. 37.
2. Dennis Rubini, 'Sexuality and Augustan England', in *The Pursuit of Sodomy: Male Homosexuality in Renaissance and Enlightenment Europe*, eds Kent Gerrard and Gert Hekma (New York and London: Harrington Park Press, 1989), p. 357.
3. See the *Sessions Papers* for July 1749, case no. 429, for the trial of a John Cooper accused of theft.
4. Some thief-takers regularly practised extortion. See Ruth Paley, 'Thief-takers in London in the Age of the McDaniel Gang, *c.* 1745–1754', in *Policing and Prosecution in Britain, 1750–1850*, eds Douglas Hay and Francis Snyder (Oxford: Clarendon Press, 1989), pp. 301–40.

CHAPTER FIVE

Willing and reluctant Ganymedes

During the September Sessions in 1732 William Curtis, aged twenty, came to the Old Bailey to prosecute John Ashford. The charge was sodomy. The judge was the London Recorder, Baron Thompson, who had convicted the young Dutchman Peter Vivian two years before.

Curtis told the court how, in 1728, when he was sixteen, he had come up to London from the country and entered the service of Mr Nutts, a printer in the Old Bailey area. Six months later Ashford also came to work for Mr Nutts and, as was customary at the time, the two servants shared a bed. Curtis testified that the prisoner kissed him, called him 'Dear Billy', and then one night attempted to sodomize him. On that occasion Curtis escaped from the bed with a torn shirt which his mother later mended. However, Ashford bribed him with money and promises of an inheritance and so overcame his resistance. Thereafter he had buggered him regularly for eighteen months before Curtis told a woman named Hannah Unwin what was happening. At her urging he left Mr Nutts's house, only to become what we would now call a rent boy. In this way he got to know other mollies and was soon augmenting his income by informing on them. Finally he went to the magistrates Sir John Gonson and Justice De Veil to inform on Ashford. Asked why he had kept quiet for so long, he replied that he 'was an ignorant country Lad and did not know the Greatness of the Crime'. Furthermore, he said Ashford had paid him three shillings a week and had given him presents, including all the clothes he wore.

Curtis did not win the sympathy of the judge or the jury when he repeated these excuses in the Old Bailey. He was damned still further when other witnesses came forward to say that when he had worked for Mr Nutts he had been idle and was known to tell lies. Ashford, who admitted he had given Curtis money and presents, hardly needed to make a vigorous defence. Curtis was clearly an unreliable witness whose uncorroborated testimony could not be relied upon. Nor was he able, so long after the supposed event, to provide any of the material evidence necessary before a man could be convicted on the capital charge of sodomy. Inevitably, Ashford was acquitted.[1]

If William Curtis had not won immunity as an informer he would have been liable to prosecution himself. As he was sixteen when the affair with Ashford began, he was equally guilty because, according to the law on sodomy, 'if the victim was under fourteen years of age, it was not a felony in him but only in the aggressor; if both were of the age of discretion (above fourteen years of age) – it was a felony in both'.[2]

It is perhaps surprising that Curtis was so frank about his role as Ashford's catamite. His candour, together with his statement that when he came to London he was an 'ignorant country Lad and did not know the Greatness of the Crime', suggests there was some discrepancy between official pronouncements about sodomy and the popular conception of it, particularly in regard to adolescents. In a previous age sex between men and boys was sometimes condoned because the boys were seen to be substitutes for girls and those who exploited them as not true sodomites. It has been suggested that this older notion lingered on into the eighteenth century.[3] If this is true, it would explain Curtis's insouciance, as well as the apparent lack of concern felt by others, about his seduction and role as a Ganymede. There is no record that Judge Thompson was moved to make any comment about the behaviour of anyone in this trial, though at some of the local assizes the judiciary are known to have expressed dismay about the corruption of minors.[4] However, the London Recorder probably regarded the Rex v. Ashford case as routine. In the twenty years under review here, the greatest number of prosecutions for sodomy, or attempted sodomy, which were heard in the Old Bailey were brought by boys in their teens.

At the May Sessions in 1735 Henry Wolf was indicted for a sodomitical attack on John Holloway, a boy who worked for a brandy merchant in Goswell Street in the City.

Holloway told the Old Bailey that recently he had been on an errand for his master. When he got to Bishopsgate he was not sure of the way so he asked Wolf, who invited him to come and have a drink. Over the next few hours Wolf took him to different places of entertainment and made repeated sexual overtures which were constantly interrupted. For example, in a tavern where Wolf bought Holloway a pint of wine, the serving girl noticed him fumbling with the boy's clothing and he had to stop. Again, when Wolf took him down an alley, they were interrupted by a passer-by. Wolf kept him with him by giving him little presents such as a nosegay and a penny custard. Finally he took him to Bedlam to watch the mad folks. There, in the 'House of Office' Wolf persuaded the boy to submit to fellatio, after which he let him go.

Subsequently, Wolf called several times to see Holloway at his master's house, eventually persuading the boy to meet him on a Sunday. By that time Holloway had told some of his friends what was happening and three other boys accompanied him when he went to keep his appointment. When Wolf saw them all he tried to run away but the boys chased after him and handed him over to a constable.

None of these boys appeared to support John Holloway's story; nor did any other witness. Sir Edmund Probyn, a judge considered by his contemporaries to be both 'learned and lucid', decided to direct the jury not to accept the uncorroborated testimony of a boy who, by his own admission, had made little effort to get away from his supposed seducer.[5] Therefore Henry Wolf was acquitted.[6]

In the next case the judge was the Lord Chief Justice Sir William Lee, renowned for his meticulous application of the law, much of which he was reputed to know off by heart.[7]

In the Sessions for April and May 1742 William Nichols was tried for sodomy. The indictment stated that Nichols assaulted Thomas Waldron 'and him did carnally know, and upon him, that detestable Crime call'd Buggery did commit and do'. Thomas Waldron was a thirteen-year-old waif. He testified that he and the prisoner shared a bed in the St Martin's Workhouse where, he said, 'at about 2 o'clock in the Morning when all People were asleep, he us'd to give me Small-beer and Bread, and then he etc.'. At this point an unusually reticent reporter of the trial stopped short, taking up the story again when the boy 'gave a particular Account of the Prisoner's Behaviour, and being ask'd a Question which the Law in such Cases makes necessary, answer'd in the Negative'. Presumably the judge had asked for exact details of what the prisoner had done to the boy, in order to find out whether penetration and emission had taken place. Two witnesses spoke in support of Thomas Waldron's story. One of them was his mother, who 'gave an Account of his Complaints'. The other, James Robinson, testified that he 'lay in the same Bed with Waldron and the Prisoner, and confirmed some Part of the above Deposition'. However, no one offered the incontrovertible proof of sodomy necessary for a conviction, so Nichols was acquitted, 'there not being sufficient Evidence to convict the Prisoner upon this Indictment'. This did not mean that Chief Justice Lee thought Nichols was innocent; one prosecution having failed, he ordered the defendant 'to remain in order to be tried for Assault'.[8]

The second trial is not recorded in the *Sessions Papers*. Nor does the name of William Nichols appear in any of the lists of convicted prisoners for 1742, so perhaps he went free. The contest between him and a young, unsophisticated lad was certainly unequal. If we are to believe James Robinson, who was in the same bed as the two of them, Nichols did not expect protest from any quarter and was probably surprised to be prosecuted at all.

Later on in 1742 yet another young boy came forward with a sorry tale to tell. Yet it is unlikely he would have told it, had he not been compelled to do so by the wife of his master. During the December Sessions William Porter indicted Thomas Pryor for making a sodomitical attack on him. Porter ran errands for Mr Greener, a leather-dresser near Leicester Fields. Pryor was Greener's apprentice.

Mrs Greener, having raised the alarm, did not appear at the Old Bailey 'out of modesty'. Instead her husband explained how the prosecution had come about. He said his wife had heard noises in the room overhead one night and had asked why the bed creaked so, to which he had replied that it was an old bed. The noise continued and Mrs Greener went upstairs to investigate. She interrogated the two boys and what she learned from William Porter confirmed her worst suspicions.

In court Porter gave evidence as follows: 'The Prisoner did wrong to me two or three times one Night – I do not know what Month it was. I believe it was in Winter.' The judge asked, 'What did he do to you?' Whereupon the same reticent shorthand writer who had reported the Nichols trial tells us 'Porter gave Evidence of a Penetration, but in such Language as is not fit to be committed to Paper.' Asked why he had not resisted though he appeared to be as strong as the prisoner, Porter replied that he had not striven 'because he [Pryor] would do it'. He admitted that he had not told anyone until he was questioned by his mistress a week previously, but denied he was a willing partner, repeating again that Pryor 'would do it'.

The rigorous questioning of Porter in this trial shows that the judge and jury were more interested in his role in the events he described than in the alleged aggression of Pryor. The implication of pursuing this line of enquiry is that if it could be ascertained that the errand boy had agreed to sodomy, then the apprentice was hardly to blame for taking advantage of him. No one stood up for Porter. Even the absent Mrs Greener appears to have been more shocked by her discovery than sorry for Pryor's victim.

Mr Greener, on the other hand, appears never to have been particularly concerned about what was going on in the bedroom above his own. He fended off his wife's questions about the creaking bed as long as he could and although he agreed to represent her at the trial, once there he completely subverted the case against his apprentice. Having described how his wife came to make her discovery, he told the court that Pryor had been with him for eleven months, and that 'he behaved very well till Michaelmas last'. Then, his master continued, 'I found he got acquainted with a Gang of young Wenches', adding 'He did not neglect my Business till the Princess's Birthday.' So the jury was left with an image of Thomas Pryor as a lusty, basically heterosexual young man, who had indulged in sodomy because he was tempted by a girlish boy who could have resisted his advances but did not. He was declared 'Not Guilty'.[9]

Sir William Chapple, who directed the jurors to reach this verdict, was sixty-five years old in 1742 and an experienced member of the judiciary. Five years earlier he had been appointed a puisne judge in the Court of King's Bench, where he carried out his duties with 'credit and distinction'.[10] One has no reason to suppose therefore that his colleagues would have found him at fault in refusing to convict Pryor.

In the ten years up to the end of 1742 juries at the Old Bailey had acquitted four men accused of engaging in sodomitical practices with young boys. The judges who directed jurors to bring in verdicts of 'Not Guilty' in the various trials had all reached the upper echelons of their profession, one of them being the Lord Chief Justice. It is reasonable to suppose, therefore, that in trials involving minors, senior figures in the judiciary, as well as those members of the general public called for jury service, worked according to an unwritten consensus that although sodomy was bad, some manifestations of it were not as bad as others.

However, there was no consistency in the treatment of suspected sodomites in the Old Bailey. Much depended on the impression created by the prosecutor and the defendant when they appeared in court. This was as important as the supposed facts of the case, as the following trial illustrates.

During the July Sessions in 1749 Richard Spencer was indicted for making a sodomitical attack on William Taylor, a seventeen-year-old apprentice. Like William Curtis, Taylor was a country boy. He had been sent by his parents in Herefordshire to learn a trade in London.

At the Old Bailey Taylor told the court that he was leaning over the hatch of his master's shop in Noble Street (not far from St Paul's) when Richard Spencer came by, shook him by the hand and asked him if his master was at home. Finding he was not, he invited Taylor to have a drink at the Bell, opposite. At first the boy refused, but he joined Spencer a little later, after he had beckoned to him from the tavern window. Spencer had begun by speaking about some business worth £200 which concerned Taylor's master, but soon he began talking about sex and told the boy he 'wanted to f—— him'. Then he offered to take him by coach down to Herefordshire and let him get 'as drunk as an Owl all the Way'. Over two pints of beer, Taylor resisted all Spencer's overtures. Finally he went out to find a constable. He returned in two or three minutes with this officer and 'a great Mob came about'.

'The Constable took hold of [Spencer's] Arm, and ordered him to pay for what he had. The Prisoner flung down three Pence and the Constable gave him a Kick or two on the Back-side, and called him a Black-guard old Rascal for making such an Attempt on a Boy, and turned him out of the House.' Taylor, 'not thinking this punishment enough', ran after Spencer, brought him back and had him arrested.

George Rouse, Taylor's master, appeared as a witness. He told the court that after Spencer's arrest he had gone to see him, to find out

about the so-called business concerning himself, whereupon the prisoner had produced nothing more than a written charity appeal.

John Godwin, the constable, confirmed that Taylor had told him the
same story as he told the court, while the Alderman who first examined
Spencer also confirmed that the boy gave the same account of what had
happened when he questioned him.

Spencer did not deny the charge. In his defence he claimed that he
was 'out of his senses' at the time. He told the court that he received
charity from ladies and gentlemen 'through the Recommendation of Dr.
Mead, under whose Hands he had been, and who found him incurable'.
Spencer did not say whether the treatment he had received had included
any attempt to change his sexual orientation. If so this would have been
a pioneering effort on the part of any eighteenth-century medical practi-
tioner. Obviously, though, Dr Mead regarded Spencer as worthy of help
and sympathy.

This was not the view taken by the jury, who declared Spencer
'Guilty', after which sentence was passed upon him by Baron Parker,
who decided not to be lenient with this offender, although he did not
have a reputation for being unduly severe. Thomas Parker was an
average member of the judiciary, described by legal historians as 'useful'
and by his friend and patron, Lord Hardwicke, as a judge who had
'gained a very high Character for Ability and Integrity since his Ad-
vancement to the Bench'.[11] He told Spencer that his punishment would
be to stand in the pillory for one hour, spend a year in Newgate and pay
a fine of one shilling. In addition he and two others had to provide £80
security for his good behaviour for one year more. Spencer was to
provide £40 of this sum himself and the two guarantors £20 each, and
he must stay in prison until the whole amount was found.[12] This last
stipulation, for a man who existed on charity, was especially harsh, but
it was probably made with the intention of keeping Spencer off the
streets of London for as long as possible.

Richard Spencer would never have found himself in the Old Bailey at
all if the constable called by William Taylor had been allowed to deal
with him in his own way. Whether men were prosecuted for sodomitical
practices was largely a matter of chance because law officers such as
this constable, as well as members of the public, were used to
adminstering what they thought of as rough justice, on the spot. This
helps to explain why there were lengthy periods in which there were no
sodomy trials in the central criminal court.

Once this particular prosecution was made, a conviction was by no
means inevitable. It would have been possible for the judge and jury to
have accepted Spencer's excuse that he was out of his senses when he
tried to seduce Taylor. Pleas of insanity were allowed in eighteenth-

century trials and the criteria for accepting them were less rigorous than they have been since the 'McNaughten Rules' were adopted in 1843. In 1736 Roger Allen, accused of instigating a riot over the Gin Law, was acquitted because a plea was made for him 'that at certain Times he was out of his right Mind'.[13]

Spencer had not laid hands on Taylor, unlike Henry Wolf who finally persuaded John Holloway to submit to fellatio, but whereas the brandy merchant's errand boy had found no one to speak for him, Taylor was better organized and came to court supported by his master and two other reputable witnesses – not that these witnesses were able to add anything to the story told by the prosecutor, because they had not heard Spencer talking to him.

William Taylor's prosecution succeeded partly because it was presented and supported efficiently. Fundamentally, however, the court reached its decision for subjective reasons. The jury was swayed by emotion in condemning Spencer, as was the judge in passing sentence upon him.

Taylor created a good impression on the jury and it is easy to see why he did so if we compare him with the young plaintiffs in earlier cases. He was not greedy or ungrateful, like Curtis; nor was he to be seduced by a penny custard and a nosegay, like Holloway. He was forthright and calm, unlike the pathetic and hysterical Porter. He was confident and did not become confused when giving evidence, in contrast to the much younger workhouse boy, Thomas Waldron. In short, Taylor struck the jury as being a respectable lad, righteously indignant about an affront offered him. He won his case because he had won the jury over by his personality, not because the evidence he presented was any stronger than that offered by other young persons whose cases have been described here.

As for the judge's sentence, in 1749 the authorities and the general public in the capital were concerned about a rising crime rate. This was mainly a matter of an increase in robbers, such as Henry Fielding was to describe in his *Enquiry* in a couple of years' time.[14] No one appears to have been especially worried about sodomites. Nevertheless, fear produced a determination on the part of the judiciary to lock up as many malefactors as possible. Baron Parker was encouraged to give Spencer a particularly stiff sentence by a climate of opinion that discouraged leniency towards any convicted person.

Notes

1. *Sessions Papers*, September 1732, case no. 85.

2. Leon Radzinowicz, *History of Criminal Law and its Administration*, 5 vols (London: Stevens, 1948–86), 1: 632.
3. Randolph Trumbach, 'Sodomitical Assaults, Gender Role and Sexual Development in Eighteenth-Century London' in *The Pursuit of Sodomy*, eds Kent Gerrard and Gert Hekma (New York and London: Harrington Park Press, 1989), p. 419.
4. *The Trial of Richard Branson for an Attempt to commit Sodomy on the Body of James Fossett, one of the Scholars belonging to God's Gift College, in Dulwich. Tried at the General Quarter Sessions of the Peace; held at St. Margaret's Hall in the Borough of Southwark, January 18, 1760* (London, 1760).
5. Edward Foss, *A Biographical Dictionary of the Judges of England, 1066–1870* (London, 1870).
6. *Sessions Papers*, May 1735, case no. 50.
7. John Campbell, *Lives of the Chief Justices of England*, 3 vols, 2nd edn (London, 1858), 2: 213ff.
8. *Sessions Papers*, April/May 1742, case no. 21.
9. *Sessions Papers*, December 1742, case no. 27.
10. Foss, op. cit.
11. Ibid.
12. *Sessions Papers*, July 1749, case no. 472.
13. *Memoirs of the Life and Times of Sir Thomas DeVeil* (London, 1748).
14. *An Enquiry into the Causes of the Late Increase of Robbers etc. with some Proposals for Remedying this growing Evil in which the present reigning Vices are impartially exposed; and the Laws that relate to the Provision for the Poor, and to the Punishment of Felons are largely and freely examined* (London, 1751).

CHAPTER SIX

Consenting adults

As most prosecutions in the eighteenth century were brought by persons who claimed to be the victims of a crime, it rarely happened that consenting adults who engaged in so-called sodomitical practices found themselves in court. Their indictment depended on the unlikely event of being detected *in flagrante* by a constable or righteous member of the public, who insisted on the law taking its course. However, the few men who were tried at the Old Bailey between 1730 and 1751 for mutual sodomy were all convicted and were usually put in the pillory and imprisoned, even though a way was found of not sending them to the gallows, no matter what the evidence was against them.

Eleven years after William Holiwell was discovered in St Paul's having sex with a waterman, one of the City constables, Robert Pert, came upon a similar scene, this time in the courtyard behind the chapter house of the cathedral. As in the earlier case the two men involved were not charged with the capital crime of sodomy, though Constable Pert believed he had witnessed this. In order to make a conviction more likely, John Deacon was accused of making a sodomitical attempt on Thomas Blair, and Thomas Blair was accused of consenting to the deed.

When the defendants came up for trial at the Old Bailey during the January Sessions in 1743, Robert Pert testified that he had discovered them between midnight Sunday and 1 a.m. Both had their breeches down and, when challenged, said that they had come into the church-yard to relieve themselves, but Pert could not believe that because, as he said later, they 'were so close that if he had had the Presence of Mind to put a Hand between them he could not have done it'. So he called his partner Peter Line and they arrested the pair. Constable Line told the court he had seen Blair loitering near St Paul's earlier that same night, at about 10.30 p.m., though Blair denied this.

Blair, who was described as 'well-dressed and genteel', claimed he was a 'Master of Languages'. He sent for some people to speak about his character, including his landlord, but no one came to the Old Bailey on the day of the trial. Deacon, who was a servant with a Mr Reeves in Bankside, was able to call on a fellow servant Mary Appleby, who told the court, 'he was ever accounted a very honest young Fellow'. How-ever, she had not known him very long. Before being employed by Mr Reeves, Deacon had worked as a porter for a druggist.

Sir Martin Wright, a King's Bench judge who presided at this trial, was persuaded by the evidence of the main prosecution witness, Constable Pert, to direct the jury to find Blair and Deacon guilty. When this verdict was brought in, he sentenced both men to stand in the pillory for one hour at Cheapside and thereafter spend six months in gaol.[1] Unlike Judge Page, who had tried William Holiwell and William Huggins in 1730, he did not distinguish between the prisoners in deciding their punishment, nor did he impose a fine of any kind. So, by the standards of the day, the convicted men were not treated with unusual severity.

Like the majority of defendants in trials at the Old Bailey, John Deacon and William Blair disappeared from the records after their hour in court. We do not know how (or even if) they lived after they had been publicly proclaimed sodomites. Just occasionally, however, our curiosity about such men is at least partially satisfied, as it is with Richard Manning, whose career we glimpse on three occasions over a period of eight years.

During the January Sessions in 1745 Sir Martin Wright was again the judge at the Old Bailey when Richard Manning came before him, accused of 'laying Hands on John Davis with an Intent to commit the detestable Sin of Sodomy', while Davis was accused of 'unlawfully and wickedly permitting and suffering Richard Manning to lay Hands on him' for the same purpose.

The chief witness for the prosecution was Sarah Holland, wife of the landlord of the Mermaid Inn in Great Carter Lane. She testified that on New Year's Eve 1744 the prisoners came into the Mermaid between nine and ten at night. She 'did not know but they might be country Gentlemen'. After a bit she ran into the room where they were sitting and asked them if they wanted a fire, but they said they did not. Something about them aroused her curiosity and she went into the bedroom next door, where her husband was in bed. Going to the glass of a partition between the rooms she saw the defendants 'sitting facing one another with their Knees jammed together', and told her husband she believed they were sodomites. Peering through a thin curtain which covered the partition, she watched as they kissed one another and, looking again, saw 'Manning's Hand in Davis's Breeches' and then that Davis 'had his Hand in Manning's Breeches'. At that point the two men, noticing a candle in the room where Mrs Holland was, got up and came to the partition to see if they could discover 'the Shade of any Body'. Mrs Holland kept back and out of sight, so they sat down again and continued to fondle each other.

Mrs Holland then called Robert Wright, a lodger, and said, 'I have heard talk of Sodomites, and believe there are some here.' Wright told her he had 'not Patience' with such a matter. Nevertheless she persuaded him to join her in spying on the men through the glass in the bedroom. Mrs Holland told the court she next saw the prisoners 'acting as Man and Woman – I saw them act as such'. Asked by Judge Wright, 'Was Manning's Back or his Face to Davis?' she replied, 'I believe his Face.' She also summoned other customers who were in the Mermaid to look with her, one of whom came into the bedroom. Finally she could bear it no longer and shouted at the prisoners. They jumped up and Davis rushed out of the room, panic-stricken, though Manning remained cool.

In court Manning declared that Davis had told him he thought he was 'clapped' and had opened his breeches so that Manning, who laid claim to some medical knowledge, could see whether he was or not. A similar defence had been used once before by George Whittle in 1726 when he argued in the Old Bailey that he was not running a molly house in the tavern of which he was the landlord. Instead he claimed that the prosecution witnesses at his trial had received a mistaken impression of what was really a clinic, held in one of the rooms in the Royal Oak by young surgeons who treated patients for the pox there.[2] Whittle's defence was successful, but Manning's was of no avail because Davis had admitted everything. This was made clear in the evidence given by the Mermaid customers, whom Mrs Holland had persuaded to accompany her as witnesses.

Edward Morey, who was drinking in the tavern that night, confirmed that he was called into the bedroom by Mrs Holland, who pulled aside the curtain covering the partition, so that he saw the two men sitting face to face with their knees close together. He then went into the yard to see if he could get a better view from the window there. Mrs Holland meanwhile called out 'Nasty Fellows!' 'Vile Rogues!' whereupon Davis ran into the yard. When he met Morey, he pleaded with him, 'For God's sake let me go, or I am ruined', adding that this was the first time he had committed such a crime. Manning, though, denied everything and became angry.

Robert Wright, the lodger, confirmed that he had looked through the partition and saw the two men in a compromising position. Davis was so terrified that he could not pull up his breeches properly when told to do so. He laid all the blame on Manning for what had happened.

Jonathan Green, another customer, gave evidence that Mrs Holland had come into the room where he was and said that there were two sodomites in the inn. Green said, 'God Forbid!' He saw Davis with his breeches unbuttoned who begged him to intercede with the landlady to let him go. Green had replied, 'Friend, if you had brought a Girl into the House, I would have interceded for you both to go, but as it is, let the Law take its Course.' As for Manning, Green told the court that 'he looked like an old Rat in an iron Cage. He did not make any attempt to go away.'

In his own defence at the Old Bailey, Davis said he was 'so much in licquor' on New Year's Eve that he did not know how he came to be in the house. To this Mrs Holland said that he and Manning were both sober. Davis, who was a servant, called three witnesses to speak for his character – his employers and another fellow who lived on the premises.

Joseph White, who owned the Leghorn Warehouse in Leadenhall Street, said he kept Davis to clean knives and run errands. He added that he had seen him 'drunk but once, but then he was mad'. Next John Fort, White's partner, testified that Davis was 'the best servant they had ever had'. Lastly William Franklin, who had shared a bed with Davis for sixteen months, said he 'never saw any unhandsome action by him' in that time.

No one came to court to speak for Richard Manning.

The jury found Davis and Manning guilty.[3] Then Judge Wright pronounced sentence. He told them both they were to be whipped.[4] This was an unusual punishment for anyone convicted of attempted sodomy, though it was regularly meted out to rogues. However Sir Martin had a reputation for independent decisions.[5] He may well have thought that Manning, at any rate, was hardened and disreputable. That graphic phrase Jonathan Green used to describe him ('an old Rat in an iron Cage') suggests he was unlikely to make a good impression on any judge. As the Old Bailey reporter did not record the sentence in the *Sessions Papers*, we cannot be sure that Davis or Manning were not sent to prison as well, and from what we learn of Manning later it is possible that he, at any rate, was.

This case, in which a judge decided on a punishment so different from the one he had imposed on Blair and Deacon the previous January, illustrates how unpredictable was the fate of sodomites who found themselves in court in the eighteenth century. For that matter, Manning and Davis would not have been prosecuted had it not been for the energetic endeavours of Mrs Holland, who displayed such a mixture of prurience and moral outrage on 31 December 1744. Her husband, on the other hand, seems to have been singularly unconcerned, staying in bed throughout the uproar. He was awake when his wife told him she thought they had sodomites in the house, but thereafter might have been dead for all the interest he showed as various customers and the lodger came into his bedroom to watch the scene beyond that glass partition.

We next meet Richard Manning a year after he and John Davis were convicted. In the January Sessions for 1746 he came to the Old Bailey again, this time indicted for making a sodomitical assault on Thomas Waldale, who was the porter at Serjeants Inn.

Speaking as the prosecutor, Waldale told the court he had opened the gate of Serjeants Inn to let in a Mr Hulbert and his lady. While he was waiting for their coach to come up, Manning approached, shook his hand and 'tickled it', though Waldale had never set eyes on him before. Manning said he did know him, however, and put his hand on the waistband of Waldale's breeches. Waldale said, 'I know nothing at all of you', whereupon Manning 'unbuttoned his Breeches and let them fall half way down his Thighs'. The two men were standing in the middle of the gateway and Waldale asked Manning to walk further inside, so that he could shut the gate but Manning said, 'I will stand here.' Waldale then called his wife and at the same time Mr Hulbert appeared and said, 'What is the matter?' To which Waldale replied, 'Sir, he is a Molly, a Sodomite, or a Devil. I know not what to call him.' At this Mr Hulbert had his own man lock the gates while the porter fetched a constable.

Richard Manning's version of events was different. Defending himself in the Old Bailey, he said, 'I was just out of Jail. This Man, the Prosecutor is as great a Villain as ever appeared in the World. I was coming down Fleet Street. "So Molly", says he. I said, "I never mollied you." My Lord, I never laid Hands upon him, nor touch'd him. I never touch'd the Man in my Life.' He was not believed.

After the jury had found Manning guilty, Sir Thomas Denison, a judge highly esteemed by Lord Mansfield, pronounced sentence.[6] He told the prisoner, 'You have been indicted for as great an Offence as can be committed. Of this you are now convicted and your Case is still worse, as we are now informed you have before received Judgment for a like Offence. The Court now sees you are not easily reclaimed.' 'As a Terror to all Others', Manning was sentenced to stand in the pillory opposite Serjeants Inn for one hour, followed by twelve months in gaol. He was also fined one shilling, with these words from the judge, 'If you were able, they would not set so small a fine upon you.'[7]

Unlike most of the other defendants we have met so far, and unlike himself at his first trial, Manning was convicted in 1746 on the uncorroborated evidence of one man. Furthermore, the story he told in his own defence has the ring of truth. It is easy to imagine how, after he had been publicly flogged as a sodomite, he was taunted by the porter at Serjeants Inn. Waldale's description of what happened is less convincing because it does not seem likely that the experienced Manning, who a year before had been so self-possessed in the Mermaid, would force himself upon someone who rejected his advances from the outset. However, he was a practised liar, so one cannot be sure if, ironically, he was telling the truth on this occasion.

Judging by the fact that Manning was only fined a shilling, he had come down in the world since he bought drinks for Davis in the

Mermaid and was taken by Mrs Holland for a gentleman from the country. This is not surprising, as he had spent most of the interval in prison, where what little money he had would have gone in procuring bedding, extra food and paying garnish to his gaolers. He was to sink still further before he appeared at the Old Bailey yet again. Six years later he was charged with what was obviously an amateurish attempt at theft.

During the October Sessions in 1752 Richard Manning appeared a third time at the Old Bailey, indicted for stealing a silver watch worth forty shillings from the person of James Stevens on 15 August. Any defendant convicted on such a charge as this was subject to the death penalty as the theft amounted to grand larceny, added to which the claim that the deed was carried out *clam et secrete* (privily and secretly) would be regarded as an aggravating circumstance.[8] The judge at this trial was once more Sir Thomas Denison.

The prosecutor James Stevens told the court that he was crossing St James's Park at 10 p.m. on 15 August and decided to sit on a bench. It was clear moonlight. The prisoner, who was sitting on his left, edged closer towards him and Stevens felt him twitch the firing of his watch before running away. Manning stumbled and fell as he ran but got up again, calling out 'Jack, Jack', though this person, whoever he was, ignored his cry. Meanwhile a man named Edward Wheeler had come to the prosecutor's assistance. He caught up with Manning and took him to the St James's guardhouse.

Edward Wheeler testified that on the way to the guardhouse he saw Manning transfer a watch from his right hand to his left. Challenged by Wheeler, he dropped it and the glass broke.

As he had done at his previous trials, Manning denied there was any truth at all in the prosecution case. He told the court that on the night in question he had just parted from a friend at the edge of the park and was walking on, when he saw Stevens and another man, sitting close together on a park bench. A little later Stevens had crossed his path and asked him if he had been sitting by him. He replied that he had not. Stevens had then told him he had lost his watch and Manning had said he knew nothing about it.

Judge Denison did not believe Manning's story in 1752, any more than he had believed the one told him in 1746. He directed the jurors to find the prisoner guilty of theft, but not 'privily and secretly', and this verdict having been reached, he refrained from sentencing Manning to death. Instead, he told him he would be transported for seven years.[9]

This is the last we hear of Richard Manning. A thorough search through the *Sessions Papers* for the next seven years reveals that he did not return to England within that period, or that if he did, he was not caught – which is as well, or he would hardly have escaped being hanged after all.

Judge Denison, who did not condemn Manning to death, nevertheless transported him for far longer than he had earlier sent him to prison when he was convicted of 'as great an offence as can be committed'. This was because, notwithstanding all the rhetoric piously reiterated by Sir Thomas and others, property crimes regularly attracted the harshest penalties.

The steady decline of Richard Manning over nearly eight years enables us to confirm what we would have suspected anyway about the life of an unequivocal homosexual in the eighteenth century. We do not know which section of society Manning came from, but he laid claim to some medical knowledge. So it is possible that, like Blair who said he was a master of languages, he had more education than the servants he picked up for casual sex. He was certainly articulate. However, no matter what his social position was originally, he became a lonely outsider once he was branded as a habitual sodomite. He had no friends when he needed them. Even the man he called upon to help him in St James's Park ignored his cries. No witnesses came to speak for him at his various trials, any more than they had for Blair and Holiwell. He lacked the varied talents and engaging qualities of John Cooper, who knew how to make money out of his sexual predilection and who, as long as he stayed young and attractive, would earn a certain admiration from the denizens of Drury Lane for the panache with which he played his role as the Princess Seraphina. Manning, who looked like an 'old Rat in an iron Cage', was driven at last to raise cash by becoming a somewhat clumsy pickpocket. When called to account he faced the world with angry defiance and bare-faced lies. The most he could hope for in that world was that its inhabitants would ignore him as Mr Holland was inclined to do, or that when he was unlucky, as he was all too often, he would not find himself at Tyburn.

Notes

1. *Sessions Papers*, January 1743, case nos 104 and 105.
2. *Select Trials for Murders, Robberies, Rapes, Sodomy ... To which are added, genuine Accounts of the Lives ... of the most eminent Convicts*, 4 vols (London, 1742), 2: 369–72.
3. *Sessions Papers*, January 1745, case nos 142 and 143.
4. This punishment is noted in the cumulative list of persons convicted for 1743, by means of a 'W' against the names of Manning and Blair. Such lists, which are published in the *Sessions Papers* volumes, do not cite additional penalties imposed, such as prison terms and fines.

5. John Cambell, *Lives of the Chief Justices of England*, 3 vols, 2nd edn (London, 1858), 3: 69.
6. Campbell, 3: 265–6.
7. *Sessions Papers*, January 1746, case no. 87.
8. Leon Radzinowicz, *A History of Criminal Law and its Administration*, 5 vols (London: Stevens, 1948–86), 1: 636–7.
9. *Sessions Papers*, October 1752, case no. 408.

CHAPTER SEVEN

Racial prejudice

Good or bad luck largely determined the lives of homosexuals in eighteenth-century London. Six months after Richard Manning and John Davis caused such an uproar in the Mermaid, the clients of the Talbot in the Strand reacted rather differently from Mrs Holland and her customers, when told that sodomy was being enacted on the premises.

During the July Sessions at the Old Bailey in 1745 John Mullins, who was Irish, accused John Twyford, a naval man, of making an assault upon him, so that he 'the detestable Sin of Buggery did commit and do'. Mullins told the court he was near the Fleet market when he saw a press gang coming along. As he was looking for a way of escape, a gentleman standing nearby assured him, 'They will not press any Irishmen,' to which Mullins replied, 'I believe they will press anything.' At this the gentleman, who said he was a sea officer, invited him to have a drink and they went to the Plough nearby. Twyford paid for the drinks and then suggested they go on to the Talbot in the Strand. There Mullins had many more drinks and agreed to take a bed at the inn for the night. He said he 'woke up to find the gentleman buggering' him. He 'hollered' and started to beat his attacker, whereupon other people from the inn came to see what was going on.

One of these customers, named Oliver Penn, came to the Old Bailey as a somewhat sceptical witness for the prosecution. Penn said he had told Mullins he was not a boy, 'so how could such a Thing be acted to you without you was as willing as the Other?' With this testimony the case against the prisoner rested, as no one else from the Talbot took the time to come to the Old Bailey at all.

The judge at this trial was the recently knighted Sir Thomas Burnet who, after a riotous youth (embarrassing to his father, the bishop), had settled down to the law and was now a respected and conventional member of the judiciary. As Mullins could not provide the evidence necessary to prove a charge of sodomy, Sir Thomas had no hesitation in acquitting Twyford. He then remanded him until the next sessions when he was supposed to be tried for the lesser offence of making a sodomitical assault.[1] However, this trial does not appear to have taken place, possibly because Mullins lacked the money to take the case further.

There are a number of possible reasons why the customers at the Talbot were unconcerned about the supposed rape of John Mullins. They may have been less respectable than Mrs Holland's clientele at the

Mermaid. Some of the taverns in the Strand had a shady reputation. The Crown, for instance, doubled up as a bawdy-house where, four years later, seamen who claimed they had been bilked would start a major riot.[2] The area was popular with sailors and Twyford may have been among friends disinclined to act against him, no matter what he had done. Furthermore, the fact that Mullins was Irish would not have been a point in his favour. During most of the eighteenth century the number of Irish immigrants convicted on capital charges and hanged was equal to the number of all other immigrants in London who were executed, put together.[3] This state of affairs made many people suspicious of men with Irish accents, especially if they had no visible means of support. If Oliver Penn was one of these, it would account for his reluctance to believe that Mullins was the innocent victim he claimed to be.

Racial prejudice may also have played a part in the case of Michael Levi, a young Jewish street trader, who was brought to the Old Bailey during the May Sessions of 1751, charged with committing sodomy on Benjamin Taylor, a twelve-year-old schoolboy.

Young Taylor told the court that, one evening before Lady Day, Levi had asked him to help carry boxes from his stall to the room he lived in, which was up the yard near the Baptist's Head, an alehouse in Holborn. When the task was done, Levi, who lived alone, locked the door, flung the boy face down on the bed, unbuttoned his breeches and sodomized him. The boy, who was a confident and articulate witness, gave the court explicit details about what had happened to him, sufficient to show that penetration and emission had taken place. He said the episode lasted about fifteen minutes. Taylor informed no one of what had occurred until a week before the trial, when he told a schoolfellow named Roberts, who told his father who then told another boy's father.

The judge at this trial was Sir Thomas Denison, who had twice convicted Richard Manning. On this occasion he cross-examined the prosecution witnesses very carefully, beginning with Taylor. He asked him if he and the prisoner had ever quarrelled, to which the boy replied that Levi had once accused him of stealing a penny, but found nothing when he searched him. Then when the boy's father, John Taylor, confirmed that Benjamin had told him exactly the same story as the one just given in court, Judge Denison asked, 'Did you search your son to see if there were any marks of violence upon him?' Whereupon Mr Taylor admitted, 'I did not.'

After this Thomas Lambard, another schoolboy aged fourteen, started to tell the court that two months earlier Levi, using the same excuse about carrying boxes to his room, had entrapped him as he did Benjamin Taylor, thereafter using him in an identical fashion. However, at this point Judge Denison prevented this witness from going into detail about what had happened, because the charge he was making was not in the indictment.

Thomas Lambard senior also came to the Old Bailey to confirm that he had questioned his son about Levi and heard his story, after 'the affair' with Benjamin Taylor was being talked about. Finally, on the prosecution side, Mr Tidmarsh, who lived in the same neighbourhood as the other witnesses, gave testimony, in which he said he believed that Levi 'had practised sodomy' on his son, Samuel Tidmarsh, a year earlier.

It was then the turn of Levi to speak in his own defence. The reporter at this trial, who never, as a rule, commented on anyone's personal appearance, noted that the defendant wore a red waistcoat, as if this made him a singular figure in the courtroom. Apart from that minor detail there was little to be learned from Levi's presence there, for when asked how he answered the charge against him he said only, 'I know nothing of it.' Instead of pleading his own case, he relied on eight members of the Jewish community in Holborn who came forward, one by one, to speak for his character. They were reputable tradesmen and merchants, such as Samuel Jacobs, a tea-broker who organized a club of which Levi was a member. They had all known him a long time, four of them since infancy. It had entered the minds of none of them that he could be a sodomite. On the contrary, they believed him to be an exceptionally virtuous young man. The view taken by Mr Liebermann was typical of these witnesses. He told the court that he knew that Levi observed all the Jewish religious rites strictly. He also said he had questioned his servants about the defendant and they had confirmed his good opinion of him.

Reputable character witnesses often influenced the outcome of eight-eenth-century trials, but in this one the jurors decided that they believed the boys and their parents. They declared Michael Levi guilty and, as he had been convicted of a felony, Judge Denison condemned him to death.[4]

Levi was the first man since 1730, convicted of a homosexual of-fence, to be sentenced to death at the Old Bailey. In the five other trials for actual sodomy, which have been considered here, the defendants were acquitted because jurors and the judiciary adhered strictly to the rules demanding physical proof of penetration and emission. This in practice meant that the uncorroborated, verbal evidence of the victim was not enough for a conviction. If this precedent had been followed, Levi would also have been acquitted because the charge against him, that he had raped Benjamin Taylor, depended on the boy's word alone. There were no witnesses to the incident. Nor had Benjamin been exam-ined by his father, still less a doctor, to see 'if there were any marks of violence upon him'. Admittedly, two other boys claimed to have had similar experiences, but the evidence of one of them was not allowed, while in the case of the other, his father merely offered an expression of opinion about what had happened to his son.

If we seek the reason why an exception was made of Levi, various explanations suggest themselves. The story the court had heard was a shocking one, told clearly and coherently by young Taylor who, like his namesake, the apprentice who had prosecuted Richard Spencer, had never varied the telling of it. In addition, the boy was supported by a father who was prosperous enough to send his son to school. In all the trials we have considered, the probity and social status of those bringing a prosecution swayed the jurors. Twelve-year-old Benjamin Taylor belonged to a respectable family which was part of a close-knit community, made up of similar families. He was held of more account therefore than thirteen-year-old Thomas Waldron, even though the workhouse boy had produced a witness who was there in the same bed when William Nichols was alleged to have carried out a rape.

Michael Levi also belonged to a close-knit community which, judging from the representatives of it who came forward to speak for him, was equally respectable. It was a pity, though, that these character witnesses were exclusively Jewish. Jews were regarded as aliens and an Act granting them naturalization was withdrawn in 1753, after a public clamour. They were not persecuted with any great zeal in eighteenth-century England, but there was considerable anti-semitism throughout society and Jew-baiting was a sport with the mob.[5] At best Jewish and gentile communities lived side by side but did not mix. Such a situation breeds fear, suspicion and a readiness to believe the worst. Some of this suspicion probably infected the jurors so that they were biased in favour of their own kind, lending a ready ear to statements made by the Taylors, Lambards and Mr Tidmarsh.

Then Levi, unfortunately as far as proving his innocence was concerned, was a solitary young man, who worked and lived alone. Judging by his behaviour in court, he was also taciturn. Perhaps no one, not even in the Jewish community, knew him intimately. Being religious did not preclude him from being a paedophile. On the other hand, it is easy to construct a scenario in which this mildly dandified young man became the victim of malicious schoolboys, who made up stories about him being a sodomite after he had mistakenly accused one of them of theft.

Whatever the truth of the matter, Sir Thomas Denison took steps after the trial to ensure that Levi did not go to the gallows. A month later the editor of *The Gentleman's Magazine* named the men who had been pardoned since the last Old Bailey sessions, to which he added a comment that 'the report of Michael Levi was suspended'.[6] Elsewhere on the cumulative list of convicted felons in the *Sessions Papers* for 1751, someone (an earlier scholar) has pencilled in that Levi was pardoned. That leaves us with two possibilities. Either this case provides one of those rare instances in eighteenth-century judicial history when a verdict was quashed, by means of a Writ of Error,[7] or, alternatively, Judge Denison successfully pleaded for royal mercy for Michael Levi after he had sentenced him as the law demanded.

Notes

1. *Sessions Papers*, July 1745, case no. 316.
2. *A True State of the Case of Bosavern Penlez* (London, 1749).
3. Peter Linebaugh, *The London Hanged: Crime and Civil Society in the Eighteenth Century* (London: Allen Lane, 1991), p. 92, table 3.
4. *Sessions Papers*, May 1751, case no. 389.
5. M. Dorothy George, *London Life in the Eighteenth Century* (London: Kegan Paul, Trench, Trubner and Co., Ltd, 1925), p. 132. For an extensive study of conflicting attitudes to Jews see Todd Endelman, *The Jews of Georgian England 1714–1830* (Philadelphia: Jewish Publications Society of America, 1979) and Frank Felsenstein, *Anti-Semitic Stereotypes: A Paradigm of Otherness in English Popular Culture 1660-1830* (Baltimore: Johns Hopkins University Press, 1995).
6. *Gentleman's Magazine*, 17 June 1751, p. 281.
7. Giles Jacob, *Law Dictionary* (1729). Under the heading 'Records', i.e. records of a trial or judgement, Jacob explains that 'By Statute Judges may reform Defects in any Record or Process. A Writ of Error is required before changes can be made to a document.'

CHAPTER EIGHT

The advantage of taking counsel

Even before it became customary to engage a lawyer to plead a case in court, men publicly accused of being homosexual took counsel more often than any other kind of defendant, though they were still in the minority. Blackmailers preyed on the eighteenth-century gentleman living in St James's, on the tradesman in the City and on their servants, threatening to expose them as sodomites – whether they were or not. Most of these extortionists were petty criminals who were not caught because their victims usually paid up, hoping that would be the end of the matter. Even when the predators found themselves in court, they might well go scot-free, for one reason or another. However, on the rare occasions when they were convicted of attempting to deprive a man falsely of his good name, they were punished harshly. As we have seen, in 1730 Judge Page gave the blackmailers John Lewis and John Jones longer prison sentences than he meted out to any of the men convicted of sodomitical practices who came before him in the Old Bailey that year.

Lewis and Jones were brought to trial because the man they had persecuted could afford to consult a lawyer, who helped to get the pair arrested. However, it was still a novelty for either the prosecutor or the defendant in a criminal trial to seek the advice of an attorney.[1] Most of those who appeared at the Old Bailey lacked the money to do other than make their own case. As a result, many a prosecution relating to sodomy was bound to fail because the original indictment had not been framed by someone who knew the law and how it worked in practice.

The trial of George Sealey and Thomas Freeman during the September Sessions of 1736 was unusual, therefore, in that they employed a counsel to defend them against the charge that they had committed buggery together. Both men were fairly well-to-do. Sealey was a pigman. Freeman was a butcher who, only recently, had sued a Mr Turner at the Guildhall for calling him a sodomite. They were prosecuted by another butcher named Thomas Palmer with an ill reputation for enticing men into card games from which, all too often, he emerged as the winner.

Palmer told the Old Bailey that he saw Freeman and Sealey in the yard of the Bell Inn on market day. Freeman invited him to drink with them, telling him privately that Sealey 'had a good Deal of Money' and that if they could get him to play cards, they might win some of it. After a while Freeman and Sealey went down to the 'necessary house' in the basement. Palmer, fearing they were plotting to fleece him, followed them to overhear their conversation. Putting his eye to a crack in the door of the necessary house, he saw Sealey buggering Freeman.

At this point the defendants' counsel interrupted. He asked the prosecutor to expand his last statement. Palmer did, saying 'Freeman was the Patient.' After this the counsel remarked 'I see you have some Notion of these Things', and let him go on. Palmer continued his story, telling the court how he had run into the market, and, seeing two acquaintances William Vincent and William Freshwater there, called on them to act as witnesses of what he had seen. Freshwater subsequently agreed to help Palmer bring an indictment which led to the trial.

When Palmer had finished speaking, the defence counsel began his cross-examination in earnest. He ascertained that the prosecutor had been reluctant to appear against Freeman when earlier he was defending himself in the Guildhall against a charge of sodomy. He also made Palmer admit that he had known Freeman for eight or nine years, without ever suspecting him of being a sodomite before. Furthermore, he elicited that Palmer knew Freeman lived happily with a woman and had two children by her. The counsel's most telling point, however, concerned the size of the necessary house. He returned to this subject several times during the course of the trial. Apparently the place was only two feet square!

As well as hiring an able lawyer, both defendants called seven witnesses each to speak for their characters. The prosecutor also produced two men who said they believed he would not forswear himself. Finally Anne Sutton, Freshwater's mistress, and two others said the same for him.

On balance, the witnesses for the defendants made the best impression, the testimony of one of them, Nathaniel Edwards, being especially effective. Edwards was Freeman's brother-in-law. He explained how he had tried to keep the matter out of the courts because of the scandal of a trial.[2] To that end he had paid various sums of money to Palmer and Freshwater and admitted that he had been prepared to pay thirty guineas for their silence. He had also visited Sealey's home in Bushey. There he found that all his neighbours spoke well of him, and that Sealey's wife was quite sure her husband could not be guilty of sodomy.

The judge at this trial was the London Recorder, a Mr Urlin who, unlike the other justices who have appeared in these pages so far, is not mentioned in the biographical dictionaries of leading legal figures. He directed the jurors to find George Sealey and Thomas Freeman 'Not Guilty', which they did.[3]

Without the help of a defence counsel who systematically undermined the prosecution case, George Sealey and Thomas Freeman might

have been convicted. Palmer made them appear as unregenerate sodomites, much as the less fortunate Holiwell and Huggins, Deacon and
Blair, Manning and Davis were. Freeman was particularly vulnerable,
having been arraigned before on a charge of sodomy. Nor would he
have impressed the jurors as being an obviously respectable citizen,
Palmer having mentioned that he was one of the card players at the Bell
Inn who was on the look-out for greenhorns to deprive of their guineas.
He also had a mistress rather than a wife though, as the defence lawyer
surmised, this could be seen as a point in his favour, because even if the
jurors had previously met sodomites who were married, they may not
have known any who lived of their own free will with women to whom
they were not legally bound.

After this trial Palmer and Freshwater walked free from the Old
Bailey as well as the defendants, despite the fact that the judgement
against them meant that they had brought a malicious prosecution.
Having been found 'Not Guilty' of sodomy, Sealey and Freeman wished
to forget and be forgotten, as soon as possible. Even an acquittal in a
case of this sort was a stand-off rather than a victory. When Jeremy
Bentham advocated the decriminalization of homosexual activity, he
argued that the current law injured the innocent as well as the guilty,
because doubts raised about a man's sexual orientation were damaging
to him, though publicly disproved.[4]

For this reason Nathaniel Edwards had spoken openly in court about
his efforts to avoid the 'scandal of a trial'. The fact that he had no
hesitation in telling a judge and jury that he was willing to pay thirty
guineas to buy the silence of his brother-in-law's accusers illustrates
how commonplace such a practice must have been.

It was fifteen years before there was another trial at the Old Bailey
which hinged on a false accusation of sodomy. Then, at the end of
1751, when John Burk prosecuted Richard Noke, the jurors heard an
all-too-familiar tale of a misadventure that could have befallen any one
of them, as he walked through London at night. Some of the jurors may
also have found the face of Richard Noke familiar. He had been present
at the Old Bailey two years before, when he appeared as a witness in a
robbery trial.

On that earlier occasion Mary Smith, who described herself as 'an
unfortunate girl of the town', told the court that, between ten and
eleven o'clock at night on 21 June 1749, she had been knocked down in
the Haymarket by Thomas Mayo, after she refused to have a drink with
him, and that he had then stolen from her a gold ring worth eighteen
shillings. Richard Noke, who was able to identify her assailant, had
gone with her to get a warrant from a justice, as she did not know how
to serve it, after which he had taken her home and spent the night with

her in her room in Covent Garden. However, when Mary Smith gave her testimony, she did not realize that Noke had now changed sides and, instead of supporting her story, would appear as a witness for the prisoner.

Thomas Mayo, a landlord, claimed that the robbery charge against him was trumped up by a former tenant of his, named Easthoff, whom he had recently evicted from a house, and who wanted to avoid paying him for items of furniture that had disappeared from it. When Noke gave evidence he agreed that Easthoff had concocted the story of the robbery, adding that Mary Smith had been bullied into aiding and abetting him in the deception. Finally, Noke ensured the acquittal of Mayo by telling the court that he had been with Mary Smith since before 10 p.m. on 21 June until dawn the next day, so he was certain she had not been robbed as she claimed.[5]

It emerged during this trial that both Easthoff and Mayo had offered bribes to most of the witnesses. Presumably, therefore, Noke had agreed to support, in the end, the man who made him the best offer.

Noke had described himself in 1749 as a printer's compositor, a trade that gave him a semblance of respectability. No mention was made of him having any kind of employment in 1751 when, during the December Sessions, he was indicted with 'another unknown Person' of a felony, namely of falsely charging John Burk 'with perpetrating the Crime called Sodomy, and demanding Money with Intent to rob him'.

Burk, who prosecuted the case himself, told the Old Bailey that he was a servant to Mr Sam Wilson and his son in Cannon Street. On 15 November, at about 7 p.m., he was returning home from Wood Street when two men stopped him. One of them, saying he was 'a very pretty fellow', accused him of offering to commit sodomy with his companion, and told him they were going to take him before Alderman Ironside. Then Noke said he fancied Burk was 'of some character, and that he would not blast it', so if Burk would 'make him some satisfaction', they would let him go and say no more about it. Burk tried to run off but the two men knocked him to the ground. Several passersby were coming along but none of them stopped, until Mr Dimford appeared with a Mr Ward. Noke told Dimford that Burk was a sodomite but Dimford, who knew Burk well, said, on the contrary, he was 'a very sober, honest man', adding that he, Noke, had 'a very ugly Look'. The one man ran away, but Dimford and Ward took Noke before the Lord Mayor.

The judge at this trial was Sir Thomas Denison who, earlier in the year, had pondered over the fate of Michael Levi. Now he realized that on the evidence he had heard Noke could not be convicted of a felony, because he had not actually taken any money from the prosecutor.

Accordingly he directed the jury to return a verdict of 'Not Guilty', after which he remanded Noke to be tried at the next sessions for a misdemeanour.[6] In the event Noke went free because, as had happened at other trials, the prosecutor dropped the case at this point.

It is hardly surprising that John Burk decided not to go on with the prosecution of Richard Noke. If Mr Dimford had not come along to help him get this opportunistic rogue arrested, it is doubtful that he would have been able to take him to court at all. Burk was a rarity too, in being willing to bear the costs of even one prosecution. As Fielding had written earlier in 1751, many victims of crime were deterred from seeking redress in the courts because of the expense.[7] Burk had already had to pay all necessary legal fees himself. These included the cost of drawing up and copying all the relevant documents, from the original indictment to the final judgement.

The price of preferring an indictment was at least two shillings and was often over three, which were sizeable sums when whole families lived for a week on ten shillings.[8] George Sealey and Thomas Freeman would have paid about ten guineas for the services of their counsel.[9] It is doubtful whether John Burk could have afforded to take legal advice of any description, but as a result of not doing so, the indictment of Richard Noke was badly worded and the 'very sober, honest man', who hoped to bring him to justice, left the Old Bailey disappointed.

Between 1730 and 1751 twenty-two defendants appeared in the Old Bailey accused of offences that related in some way to sodomitical practices. Of these, six were charged with the capital crime of sodomy, five of whom were acquitted – or all of them if we include Michael Levi, whose original conviction appears to have been overturned. The only man hanged in the twenty-one years was Williamson Goodman who, while guilty of making sodomitical advances and attempted blackmail, was sent to the gallows because he had robbed his prey of 9s. 6d.

Among the acquittals were those of the three young bachelors charged with sodomizing adolescents. Teenage boys who claimed to be victims of a homosexual attack earned little sympathy at the Old Bailey if it was shown that they had accepted so much as a penny custard from the would-be seducer. Furthermore, although the two trials concerned with the sexual abuse of children ended in a conviction, there is no indication that anyone in the court regarded this kind of offence as more heinous than any other involving sodomitical practices.

Consenting adults convicted of being sodomites were among those most harshly treated. George Sealey and Thomas Freeman might well have suffered the same fate as the other older homosexual couples who were tried at the Old Bailey had they not been able to employ an adroit lawyer.

From the trials described here a picture emerges of the life of a homosexual in mid-eighteenth-century London. Casual sodomy committed by young single men was probably commonplace and tacitly accepted, if it took place with young effeminate adolescents. The older homosexual was viewed more sternly, even if few people wished to see him put to death. Nor was he treated more leniently if, like the loving husband, William Huggins, he was bisexual. Thomas Blair, Richard Manning and Richard Spencer, whose sexual orientation was fixed, led lonely as well as precarious lives. There is no indication that they, or any of the other defendants who appear in these pages, frequented the molly clubs or belonged to the burgeoning homosexual community.

Even John Cooper, who lived unmolested as a mollies' pimp and was admired for his convincing performances in drag, found he had no one on his side in a contest with the ex-tar whom neighbours regarded as honest-to-goodness and straight. He had but a tenuous foothold in the relatively tolerant world of Drury Lane. Moreover, his future as the Princess Seraphina was equivocal, once his youth and looks were gone. As it happens, seventeen years after Tom Gordon made off with the new suit, a John Cooper came to the Old Bailey charged with theft. On the night of 24 June 1749 he was seen leaving a coach house from where he was supposed to have stolen a cloth coat valued at ten shillings, the property of Moses Skeytts, as well as another cloth coat belonging to Joseph Barnes. After a watchman testified that he had caught the defendant with the two coats upon him, he was convicted and sentenced to transportation for seven years.[10] There is no way of telling from the records whether this John Cooper was the Princess Seraphina, but the fact that the case again involved clothes arouses some misgivings.

Apart from the various penalties inflicted on known homosexuals in the courts, they found it difficult to earn a living. The effect of the Tudor Buggery Law was to cast out from everyday society a section of the male population, not because the members of it harmed their fellow human beings, but because they were not heterosexuals.

Heterosexuals, or any man who wished to pass as one, were also put in fear by the Buggery Law. We have already seen how this was so from the cases involving false accusations and extortion that were heard at the Old Bailey during the twenty-one years which have just been reviewed.

This book goes on to say more about the plight of heterosexuals accused of sodomy, explaining first of all why it was difficult for them to obtain redress in the courts.

Notes

1. Until the 1730s lawyers seldom appeared for the prosecution and never for the defence. See John H. Langbein, 'Shaping the Eighteenth-Century Criminal Trial', in *The University of Chicago Law Review*, 50.1 (Winter, 1983), 1–136.
2. Jeremy Bentham noted that if a man imputed to be a sodomite decided 'to meet his accuser in the face of justice' the 'danger to his reputation' would still be 'considerable'. See 'Jeremy Bentham's Essay on "Paederasty"', Part II, ed. Louis Crompton in *Journal of Homosexuality*, 4 (1978): 99.
3. *Sessions Papers*, July 1749, case nos 78 and 79.
4. 'Essay on "Paederasty"'. Bentham's main argument for changing the law on homosexuality was that it encouraged blackmailers and harmed the innocent.
5. *Sessions Papers*, July 1749, case no. 490.
6. *Sessions Papers*, December 1751, case no. 33.
7. *An Enquiry into the Causes of the Late Increase of Robbers* (1751), section 8. Fielding suggested that the state met the costs of needy litigants.
8. Roy Porter, *English Society in the Eighteenth Century* (London: Allen Lane, 1982), p. 235.
9. This sum is approximate, based on the information that a poisoner in the 1750s paid thirty guineas for three counsels to defend him. See Douglas Hay and Francis Snyder, *Policing and Prosecution in Britain 1750–1850* (Oxford: Clarendon Press, 1989), p. 23.
10. *Sessions Papers*, 5–10 July 1749, case no. 429.

PART IV
Victims of malice

CHAPTER NINE

Blackmail and the fall of Samuel Foote

Towards a law on blackmail

The laws and official rhetoric condemning homosexuals inevitably produced a blackmailers' charter which was bad for heterosexual men as well. Accusations of sodomy were easily made but not easily gainsaid, for there needed to be no material evidence of the offence – no misappropriated objects as in theft, no corpse as in murder. As Jeremy Bentham pointed out, 'For a man to bring a charge of this sort against any other man without the possibility of its being disproved there needs no more than for them to have been alone together for a few moments.'[1] Yet legislators were painfully slow in devising a law that attempted to deter those who terrorized their fellow men by threatening to call them sodomites.

A major problem arose because the concept of blackmail in its modern sense did not exist for most of the eighteenth century. When that term was used at all it referred to the protection money exacted by raiders from farmers and others living in the Border country. To deal with this crime an Act had been passed in 1601 whereby not only the predator but also the victim, who gave in and paid the money or goods demanded of him, could be charged with felony.[2] For a long time after that blackmail was deemed a species of robbery and very little account was taken in law of the psychological damage suffered by anyone menaced with the loss of his good name.

As a result, if a man threatened with a charge of sodomy decided to prosecute his accuser, he often indicted him for extortion and tried to prove in a court of law that the man charged was a thief. This kind of case might well fail, as Francis Godelard discovered after his encounter with John Casey in 1721. Casey had approached him one night near the end of the Mall, demanding his money and watch. Godelard had no watch and only one shilling on him, so the frustrated Casey started to beat him up. The noise brought two soldiers on the scene, whereupon Casey pointed to Godelard, saying, 'He wants to bugger me; take him prisoner!' The soldiers were unconvinced and Casey was arrested. At his trial, however, his threats were discounted and he was acquitted because it could not be proved that he had stolen anything.[3]

Threats to charge a man with sodomy were for the most part verbal, but if menaces of any kind had been made in writing the prosecutor could use the 1723 Waltham Black Act. A section in that catch-all piece of legislation made it a crime 'knowingly sending any letter [signed or unsigned] demanding money, a remission, or any other valuable thing'.[4] This clause had been included in the Act not to protect the victims of homosexual blackmail but because extorting money through the mail became a common offence in the eighteenth century.[5] Some of the letters, in which the aggrieved writer threatened to set fire to the recipient's hayricks or house unless he paid up, are seen now to have been a form of social protest.[6] Punishment for the offence was severe and could be death, as it was for Jepthah Big who was convicted and hanged in 1729.[7]

However, the practice of using the postal system to menace the powerful continued apace. So in 1754 a further law was passed, strengthening the clause in the Black Act.[8] From then on, sending any threatening letter became a crime, even if the writer of it made no demands.

Nevertheless the difficulty of proving in court that a defendant had written the letters he was accused of sending could make it hard to obtain a conviction. The 3rd Duke of Marlborough faced this problem in 1758. In that year he received a number of anonymous letters threatening him with assassination unless he paid the writer anything from two to three hundred pounds. Marlborough went to keep two appointments with the extortioner, first in Hyde Park and then in Westminster Abbey. On each occasion he met a Mr Barnard, but the latter refused to speak. Barnard was finally arrested and tried under the Waltham Black Act. The Duke briefed William Davy, who had had a reputation for being a very able attorney ever since his successful prosecution of the notorious Elizabeth Canning five years earlier. Nevertheless Barnard, who could produce good character witnesses, was acquitted because of insufficient evidence.[9]

It was rare for anyone receiving letters accusing him of sodomitical practices to prosecute the writer. In order to avoid the publicity of a court case he was far more likely to pay the sum of money demanded of him and hope the predator would not become too rapacious. However, if his accuser went to the length of indicting him, the victim could use the Black Act to lodge a counter-charge of malicious prosecution, though before he did that he had to stand trial himself and clear his name, after which he might well decide that seeing his persecutor punished was not worth the continued publicity (to say nothing of the expense) a second court case would bring.

Furthermore, it was very unusual indeed for a man who succeeded in showing he had been falsely labelled a sodomite to be awarded damages. The notebooks Lord Mansfield kept of cases he heard record just one instance. It was a trial for defamation held at the Croydon Assizes in August 1781. Apparently, during a scuffle at the May races Lewis George Dive had decided that John Howe wanted to bugger him and said as much. As he refused to retract his statement, Howe had taken him to court where the verdict went his way and he was awarded damages of £500.[10]

Before that a number of cases involving accusations of sodomy, heard during the 1770s, produced judgements which indicated a wish to take into account the mental agony endured by a man faced with the threat of being falsely proclaimed a homosexual.[11] Judge Ashhurst expressed this new awareness in 1784 when he told the court at the end of the R. v. Hickman trial, 'a threat to accuse a man of having committed the greatest of all crimes is a sufficient force to constitute the crime of robbery by putting in fear [...] to most men the idea of losing their fame and reputation is equally, if not more terrific than the dread of personal injury'.[12] Twelve years later he was still proselytizing for this point of view when he declared 'Terror is of two kinds: namely, a terror which leads the kind of the party to apprehend an injury to his person, or a terror which leads him to apprehend an injury to his character.'[13]

Not all judges were willing to accept the principle of constructive robbery enunciated by Judge Ashhurst. It was still being questioned in 1802.[14] The arguments dragged on, and it was 1843 before a Libel Act specifically offered protection from those publishing 'or threatening to publish a libel' damaging to an individual's reputation 'in order to extort money or some other valuable thing'.[15]

However, none of the legislation passed could alleviate the misery suffered by anyone who faced an accusation that he was a sodomite. While homosexuality was considered a crime, as Jeremy Bentham argued, even if the accused proved his innocence, 'the well-seasoned perjurer' would 'have finally the advantage over him', for 'whether a man be thought to have actually been guilty of this practice or only to be disposed to it, his reputation suffers equal ruin'.[16]

The fall of Samuel Foote

Just how much of an ordeal it was for an man to stand trial for sodomy, even if he was acquitted, can be seen from the experience of Samuel Foote who, in 1776, was indicted 'for Assaulting John Sangster, with an Intent to Commit Buggery'.[17]

Sangster had been taken on as Foote's coachman in November 1775 and remained in his employment until the following May. Foote was a satirical dramatist who acted in his own plays, latterly at the Haymarket Theatre, of which he became a manager in 1767. Almost forgotten now, Foote has been called the Oscar Wilde of his day.[18] Like Wilde, he was over-confident and incautious, as well as being a famous wit who went everywhere and made many friends in London society. He also made enemies, notably the raffish Duchess of Kingston, whom he guyed as Lady Kitty Crocodile in a comedy called *A Trip to Calais* first written in 1775. About to face trial for bigamy, she objected vociferously and Foote had to suppress the play. But then he revised it and put it on again, calling it *The Capuchin*, with the Rev. Dr Jackson, the Duchess's friend and adviser, featuring as the central character, Dr Viper.

Dr Jackson, a newspaper editor, was a dangerous man to antagonize. On 13 May 1776 he published a scurrilous piece in his own journal *The Public Ledger*, suggesting that Aristophanes (a name commonly applied to Foote) was addicted to sodomy and preferred love in a stable to love in a boudoir. The reference to the stable was the first indication that Dr Jackson and the Duchess had now joined forces with Jack Sangster, the actor-manager's former coachman. Foote prosecuted Dr Jackson for libel and won his case.[19]

However, the campaign against him continued, with rumours flying round London that he was soon to face prosecution for an odious assault. When the season at the Haymarket opened that spring, Foote went on stage to assure the audience that he would clear his name. Then he tried to carry on as usual.

The crisis came on 8 July when Sangster preferred a Bill of Indictment at Hick's Hall, accusing his former employer of trying to sodomize him. As soon as this happened, Foote's friends rallied round, including two royal dukes, Edmund Burke and Joshua Reynolds because, as they said, 'if loose charges of this abominable nature were once permitted quietly to take footing in the practice of the world ... no man who kept male servants in his house would be safe from calumny'.[20] It was also pointed out that discontented servants might 'become mere instruments in the hands of others'.[21] For although the involvement of the Duchess and Dr Jackson in this prosecution was never conclusively proved, no one ever doubted that it had been organized and financed by them. Sangster would later admit in court that his legal expenses had been met by 'a stranger' who had come forward on 23 May, offering his support.[22]

The trial was held in the court of King's Bench on 8 December 1776, with Lord Mansfield as the judge and a special jury 'of gentlemen of Middlesex County'.[23] It attracted a good deal of publicity, not only because Foote was well known, but because his feud with the Duchess of Kingston was common knowledge and the Duchess herself had featured spectacularly in a trial in Westminster Hall in April, when a jury of her peers had decided she was indeed a bigamist.

Foote could not face attending his trial himself. Nor did he have to. As he had obtained bail, current practice allowed him to stay at his Suffolk Street house while his attorney fought his case for him. As prosecutor, Sangster told his story first. He gave a highly graphic account of how Foote had tried to persuade and then bully him into buggery in England and Ireland over a period of four months and how, in disgust and rage, he had decided to leave his service within hours of an episode which had occurred in London on 1 May.

For many years Foote had regularly gone to town on that date for a meeting with the players at the Haymarket, and the coachman began by describing how he had driven his employer from his house at Northend to the theatre as usual. He was very specific about the occasion, and Lord Mansfield noted down pretty well everything he said, beginning as follows:

> The carriage was ordered to the door at Northend [on] 1st May at 10 o'clock, We got to town [at] a quarter before 11. Defendant went on stage & continued there about an hour & 1/2. A woman inquired for Mrs. Garner [&] desired me to ask, which I did. As I opened the door to go on stage out of the house, Defendant said, 'John, where are you going?' [I answered] 'A gentlewoman at the door asks if Mrs. Garner is here & I am going to inquire'. He said, 'Bid her go round the other way'. I turned about directly. Defendant walked with me to the hall door where she stood. He gave her the answer himself. When the door shut, he went upstairs. In 5 minutes [he] rang the bell. I ran upstairs into the drawing room where he stood, which was going to be fresh-papered. The paper lay in the window. 'John', said he, 'this is the paper?' 'I don't know', I said, 'I'll ask the maid'. I went to the stairs and called out, 'Nanny'. She answered. I came back to the drawing room. Defendant bid me come into the dining room & take down these books. I went in, he said, 'Take these books into the country'. He kept looking at the book & often asked, 'John, are you quite well of the measles?' & turning round & laughing in my face [he] called, 'John, reach me this', seeming to mean a looking glass. While I stood up to take down the glass, he shut & as I found afterwards locked the door. He called out, 'John, I don't mean that it is of no consequence'. Defendant stood with [his] back to the door, laughing & grinning in my face. [He] said, 'Have not my servants been good to you, while ill of the measles?' 'They have', [I said] & [he] said, 'Have not I taken a great deal of care of you? Giving you physic & things?' I thanked [him]. He said, 'The best recompense you can make is to let me have a fuck at you'. I said, 'What do you mean by that?' 'Don't you know?' 'Yes', says I, 'I had sooner be hanged. I am very much surprized [sic] a man like you would offer such a thing to a servant. I did [not] know you was such a person

before I came. Had I known you was such a person I would not
have lived with you for 100 guineas a year'.[24]

The scene did not end there. As Sangster described it, Foote tried first to
argue him out of his objections and, when that failed, manhandled him,
seizing his testicles and holding them 'so fast [they] were swelled many
days'.[25]

So far the court had heard a dramatic tale with graphic touches to
make it plausible. However, when it was the turn of the defence witnesses to testify, players from the Haymarket Theatre affirmed that,
although they had gathered at noon on 1 May for the meeting, Foote
did not arrive. At 2 p.m. they received a message that he was not
coming to London at all that day. The court was also shown a copy of
the *Morning Chronicle* with a notice telling all concerned that the
meeting had been postponed until 6 May. It was impossible for Sangster
to say that he had merely made a mistake about the date because it was
on record that on the day the meeting was finally held he had gone to
Sir John Fielding to charge Foote, and had given that magistrate precise
details of the circumstances and time of the supposed assault.

Almost from the beginning the trial went the defendant's way. The
longer Sangster had gone on speaking, the less convincing he had
sounded. He did not know when to stop, and over-elaborated. So
having made it appear that Foote's supposed homosexual advances on 1
May had come as a shock and a surprise, he went on to describe
another occasion four months earlier in Ireland which had convinced
him that his employer was a sodomite with designs on him. Yet he had
made no effort to look for another job then, nor, according to other
servants of Foote, had he left voluntarily in May. They testified that he
was drunken and abusive and had been turned off. Nor did anyone else
come forward to support the accusations he made about the actor-
manager. Admittedly it was never made clear where Foote spent 1 May.
One of his servants said he spent the whole of that week at Northend,
while another testified that he had driven his employer to the house in
Suffolk Street that day and had left him there.[26]

However, nothing was made of this conflict in the evidence when
Lord Mansfield summed up. In a forceful speech, that was widely
reported in the press, he laid particular emphasis on two factors. First
of all he spoke of Sangster's mysterious financial backer. 'Here a man
takes up the Prosecution' he told the jurors, 'who is a stranger to the
Prosecutor, does not know him, and never meddled with the affair till
the 23rd. of May – Who is that man? Is he a friend to Justice, or an
enemy to Mr. Foote?' Then, aware no doubt of the alleged part played
by the Duchess of Kingston and Dr Jackson in the charges made about
Foote, he added, 'I expected to have heard of the real person who acts

behind the curtain.' Secondly, the Lord Chief Justice seized on the fact that Sangster had got his dates wrong. This, he told the court, was heaven-sent, 'For the Providence of God interposes for the Prosecutor to fix on such a day as Mr. Foote did not go to town, though he had done it for many years back – and in such cases it can only be by providential means, or the Prosecutor's contradicting himself in evidence, that the innocent escape the ruin of their reputation and welfare.'[27] This speech was mainly for the benefit of the journalists and their readers, as Lord Mansfield admitted. To the jurors he concluded by saying, 'You are in possession of the Evidence, you are masters of the whole matter and will, I do not doubt, do you duty.'[28] Whereupon the jury, without leaving the courtroom, found the defendant 'Not Guilty'.

The trial of Samuel Foote in the last quarter of the eighteenth century differed greatly from the trial of Oscar Wilde at the end of the next century, not least in that few people, apart from the prosecutor and his backers, wished to see the defendant convicted. Indeeed, a number of people had various reasons for wanting Sangster to lose his case. Those men among Foote's friends who kept servants had immediately seen the danger to themselves if loose charges of the kind the coachman had made were not speedily and comprehensively quashed. Foote's own servants and the players at the Haymarket had nothing to gain by seeing their employer sent to gaol. At the trial they all stood by him and the Lord Chief Justice, who was fully aware of the machinations of the Duchess of Kingston and Dr Jackson, was on the side of the defendant.

Nevertheless this story does not have a happy ending. When Arthur Murphy, Foote's friend, drove from the King's Bench to Suffolk Street to tell him of the verdict, he found he had collapsed and was lying 'extended on the floor'.[29] He seems to have had a minor stroke. He recovered from this and went back to the stage but he looked ill and his performance lacked energy and spirit. He was depressed because the rumours about him had not ceased. Dr Jackson was still busily at work. After the trial a second attack on his enemy, which he had written under a pseudonym, circulated in London. This consisted of twenty-nine pages of verses entitled *Sodom and Onan, a Satire, Inscribed to ———— Esq.*, with Foote's portrait on the frontispiece. The work was both nasty and comprehensive. It hinted yet again that the actor pursued his amours in the stable in a couplet which read:

> In splendid Mansion finding no resource,
> Fain he'd defile the Chamber of the Horse.

It then went on to make barely veiled references to other supposed sodomites, including Lord George Sackville-Germain and Peregrine

Bertie, Duke of Ancaster. Most importantly, it suggested that Foote's trial had been rigged since:

> ... the Laws leave Avenues
> Which powerful Sod'mites frequently abuse;
> Tamper with Gold, and terrify with Threats.[30]

Foote was utterly unnerved and physically debilitated by the virulent campaign that had been waged, and was still being waged against him. He sold his share in the Haymarket Theatre and then gave up acting entirely after a second stroke. When he had made another partial recovery, he decided to go and stay in France. However, while waiting to embark at Dover, he was struck down again and died on 20 October 1777, less than a year after the trial that had ruined his life.

Sangster went unpunished. Foote never contemplated charging him with making a malicious prosecution after the King's Bench jurors decided that the coachman was lying. For this actor, who fed on popular acclaim, the thought of yet another Pyrrhic victory was more than he could bear. Once doubts about his sexual tastes had become the talk of the town, not even a powerful Lord Chief Justice could dispel them, with the result that opinion is still divided about Foote's sexual orientation.[31]

It does not help us in coming to a decision if we look at the way he lived. He was unmarried, and for many years the handsome Sir Francis Blake Delaval was 'his very intimate acquaintance and inseparable companion'. But there was also talk of a washerwoman who was his mistress and he had at least two sons.[32] Now the question has been raised, it is impossible for us to say whether he was heterosexual, homosexual or bisexual. It was equally impossible for the general public in 1776. Yet, whatever the truth of the matter, this uncertainty does not alter his status as a pitiable victim of a bad law.

Jeremy Bentham could well have been thinking of Foote when he wrote in his essay on 'Paederasty' that in trials of men eventually acquitted of homosexual offences 'the well seasoned perjurer' was the ultimate victor. As long as the Buggery Law remained on the statute books it was impossible to devise any legal measure whereby a man could escape unscathed once he had been publicly accused of sodomy.

Of course not everyone who found himself in that situation let himself be crushed as easily as Samuel Foote. If, however, the victim of a sustained attack to expose him as a sodomite was determined to overcome his enemies, he had to be not only resolute and rich, but also ruthless. Such a man was Edward Walpole.

Notes

1. Jeremy Bentham, 'Essay on "Paederasty", introduced and edited by Louis Crompton, *Journal of Homosexuality*, 3 (1978), 383–405 and 4 (1978), 91–107, 4: 99.
2. 43 Eliz. c. 13, preamble and s. 2.
3. *Select Trials for Murder, Robberies, Rape, Sodomy ... From the year 1720 to 1724*, 2 vols (London, 1734 and 1735), 1: 152–3.
4. 9 Geo. 1, c. 22.
5. Leon Radzinowicz, *A History of Criminal Law and its Administration from 1750*, 5 vols (London: Stevens, 1948–86), 1: 73.
6. E. P. Thompson, 'The Crime of Anonymity' in *Albion's Fatal Tree*, ed. Douglas Hay (London: Peregrine Books, 1975), pp. 255–308.
7. William Jackson, ed., *The New and Complete Newgate Calendar*, 8 vols (London, 1818), 2: 206–9.
8. 27 Geo. 2, c. 15.
9. H. W. Woolrych, *Lives of Eminent Serjeants-at-Law*, 2 vols (London, 1869).
10. James Oldham, *The Mansfield Manuscripts and the Growth of English Law in the Eighteenth Century*, 2 vols (Chapel Hill: University of North Carolina Press, 1992), 'Crime and Tort', p. 851.
11. R. *v.* Jones 1776 and R. *v.* Donnally 1779. See W. H. D. Winder, 'The Development of Blackmail', *Modern Law Review*, 5 (1941), 26.
12. R. *v.* Hickman, quoted by Winder, p. 26.
13. R. *v.* Knewland, quoted by Mike Hepworth, *Blackmail: Publicity and Secrecy in Everyday Life* (London: Routledge, 1975), p. 13.
14. In R. *v.* Elmstead three out of twelve judges did not consider the R. *v.* Hickman decision was binding. See Winder, p. 27.
15. Quoted Hepworth, p. 14.
16. 'Essay on "Paederasty"', 2: 100.
17. Oldham, 'Crime and Tort', pp. 1004–9.
18. Rictor Norton, *Mother Clap's Molly House: The Gay Subculture in England 1700–1830* (London: Gay Men's Press, 1992), p. 180.
19. PRO, KB 1/20, no. 10.
20. William Cooke, *Memoirs of Samuel Foote*, 3 vols (London, 1805), 1: 228.
21. Ibid.
22. Oldham, p. 1007.
23. *London Chronicle*, 7 December 1776.
24. Oldham, p. 1004.
25. Quoted by Oldham, p. 1006.
26. Oldham, p. 1008.
27. *Lloyds Evening Post*, 9–11 December 1776. Also reported in the *Annual Register*, 1776, p. 199.
28. *Lloyds Evening Post*, 9–11 December 1776.
29. Cooke, pp. 232–3.
30. Reverend Jackson, *Sodom and Onan, a Satire, Inscribed to ——— Esq. alias the Devil upon two Sticks* (c. 1776). Written under the name of 'Humphrey Nettle'.
31. Norton, pp. 174–84.

32. John Bee, *The Works of Samuel Foote, Esq., with ... An Essay on the Life, Genius and Writings of the Author*, 3 vols (London, 1830), 1: clxiii.

PART V

Edward Walpole and the conspirators

CHAPTER TEN

Taking sides

A patron and his protégé

Early in the winter of 1750 an Irish boy of eighteen years walked along Pall Mall looking for the house of the Honourable Edward Walpole, son of the late first minister. The boy's name was John Cather. He was tall and 'very fair', with a clear complexion.[1] He had recently arrived from Dublin where he had once met Walpole, who had offered to employ him if he ever came to London.

Cather was said to be the son of a farmer in Donegal, now dead, whom he used to help labouring in the fields – the only work he is known to have done.[2] Even so he did not think of himself as being on a par with the Irish migrants who came over every summer to help with the English harvest. He could read and write and had the advantage of belonging to the Protestant minority in Ireland. All the time he remained in London he would be described in official documents as a 'gentleman'.[3] He had very little money but tooks pains with his appearance, and had hopes of bettering himself, once Walpole took him into his service.

Cather found the place he was looking for, opposite the shop of the court clockmaker, Vulliamy, and directly in front of what had been the London home of the old Duchess of Marlborough. It was a new house, built in the Palladian style a decade or so earlier.[4] Inside it was, according to the owner's brother, 'filthy and casually run'.[5] Unlike Horace Walpole, Edward was careless about his domestic arrangements, but he was an attentive father, all the more so because Dorothy Clement, the mother of his four young children, had died some twelve years before. Walpole found his high-spirited son difficult to manage, but delighted in his three little girls.

Cather knocked on the door and was admitted. Soon he was led upstairs into a room where Walpole was sitting, surrounded by musical instruments, which included a variation on the bass viol that he had invented himself and called a pentachord.[6] Walpole had not set eyes on the boy for two or three years, but he remembered him and received him cordially. However, he did not offer him a job. Instead, he said he would give him a recommendation if he found a place elsewhere.

Walpole was forty-four in 1750 and had already been living in semi-retirement for over ten years. Earlier his father, Sir Robert, had launched

from a drawing by Rosalba.   Etched by Edwards.

SIR EDWARD WALPOLE, K.B.
M.P. FOR YARMOUTH FROM 1754 TO 1768.
C. Muskett, Norwich

10.1   Sir Edward Walpole (1706–84). From the Rosalba portrait painted when
he was on the Grand Tour in 1728–30 and called by ladies in Italy 'the
handsome Englishman'.

him on a political career, in which he had been thoroughly ill at ease, so that he had resigned in 1739 from all his public appointments.[7] Reluctantly he carried on as a back-bencher in the House of Commons because, as he told the Duke of Newcastle in 1747, he considered it his duty to be of 'service to the Government'.[8] As long as the Duke was in power he could rely on Walpole's vote, though his supporter rarely spoke in the House of Commons. In return for Walpole's loyalty, the Duke tried to meet his many requests for places or commissions for his protégés.

Over the years Walpole helped a large and heterogeneous collection of people. One of them was his old tutor Styan Thirlby, a spasmodically brilliant and chronically alcoholic scholar, to whom he gave a home for a time, before finding him a small sinecure.[9] Another less problematical charge was Peter Platel, an impoverished clerical friend, on whose behalf Walpole wrote seven letters between 1745 and 1749, until he secured for him a comfortable church living at Ashburton in South Devon.[10] Other men he helped included a carpenter, a master sweep and a fair number of struggling artists.

Walpole was particularly sympathetic to this last group as he was an artist himself, a gentleman amateur. He sketched intermittently and could catch a likeness. When over forty he took up painting for a while. He also wrote occasional verses and essays, though he rarely published these, and never under his own name. Above all he loved music and here, if anywhere, his real talent lay. According to his brother, he 'composed admirably, particularly in a melancholy church style'.[11] His preferred instrument was the bass viol, which he played in a small group, led by the Prince of Wales at Leicester House, even though going there meant that he had to overcome a distinct aversion he had to fashionable society, as well as avoid getting involved in opposition politics.

Walpole often took considerable time and pains to promote other men in their careers, but did not as a rule finance them out of his own pocket, though he was rich. Sir Robert had obtained lucrative sinecures for both his younger sons, which would enable them to live well for life. Edward Walpole preferred to help men to help themselves. The most famous instance of how this system worked in practice concerned Louis Roubiliac. When Roubiliac was young and still unknown, he found Walpole's pocket book lying on the ground in Vauxhall Gardens one evening. He returned it, whereupon Walpole gave him a reward and took him to the studio of a leading sculptor of the day, Henry Cheere. In due course Cheere introduced the young man to Jonathan Tyers, who commissioned him to make the statue of Handel which was to make his name.[12]

Not all Walpole's attempts to set an artist on course ended so well. Sometimes the fates were unkind. When an indigent gentleman, James Deacon, decided to become a professional painter, Walpole went to great trouble to secure a commission for him to paint a miniature of George II, a monarch who detested sitting for portraits. Alas, before Deacon had even been paid for this work, he was called to the Old Bailey that April day in 1750 when gaol fever infected the entire court, killing the judge, jury, all the trial lawyers and a score of others – Deacon among them.[13]

Walpole was not a collector. He rarely commissioned works of art himself. He acted on impulse when he helped someone, and he could be capricious. Such was Laetitia Pilkington's experience. In 1739 Mrs Pilkington left Dublin and came to England, where she hoped to make a living by writing, her initial plan being to publish her poems by subscription. In her *Memoirs* she describes how, within a few months of arriving in London, she was 'in great distress, and knew not what to do. Having heard Mr. Edward Walpole was a very humane gentleman', she goes on, 'I wrote to him, and he sent me a letter by return, wherein he promised to wait on me the next evening.' He duly arrived at her lodgings and sat with her three hours. 'At the end of which time' she writes, 'he told me he did not know how he could possibly be of any service to me. I told him I had some Poems, which I intended to print by Subscription, and, if he would do me the honour of promoting it, it was all the Favour I desired.' Mrs Pilkington did not know that Walpole avoided clubs and drawing rooms, and was also incorrigibly forgetful. So she was surprised and dashed when he answered that, if he undertook such a task, 'he should certainly neglect it'. Her spirits rose, however, when her visitor said he would give her something and produced five guineas. But then, to her dismay, 'the gentleman took a second thought, and put the Guineas in his purse again', telling her that 'it was not convenient to part with them'. She concluded her account of this episode with the tart comment that such was 'his constant answer to every person, as I have frequently observed, when those whom he chose for Friends and Companions wanted but the smallest Assistance from him'.[14]

This anecdote suggests that Walpole's reputation for philanthropy was a mixed one. Mrs Pilkington's *Memoirs*, first printed in 1748 and reprinted the year Cather came to London, were a *succès de scandale*. Her strictures on Walpole would have been fresh in readers' minds. Not everyone would have believed her, of course. Her sensational autobiography is crammed with libellous stories about those who had slighted or insulted her. It was not in her nature to be dispassionate, but in so far as one can check her anecdotes, a surprising number of them turn out to be based on fact; many of her grievances were real enough. Furthermore, she had almost total recall of conversations and events. When she said Walpole's rejection of her was typical of him, she had the experience of her ex-husband to go on. Matthew Pilkington had been encouraged by the first minister's son, and spent many weary months in London, hoping he would do something for him, only to be disappointed in the end. There is also a suggestion in her story that, before 1750, there were other Irish people, apart from herself and her husband, who had reason to harbour a grudge against Walpole. This is worth bearing in mind, because from such small beginnings feuds can arise.

Walpole was quite well known among the Irish, in Dublin as well as in London. During his brief excursion into public life he had been a secretary to the Duke of Devonshire, Lord Lieutenant of Ireland. Even after he gave up this post in 1739, he crossed the Irish Sea often, so as to stay with the friend he had made on the Grand Tour, Gustavus Hamilton, Viscount Boyne.[15] The Irish soon noted the various material benefits that came the way of the young Viscount and his dependants, as the result of a friendship with the son of England's first minister. Through Sir Robert, Edward secured the post of Commissioner of Revenue, at £1000 p.a. for Lord Boyne, as well as other sinecures for his relatives.[16] It was during one of his visits to Ireland that Walpole had been approached by Cather, who told him that he was the son of one of Lord Boyne's tenants, and that he wanted to work in England. At this time Cather could have been no more than fifteen, because Walpole had no reason to go to Ireland after 1746, the year in which Lord Boyne died prematurely.

After his disappointing interview Cather was not too discouraged. He went looking for work in another gentleman's household, as he had been advised to do, assured that he could use Walpole's name as a reference to help him find a place. He was not without acquaintances in London, mostly Irish, trying to make their way in the English capital, like himself. He found lodgings in Maiden Lane, where rents were cheap because the area, Covent Garden, was disreputable. The street had long been a favourite with strangers to London. Twenty-five years earlier Voltaire had stayed there. In Cather's lodging house there were at least two other Irishmen, Andrew White and John Brownsmith, who earned a living on the fringes of the legal profession.

Walpole was the only English gentleman Cather knew, however, so throughout the winter he went back to the house in Pall Mall regularly. The weather was unusually warm. It had been so for eight months, with temperatures higher in the south of England than they were in Naples.[17] In February there was a minor earthquake. This was followed, over the next few weeks, by two more. These toppled some church steeples,

whereupon fashionable folk began leaving town.[18] Cather was not finding it easy to get the sort of work he wanted. Some of the large houses
he went to were deserted. Then spring came and Cather returned to Pall
Mall in high spirits. He had heard of a place, and carried a letter asking
Walpole to recommend him.

Walpole's manservant William Collier took the letter up to his master,
who called Cather in. There were no witnesses to the scene that followed,
but apparently something happened to make Walpole furiously angry. He
refused to give Cather a recommendation, and forbade him ever to come
to the house again. As we shall see, Walpole would eventually say why he
acted the way he did and, as we shall also see, Cather thought he had
been very badly treated. For now it is sufficient to say that it was not
unusual for Walpole to lose his temper and act precipitously. His son
Edward, his brother Horace, the children's aunt Jane Clement, and the
Prince of Wales were all guilty of relatively minor offences that provoked
Walpole's rage, and an impulsive decision to sever relations with them.[19]
Usually he cooled down after a while, and a conciliatory overture, or the
mediation of well-disposed friends, led him to change his mind again.
Cather had no way of knowing this, and was himself a vain and hot-
tempered man. According to a compatriot who had known him in Donegal,
his violent quarrels with his widowed mother had shocked all the neighbours.[20] He had eventually left home without being reconciled to her.
Now he left the house in Pall Mall as angry as the man who had thrown
him out, filled with a resentment that only burned more fiercely as the
days and weeks went by. The two men never set eyes on each other again,
though neither was allowed to forget the other.

The indictment

At the beginning of April 1750 Walpole received a letter from Daniel
Alexander. He did not know this correspondent, who turned out to be
'a Hackney Writer to a Gentleman of New Inn'.[21] The letter contained
disturbing news. Cather intended to prosecute Walpole for attempting
to rape him. Alexander had been asked to take on the case, but as he
respected 'him and the Walpole Family, he had declined proceeding in
that Cause till he had first acquainted him with it'.[22] When he read this,
Walpole froze. He kept the letter but claimed he did not answer it, nor a
second one that arrived shortly afterwards, wherein Alexander wrote of
'having it in his Power to serve Mr. Walpole in the Affair', which he
declared he would do 'if he would permit him'.[23]

Soon afterwards Alexander came to see Walpole and offered his
services in person. His visit was followed by one from Walter Patterson,

who said he was Cather's attorney. He informed Walpole that 'a Bill of Indictment was, or soon would be, preferr'd against him, if not timely prevented'.[24]

These initial conversations with Alexander and Patterson, both of whom thought it was best if the case did not reach court, persuaded Walpole that the whole purpose of the threatened prosecution was to get money from him. As his two visitors were Irish, he also decided they were colluding with Cather, in the hope of sharing the proceeds if, as they suggested, he compromised the matter, that is, did a deal.

So far Walpole had kept his troubles to himself. He did not confide in any of his friends and, as yet, saw no reason to consult a lawyer. He was under no illusion, however, about the seriousness of the predicament he was in. In the upper echelons of society, a limited tolerance of homosexuals depended on their never becoming embroiled in a public scandal. Under those circumstances Walpole's social equals might deal in their own way with one of their number whose sexual behaviour they thought was reprehensible. Hence Viscount Bateman who, Horace Walpole said, 'debauched' boys, was forced by his wife's relatives to agree to a separation.[25] If it came to the point, Edward Walpole might escape being put on trial by going abroad, after which he would probably have to spend the rest of his life there. Alternatively, he might live in self-imposed exile in his own country, as William Beckford was to do later at Fonthill. At all events he faced ostracism by polite society unless he could dispel any widespread belief that he was a sodomite.

Nevertheless, Walpole was in a fairly strong position. As far as one can tell, there had been no rumours that he was given to sodomitical practices, until Cather said he was. He was not married, but that was not unusual. He could have been one of a number of eighteenth-century gentlemen who did not consider marriage essential to happiness. Certainly when he was young he found girls attractive.

When he was twenty-two and just down from Cambridge, he may even have gone through some kind of wedding ceremony with the daughter of John Hollings, a physician who lived in Pall Mall. Margaret Hollings, the girl in question, published a verse letter saying this was so, and that the 'Great Man' (Robert Walpole) had refused to allow the clandestine marriage to be recognized, because he wanted his son to make a better match.[26] There was more parental opposition in 1741, when Edward proposed to Caroline Howe. She was the daughter of a viscount, but penniless. On this occasion Sir Robert reluctantly waived his objections after a while but Edward, who, of all his father's children, 'loved him best', broke off his engagement to Miss Howe anyway.[27]

Unfortunately for Sir Robert, women who were heiresses or the toast of the town made his son nervous. In sexual matters, as in many other aspects of life, Edward disliked having to compete. Horace Walpole may have been thinking of this when he warned a friend that, although he would be interested and entertained when he visited Edward, he could not expect to hear anything of 'court Beauties'.[28] Early in the 1730s Edward Walpole asked Dorothy Clement to share his life, but never contemplated seeking parental permission to marry her because she was a milliner's apprentice. When he first saw her she was working in a Pall Mall shop, underneath the rooms where Walpole was lodging at the time, and he could hardly have failed to notice how beautiful she was.[29] Mrs Secker, the wife of the future Archbishop of Canterbury, once caught sight of her and said 'she never saw a more lovely creature'.[30] After Dorothy became Walpole's mistress, he 'doated on her till the day of her death', at the age of twenty-four, soon after giving birth to their fifth child.[31]

The available evidence points, therefore, to Walpole being heterosexual, and an unlikely perpetrator of homosexual rape. At the beginning of his contest with Cather, he appeared to behave with all the confidence of a man who knew the charge against him was baseless and as if, having nothing to hide, he supposed the boy would not go ahead with the prosecution, if his adversary stood firm.

In this belief Walpole was mistaken. In the third week in April Cather went to the Middlesex magistrates' court at Hick's Hall, St John's Street, where he preferred a bill of indictment which stated:

> That the Honourable Edward Walpole, late of the Parish of St. James, within the liberty of Westminster, in the County of Middlesex, Esq; on the First Day of March, in the Twenty Third Year of the Reign of our Sovereign Lord George the Second, King of Great Britain etc. with Force and Arms, at the Parish aforesaid, in the County aforesaid, in and upon one John Cather, Gent. in the Peace of God, and our said Lord the King, then and there being, did make an Assault, and him the said John, then and there did beat, wound, and ill treat, so that of his life it was greatly despaired, with Intent, then and there, feloniously, and against the Order of Nature, to commit that detestable and sodomitical Sin (not to be named amongst Christians) commonly called Buggery, with the said John, and other Wrongs to the said John, then and there did, to the great Damage of the said John, and against the Peace of our said Lord the King, his Crown and Dignity.[32]

On 24 April the Grand Jury met at Hick's Hall to consider this indictment and decide whether it could be dismissed, or whether it was necessary to take action. As was customary, the jurors met *in camera* and heard only the prosecution's side. On this occasion the Grand Jury passed Cather's indictment as a true bill. This meant that Walpole was notified that he would have to stand trial. It also meant that the charges against him became public knowledge. Soon the taverns and coffee houses were buzzing with talk about a certain Member of Parliament.

Walpole put the legal arrangements for his defence in the hands of his lawyer, Robert Bygrave. He then applied for the case to be removed from Hick's Hall to the court of King's Bench, by writ of *certiorari*. Such writs were not available on demand. A defendant hd to give a good reason if he wished to be tried by the highest tribunal of criminal jurisdiction in the country. Walpole would have been able to say that his counsel did not attend sessions at Hick's Hall, while the fact that he was 'a man of good reputation' would have ensured that his request was viewed sympathetically.[33] Writs of *certiorari* were expensive, but from now on Walpole spared no expense. In the end this would prove to be considerable, but from his point of view having the trial transferred to the King's Bench was well worth the effort. For one thing, a lawyer who pleaded a case in the King's Bench had to be a member of the Serjeants Inn, and was the equivalent of a modern Queen's Counsel. For another, some senior members of the court knew Walpole personally, and nearly all of them were his social equals, with whom he could feel at ease.

Once the writ was granted, Walpole was summoned to appear in the court of King's Bench during the Trinity term, to answer for 'certain Trespasses Contempts Assaults and Misdemeanours' of which he had been indicted.[34] Meanwhile he was granted bail, on providing the usual recognizances.

Edward Walpole's supporters rally to his side

Obnoxious as the miasma of publicity now surrounding Walpole was, it brought him allies, some of whom came from unexpected quarters. 'News of an impending prosecution against his brother' soon reached Horace Walpole in Twickenham,[35] where he had recently embarked on a new project, that of building 'a little Gothic castle' at Strawberry Hill.[36] Up till now the two brothers had not got on at all well. When their mother was alive Edward had resented the fact that Horace was her favourite.[37] Then, later on, it had seemed as if his father also preferred his youngest son.[38] As the years went by, Edward, who was touchy and insecure, became increasingly irritated by his equable, confident brother. It was all very understandable. He had abandoned a political career, knowing he could never be worthy of Sir Robert, whom he adored, only to find himself outshone in private life by a sibling, eleven years younger than himself, whom he did not even like. Horace was still in his early twenties when he began publishing essays and books on politics, the arts, literature and antiquities – well before *The*

Castle of Otranto and Strawberry Hill made him as famous as his father had been.

At first Edward Walpole tried to keep his younger brother in line, reprimanding him whenever he felt he had stepped over it. During the 1740s there were a number of one-sided altercations: over Horace's disposal of a family borough at Castle Rising to a friend, and his seeming presumption in making and publishing a catalogue of the pictures at Houghton, as well as a so-called attempt to choose a biographer for their father.[39] Throughout all this Horace remained irritatingly cool, regaling his particular friends with stories about 'Ned's envy' that 'overflowed on a thousand ridiculous occasions'.[40]

However, Horace was looking for an opportunity to end a quarrel that had not been of his choosing. As soon as he heard of the impending prosecution, he wrote to Edward asking if he could help. His offer was accepted and he went promptly to see his brother in London, giving him practical assistance over a period that was to last more than a year. The testimony that Horace Walpole gave at the trial of Cather and others in 1751 was instrumental in securing the conviction of at least one of the defendants, all the more so because what he had to say was confirmed by Stephen Slaughter.

Stephen Slaughter, the portrait-painter and Keeper of the King's Pictures, had painted a charming picture of Walpole's children in 1747.[41] He also knew something of Ireland, having worked in Dublin in the 1730s where he had first met Walpole. Asked to help, he readily agreed to do so.

One more acquaintance from the Dublin days who cheerfully offered his assistance was another artist, named James Worsdale. Worsdale, who was now in his fifties, had started his career as an apprentice in the studio of Godfrey Kneller, whose natural son he laid a dubious claim to be.[42] From time to time Walpole had found him commissions, including one to paint the Duke of Devonshire. There were no detectives in eighteenth-century England, but for the duration of the Cather case Worsdale created that occupation for himself, so adding to a career that was already varied. For he was not only a painter but an actor, a writer or adapter of plays, a singer of sentimental songs, a theatrical impresario and last, but by no means least, professional boon companion.

Some time in April Worsdale had been in a London coffee house when one of the men at his table, who 'did not at all know Mr. Walpole', had begun talking about him, saying he was 'guilty of Sodomy, or at least accused of that Crime'. Afterwards Worsdale went to express his concern to Walpole, who 'told him the whole Affair of his being accused by one Cather, and that he believed some others, more artful than himself' were involved. When he added that he needed to know who and where these people were, Worsdale said he would find them.[43]

Being employed by Edward Walpole in 1750 was providential for Worsdale, who was going through a bad patch in a life that had always had its ups and downs. Somewhat earlier Mrs Pilkington had come upon him loitering in a coffee house doorway, unable to go home to Mount Street because his creditors were laying siege there.[44] In good times he lived well and treated all his friends. In bad times he pawned his cutlery and ate off old playbills. He was popular, but not universally so. Mrs Pilkington (probably an ex-mistress) was resentful because he asked her to write the lyrics for his songs and scripts for his plays, without giving her any credit or adequate payment for her work.[45] The art historian George Vertue, who thought little of Worsdale as a painter, was scathing, describing him as a man who pushed himself into notoriety by 'artfulness' and 'shameless mountebank lies'.[46]

It is true that Worsdale had a habit of making himself useful to men he could make use of in turn, and he was extremely accommodating. So in previous years he had created the Irish Hell Fire Club for Lord Santry.[47] From that he had gone on to pose as the Reverend Smythe for Alexander Pope, in a convoluted story in which the poet tried to trick his foe Edmund Curll into bringing out an unauthorized edition of his letters.[48]

Worsdale was well cast as an undercover agent. He had a large acquaintance, Irish and English, reputable and raffish, while his easy, convivial manners disarmed suspicion. In addition, he was a better actor than he was a painter. In the Dublin and London theatres he scored some of his biggest successes playing women's roles. Now he began his search for Cather and his friends by visiting taverns and lodging houses in the guise of a haymaker's widow.[49]

Cather had disappeared, but before long Worsdale tracked down Walter Patterson at a tavern near Buckingham Gate, known to its regular customers as the Devil and Bag o' Nails. When discovered, Patterson was playing skittles with a couple of his compatriots, Bartholemew Dennison and John Faulkner. Posing now as Counsellor Johnson, a lawyer with a grudge against the rich, Worsdale won Patterson's confidence. Patterson told him about Walpole's attack on a young man he knew, and of his refusal to do anything for him afterwards. Patterson then said that the young man intended to make Walpole pay for the wrong he had suffered. Counsellor Johnson listened sympathetically. The two men went on drinking well into the night. There was a problem if Cather wished to proceed with a prosecution. It was hard to see where the money necessary to bring a case to court was going to come from since he had no income. Over a bowl of punch the counsellor consolidated his new friendship with Patterson, and lured him into a trap by offering to help finance the campaign against Walpole.

The morning after this first meeting with Patterson, Worsdale met a friend named Andrew White walking in St James's Park. As this friend was Irish, Worsdale asked him if he knew Cather. White said he used to lodge with him. He also said he thought he knew where he might be living now. Then, his curiosity aroused, he asked what Worsdale wanted with Cather, whereupon Worsdale told him the whole story. It did not take White long to see the advantage of helping such an influential person as Walpole, so he agreed to go and talk to Cather, if he was where he thought he was.

After a few days White came back to Worsdale with the news that he had found Cather living in Patrick Cain's house in Princes Street, Drury Lane. Cather had greeted him eagerly as an old friend and soon, in the presence of Cain, from whom he said he had no secrets, told White all about the injuries he had suffered at the hands of Walpole, and of his determination to get compensation. However, he was dissatisfied with the lawyers he had consulted, fearing that they would settle out of court, without telling him how much money Walpole had paid. This gave White the opportunity he was looking for, to arrange for Worsdale to meet Cather. He mentioned a Counsellor Johnson he knew, who he was sure would take on the case without wanting to be paid anything right away, whereupon Cather asked White to approach this liberal gentleman on his behalf.

On hearing this, Worsdale suggested that, on the following evening, White should bring Cather and his friend to a run-down place of entertainment called Cuper's Gardens on the South Bank.[50] White went back to Princes Street and issued the invitation. At first Cather said he could not come because he had no money left. So White offered to treat him and Cain. From then on everything went according to plan. As if by chance, the three men came upon the supposed counsellor strolling in the pleasure gardens. As predicted, he offered to advise Cather on what we would now call a 'No win, no fee' basis. Then he gave the young man the same assurance he had earlier given Patterson, to the effect that if in the meantime 'any Money was wanting, he would advance it to carry on his Prosecution'.[51]

Andrew White became a regular member of the Walpole team as a result of the help he had given Worsdale. He had some legal training and soon he was assisting Robert Bygrave, while at the same time keeping up his friendship with Cather and Cain. Walpole approved of the efforts made by his agents to ensure that Patterson and Cather went ahead with their plans to prosecute him. He no longer wanted the case dropped, having realized that the best way of silencing the ugly rumours about him was to establish his innocence by discrediting his accuser in open court. Furthermore, the accounts Walpole had been given of Patterson and his cronies, and of Cain, confirmed his belief that he was the target of a conspiracy. From now on he had two aims. The first was to clear his name. This was a matter of personal honour. The second was to bring every member of a dangerous gang of criminals to justice. This was a public duty.

However, there was some way to go before either of these aims could be achieved. The story continues and the plot thickens.

A visitor to Frogmore

In the summer of 1750 Walpole left London for his home in the country. On 5 June he was at his house in Frogmore, near Windsor, when a visitor from town arrived in a 'one-horse Chair'.[52] It happened to be a day when all the servants were out, except for William Collier, who answered the door. The caller asked if Mr Walpole was at home and, on being told that he was, requested an opportunity to speak with him. He gave his name as George Sandys, but refused to say anything about his business, except that 'it was a Matter of Moment which nearly related to Mr. Walpole'.[53] The manservant asked him to wait while he let his master know of his arrival. The name Sandys meant nothing to Walpole, but on learning from Collier that the man was young, genteel and spoke with an accent that could be Irish, he told him to let the visitor come up, and to remain in the room as long as he was there.

When Sandys was admitted he said he had been informed about 'the most dangerous and wicked Prosecution' mounted against 'Mr. Walpole', and had come to see him because he knew how to prevent Walter Patterson from carrying on as Cather's attorney.[54] Patterson 'owed him £150, besides Interest, on a Bond'.[55] Sandys, who confessed he 'had a pressing Occasion' for his money, showed Walpole the bond and offered to sell it to him, explaining that 'if Mr. Walpole put the Bond in Suit against Patterson', who was 'but poor', it would inevitably 'disable him from prosecuting the Cause of Cather' because he did not have the money, either to pay the debt, or to raise bail if he was arrested, and therefore 'must lie in Gaol'.[56]

Sandys had an open countenance and an engaging manner, but the mere fact that he was on familiar terms with Patterson made Walpole suspicious. The suspicion was enough. The scene that followed was brutal and short. 'Imagining some Trick and that this Fellow was one of the Villains, concerned in Cather's Conspiracy', Walpole 'collared him', at the same time ordering Collier to 'call a Constable'.[57] Sandys broke free and tried to knock Walpole down with a whip he was carrying 'which was very heavy in the Handle'.[58] Then he fled the room. Walpole and his manservant chased after him and caught up with him in the hall. Walpole grabbed 'a large Stick which stood in the Entry' and felled him.[59] Sandys got up and was running to his chair when Walpole 'felled him a second Time'.[60] After that Collier, with some of the returning servants, tied the dazed man up and 'he was carried before the Mayor at Windsor'.[61]

George Sandys was examined on four successive days during which, notwithstanding his Irish accent, he insisted he was a gentleman from Andover in Hampshire, where he lived with his father Richard Sandys Esq. Yet he could not name anyone else living in that town, nor did he know whether it had a corporation, or a Member of Parliament. So he was detained in custody in Reading gaol while enquiries were made. These showed there was no one called Richard Sandys living in Andover, but his supposed son refused to say anything further. Meanwhile he had managed to chew and swallow the bond which he tried to sell Walpole, so destroying the one piece of material evidence against him.[62]

Walpole was not to be deflected, and when questioning the prisoner proved futile, he returned to London where he paid for advertisements to be posted, describing the man who called himself Sandys, in the hope of finding out who he really was. Details were also sent to Dublin in case he was known there.

Before long a Londoner, Thomas Weekes, read the advertisement and thought he recognized the man it described. A few months earlier Weekes had gone into a shop with a bill of exchange for £45 and had drawn £10. Later he had gone back for the remaining £35, only to find that someone had forged his signature and made off with the money. Everything pointed to the forger being an erstwhile lawyer's clerk, an Irishman named William Smith, who had been with Weekes when he went into the shop on the first occasion. Smith had then sailed to Holland before he could be arrested. Now Weekes contacted Walpole, who arranged for him to go to Reading gaol. There he positively identified the man being held as Smith, who was then transferred to Newgate to await trial during the next sessions at the Old Bailey.[63]

Worsdale had never heard William Smith mentioned during any of the time he spent buying drinks for Patterson and his friends, even though he believed that, as Counsellor Johnson, he was trusted by them. He was disconcerted therefore to learn what had been happening at Frogmore. Immediately after Smith's arrest he put on his lawyer's gown and set off to meet Patterson, 'under the Pretence of consulting how to prepare for carrying on Cather's prosecution', but actually to find out whether Smith had any other motive in trying to sell Walpole a false bond, other than the obvious one of making money for himself.[64] After the meeting Worsdale came back to Walpole with the following story.

As soon as Patterson saw the supposed counsellor he told him 'that an unhappy Accident had happened which he was afraid would frustrate all their Scheme'.[65] Worsdale reacted to this news by feigning indignation, swearing 'that if they went on without consulting him in every Thing, he would have nothing to do farther in the Affair'.[66] An apologetic Patterson placated him by 'promising that in Future he would not stir one Step without his Assistance and Advice'.[67] Worsdale, apparently mollified, asked for details of the mischance Patterson had referred to, and was told about Smith's approach to Walpole and subsequent arrest. Worsdale then asked Patterson what he 'intended or expected from the Bond'.[68] 'Why,' came the reply,

> the Bond was dated three months before I came to England, and there was no such Person as George Sandys, to whom it was made payable, at the Place where Smith was to say he liv'd, nor any such Persons to be found as were the subscribing Witnesses. Therefore if Mr. Walpole had swallow'd the Bait, and brought an Action against me for the Bond, I should have proved by undoubted Witnesses that I was in Ireland when the Bond was dated, and that it was not in my Hand-writing, and he not being able to produce the Person he had the Bond from, Smith being to have gone Abroad in a few Days after, I should have had my Advantage upon him for publishing a forged Bond, by which means he must have come down on me to have stifled the Affair, lest the World should think him guilty of both Crimes.[69]

There were no witnesses to the conversation between Patterson and Worsdale, so we have only the latter's word that Smith's attempt to extract money from Walpole had not been an opportunistic, and independent, venture on his part. Worsdale's report was, however, timely because it gave Walpole a reason for disposing of Cather's attorney, before he himself had to appear in court to answer the charge of attempted sodomy.

Patterson, a native of Donegal, had not obtained a legal right to settle in England. It was possible, therefore, to have him arrested under the 1743 Vagrant Act (17 Geo. 2, c. 5), particularly if it could be shown he was an undesirable character. Accordingly, an application was made to Justice Henry Fielding, 'who granted a Warrant against Patterson on the Oaths of Mr. John Sherwood [a constable] and Mr. James Worsdale'.[70]

On the evening of 14 June Worsdale went to keep a rendezvous he had previously arranged with Cather, Cain and Patterson. They were to meet in the gardens of Somerset House. John Gray, a constable, warrant in hand, accompanied Worsdale. They watched from the window of a grace and favour apartment, where a friend of Worsdale's resided, until they saw the trio enter the gardens. Then in the half-light they went down to meet them. Gray arrested Patterson, while Cather and Cain watched dumbfounded as the affable man they knew as Counsellor Johnson identified Cather's lawyer and helped to escort him away.

Patterson was taken before Justice Fielding, who remanded him in custody in the Clerkenwell Bridewell where he was to stay until his case was heard at Hick's Hall on 14 July.[71]

The trial of Edward Walpole

On 15 June 1750, the day after Patterson's arrest, a preliminary hearing of the charges against Edward Walpole was held in the court of King's Bench. He was represented on this occasion by one of that court's attorneys, William Hughes. The indictment framed by Cather was read out, after which Hughes entered a plea of 'Not Guilty' on behalf of the defendant, who put himself upon the country. This meant that Walpole submitted himself to trial by jury. The date for the trial was fixed for three weeks hence by James Burrow, the Coroner or Master of the court.[72]

Walpole wanted a Special Jury for his trial, so William Davy of the King's Bench made the necessary application on 27 June.[73] A Special Jury differed from an ordinary one in being composed of men with higher property qualifications and presumably more education. In the event all the jurors selected for Walpole's trial were entitled to write Esq. after their names.[74] Applications for this kind of jury were granted when a cause of consequence was to be tried at the bar, especially if the appplicant was a man of good standing in society.[75] Nevertheless, a request for a Special Jury was unusual and, like a writ of *certiorari*, it was expensive.[76]

Obviously Walpole was taking no chances. He supposed that he was more likely to receive a sympathetic hearing from a jury made up of merchants and gentlemen, rather than lesser tradesmen. Conversely, Cather might expect such men to have but a slight acquaintance with hungry, hopeful Irish immigrants. Ironically, he would have been better served if he had not been a subject of the English king. A foreigner could ask for half the members of a Special Jury to be foreigners as well, though not necessarily from his own country.[77]

In theory the method laid down for selecting a Special Jury allowed both sides a say about whom was chosen, though in practice this did not always happen. The rules stated that the sheriff of the county was to bring his freeholders' book to the court on an appointed day. Then a senior officer of the court read out forty-eight names from the book 'in the presence of the Attorneys of both Sides', after which the opposing attorneys struck out twelve names each, one at a time alternately.[78] The remaining twenty-four men on the shortlist were required to appear in court on the day of the trial, when twelve of them would be sworn in.

Bygrave had agreed to take a copy of these rules, together with a notice of the trial, and give them to Cather personally. However, he did not find him. On 27 June he informed the court, in an affidavit, that he had been to Cather's lodging in Princes Street, where he saw Patrick Cain who told him that Cather had left the house some weeks before, without saying where he was going. From this Bygrave concluded that Cather 'was keeping out of the way on Purpose to prevent his being served with Notice of the Tryal in the Cause'.[79] During his conversation with Cain, Bygrave had asked who Cather's legal representatives were, whereupon Cain had mentioned Walter Patterson and another attorney named Adam Nixon. This is the first time we hear of Nixon, who came from Dublin but now worked in London. Worsdale and White had not met him, although, as we find out later, he had once written to Bygrave asking to be sent documents relevant to Cather's prosecution of Walpole. Since then, however, he had dissociated himself from the case and declined receiving any papers sent him about it.

So Cather had no legal representatives who could come to the King's Bench when the Special Jury was chosen. Patterson was incarcerated in the Clerkenwell Bridewell, while Alexander and Nixon refused to have anything to do with him.

On 2 July Bygrave returned to the court and swore another affidavit, in which he said he had now looked for Cather at all the addresses he was known to have frequented, but 'in vain'. He had also been back to Princes Street where Cain had given him a positive assurance that 'Adam Nixon and Walter Patterson were concerned with the prosecutor when the indictment was drawn up, and were still concerned'.[80] From Princes Street Bygrave had gone to Nixon's house in Warwick Court, Holborn, to serve him with notice of the trial. Not finding him at home, he had left the notice with Nixon's wife. Similar notices had been left with Patterson in the Bridewell, and at Princes Street for Cain to give Cather, if he returned there.

As Walpole's trial was now only three days off, it was decided to go ahead and strike the Special Jury without further delay. The rules allowed for this, stating that if one side failed to send a legal representative, then the Deputy Master of the court was to strike out twelve names from the shortlist of jurors 'for the Attorney who makes default', which is what happened on this occasion.[81]

The date of 5 July, appointed for Walpole's trial, fell on the Thursday after the Trinity term had ended, which may help to explain why there was no mention of it in the newspapers afterwards. However, if the aim of choosing a date for the trial, when Westminster was half empty, had been to spare Walpole unpleasant publicity when the prosecutor gave his version of events, the precaution was unnecessary. The prosecutor was absent.

Cather had not been seen since the night of Patterson's arrest. Without him, the case against Walpole collapsed, though it was not dismissed. The officers and clerks of the court of King's Bench took their places as in any other trial. The Lord Chief Justice, Sir William Lee, sat on the Bench. The Special Jury was sworn, and listened to the indictment. The Master of the court acted as prosecutor for the Crown and Sir Richard Lloyd, a senior member of the King's Bench, came forward in answer to a public proclamation calling for a person to speak 'touching the Matters in the Indictment'.[82] The only information he could provide, however, was that given him by Walpole and his lawyer.

The focal point of the trial should have been an opening speech by Cather, in which he would have explained the circumstances of the supposed attack upon him. Instead the main speech was made by Walpole in his own defence. He told the court that he was the victim of a malicious prosecution. He also claimed that he was the target of a conspiracy by Cather and others, whose sole aim had been to extort money from him. Finally he named all those who had assisted Cather, or contemplated assisting him in any way, as his fellow conspirators. In this fashion he converted a violent dispute between a gentleman and an unemployed servant into something more portentous, that is, into a conflict between a citizen defending law and order and a gang of Irish rogues who were a threat to society.

Sir William Lee accepted Walpole's interpretation of events and directed the jurors accordingly. Without leaving the room, they brought in a verdict of 'Not Guilty'.[83]

It was also placed on record that John Cather, Walter Patterson, Adam Nixon, Daniel Alexander and Patrick Cain 'did wickedly, maliciously, unjustly and without Cause, combine, conspire, contrive, and agree together, to get and procure the aforesaid Indictment, preferred and found against the said Edward Walpole, in the Manner and Form aforesaid, with an Intent and Design unlawfully and unjustly to procure Money to themselves, from the said Edward Walpole'.[84]

The conclusion reached by the court of King's Bench on 5 July 1750 forms the prologue to the next part of this history, which tells how Walpole set about taking his revenge on all the five men he had named as conspirators, as well as on William Smith, and how in the course of doing so he had to make use of virtually all the legal resources available to him. When these resources proved inadequate, as they not infrequently did, we shall also see how he and the team he employed had no hesitation in bending the law to suit their purpose.

Notes

1. *Full and genuine Narrative*, p. 4.
2. Ibid., p. 2.
3. Dr Cowell in *A Law Dictionary, or the Interpreter of Words and Terms* (London, 1727), says of the word 'gentleman': 'Under this Name are comprised all above Yeoman.'
4. *Survey of London*, gen. editor F. H. W. Sheppard (London, 1900–), 29: 378–9.
5. W. S. Lewis, *Horace Walpole: The A. W. Mellon Lectures in the Fine Arts 1960* (London, 1961), p. 26.
6. *Last Journals of Horace Walpole during the Reign of George III*, ed. G. F. R. Barker, 4 vols (London, 1894), 1: 102.
7. *History of Parliament: The Commons 1754–1790*, eds Sir Lewis Namier and John Brooks, 3 vols (London: HMSO, 1985).
8. BL, Add. MSS 32711, f. 418.
9. John Nichols, *Literary Anecdotes of the Eighteenth Century*, 9 vols (1812–15), 4: 267.
10. BL, Add. MSS 32704, f. 545, 32708, fos 369–70, 32713, f. 536, 32718, f. 234 and the *Gentleman's Magazine*, July 1749.
11. *Last Journals*, 1: 102. Edward Walpole also agreed to write the music for the hymns in his brother's play, *The Mysterious Mother*. See Horace Walpole, *Corr.*, 36: 53, letter dated 22 May 1769.
12. James Northcote, *Life of Sir Joshua Reynolds*, 2 vols (London, 1818), 1: 49–50.
13. BL, Add. MSS 32718, f. 325 and Horace Walpole, *Anecdotes of Painting in England*, 5 vols (Strawberry Hill, 1760–71).
14. *Memoirs of Mrs. Laetitia Pilkington*, ed. A. C. Elias Jr, 2 vols (Athens and London: University of Georgia Press, 1997), 1: 131–2 and 2: 509n. Information about Laetitia and Matthew Pilkington in these pages comes from Elias's annotated edition of the *Memoirs*.
15. Lord Boyne's career is summarized in *The History of Parliament: House of Commons 1715–1754*, ed. Romney Sedgwick, 2 vols (London: HMSO, 1970).
16. Chomondeley (Houghton) MSS no. 2576.
17. Horace Walpole, *Corr.*, 20: 119 and 20: 128, letters to Horace Mann dated 25 February and 11 March 1750.
18. Horace Walpole, *Corr.*, 20: 128, letter to Horace Mann dated 11 March 1750.
19. For Edward Walpole's quarrels with his son and with Mrs Clement, see Lewis Walpole Library, letters written from October to December 1766. For the quarrel with the Prince of Wales, see *Last Journals*, 1: 104–5.

Quarrels with Horace Walpole are referred to *passim* in Horace Walpole, *Corr.*, up to 22 December 1750 (20: 215).

20. *Full and genuine Narrative*, pp. 2–3.
21. *Whitehall Evening Post*, 4–6 July 1751. The editor made this fact clear when apologizing for confusing Daniel Alexander with an attorney David Alexander.
22. *Whole Proceedings*, p. 5.
23. Ibid.
24. Ibid.
25. Horace Walpole, *Corr.*, 30: 309, the satire 'Little Peggy' and Rictor Norton, *Mother Clap's Molly House: The Gay Subculture in England 1700–1830* (London: Gay Men's Press, 1992), p. 43.
26. *A Letter from a Lady to her Husband Abroad* (1728). Described in the British Library catalogue as 'purporting to be from Margaret (?) daughter of John Hollings to Edward Walpole'. Internal evidence supports this claim, though there is no external evidence. It is worth noting, though, that Edward Walpole had just been sent on the Grand Tour in 1728. Also the girl's father, who had refused to side with his daughter, was made Physician General to the Army and Physician in Ordinary to the King at about this time, which is very much what one might expect if Robert Walpole had decided to bribe him. See entry in the *Dictionary of National Biography*.
27. Horace Walpole, *Corr.*, 28: 70. Letter to the Rev. William Mason, 2 March 1773.
28. Horace Walpole, *Corr.*, 9: 14, Letter to George Montague, 25 May 1745.
29. Violet Biddulph, *The Three Ladies Waldegrave* (London: Peter Davies, 1938), pp. 13–17. The original source of this information is the Waldegrave MSS which are unavailable at present. Consult The Royal Commission on Historical Manuscripts, NRA 28249.
30. *Complete Letters of Lady Mary Wortley Montagu*, ed. Robert Halsband, 3 vols (Oxford: Clarendon Press, 1965), 3: 213.
31. Ibid. The fifth child was Charlotte (1738–89). The other surviving children were Laura (1734–1813), Maria (1736–1807) and Edward (1737–71).
32. PRO, KB 10/29, London and Middlesex Indictments, Easter 24 Geo. 2, Indictment no. 4. The GLRO also has a copy of this indictment (away for repair) which was filed at Hick's Hall, ref. MJ/SR/2938, no. 16.
33. Richard Gude, *The Practice of the Crown Side of the Court of King's Bench*, 2 vols (London, 1828), reprinted 1991, 1: 136.
34. PRO, KB 29/409, Controlment Roll.
35. *Whole Proceedings*, p. 7.
36. Horace Walpole, *Corr.*, 20: 106. To Horace Mann, 10 January 1750.
37. Ibid., 36: 16–21. Unposted letter to Edward Walpole, written *c.* 16 May 1745.
38. Ibid., 28: 70. To Rev. William Mason, 2 March 1773. Horace Walpole asked that a phrase referring to him as his father's 'favourite son' be deleted from the manuscript of Mason's *Life of Gray*, 'lest it stab my living brother to the soul'.
39. Ibid., 16–21. Unposted letter to Horace Mann, *c.* 16 May 1745. Also, 20: 41–2 and 20: 215. Letters to Mann, 23 March 1749 and 22 December 1750.
40. Ibid., 20: 41–2. To Horace Mann, 23 March 1749.

41. The portrait is now owned by the Minneapolis Institute of Arts. It is reproduced in numerous histories of British painting and also in W. S. Lewis, *Horace Walpole: The A. W. Mellon Lectures in the Fine Arts 1960* (London, 1961), p. 27.

42. For James Worsdale see *The Dictionary of Irish Artists*, ed. W. G. Strickland, 2 vols (Dublin and London, 1913); also the *Memoirs of Mrs. Laetitia Pilkington, passim.*

43. *Whole Proceedings*, p. 8.

44. *Memoirs of Laetitia Pilkington*, 1: 274.

45. Ibid., *passim.*

46. *The Vertue Notebooks*, 6 vols (Oxford: Walpole Society Publications, 1930–55), vol. 3.

47. Lord Killanin, *Sir Godfrey Kneller and his Times 1646–1723* (London: Batsford, 1948), p. 53.

48. *The Correspondence of Alexander Pope*, ed. George Sherburn, 5 vols (Oxford: Clarendon Press, 1956), III: 476n.

49. *Dictionary of Irish Painters.*

50. *Old and New London*, ed. Walter Thornbury (London: Cassells, Petter & Galpin, n.d.), 6: 388.

51. *Whole Proceedings*, p. 9.

52. *Whole Proceedings*, p. 15.

53. Ibid.

54. Ibid.

55. Ibid.

56. Ibid.

57. Ibid.

58. Ibid.

59. Ibid.

60. Ibid.

61. Ibid.

62. *Full and genuine Narrative*, p. 20.

63. *Sessions Papers*, September 1750, case no. 501.

64. *Whole Proceedings*, p. 16.

65. Ibid.

66. Ibid.

67. Ibid.

68. Ibid.

69. Ibid.

70. Ibid.

71. GLRO. Calendar for the House of Correction at Clerkenwell, 1750 (MJ/CP/P no. 169).

72. PRO, KB 28/194, Plea Rolls, Trinity 24 Geo. 2.

73. PRO, KB 1/10, Depositions etc., Trinity 24 Geo. 2.

74. PRO, KB 20/2, Posteas, Part I, Trinity 24 Geo. 2.

75. Richard Gude, 1: 136.

76. Giles Jacob, *Law Dictionary* (1729).

77. Ibid.

78. PRO, KB 1/10, Depositions etc., Trinity 24 Geo. 2.

79. Ibid.

80. Ibid.

81. Giles Jacob.

82. 'An Examined Copy of the Record' in *Whole Proceedings*, p. 21.
83. PRO, KN 20/2, Posteas, Part I, Trinity 24 Geo. 2.
84. 'An Examined Copy ... ', *Whole Proceedings*, p. 24.

CHAPTER ELEVEN

The counter-attack

In custody

Walter Patterson was tried exactly a month after being remanded in custody in the Clerkenwell House of Correction. While imprisoned, his behaviour was 'very much of the Gentleman, notwithstanding his Commitment was upon the Vagrant Act'.[1] Somehow he found the money to pay for a room in the Keeper's apartments, where a great many of his compatriots came to see him.

His case was heard on 14 July 1750, during the Quarter Sessions at Hick's Hall. Edward Walpole's counsel was present to explain why, despite appearances to the contrary, Patterson was a rogue and vagabond within 'the true Intent and Meaning' of the Act passed in 1743, 'to amend and make more effectual' the law relating to such people.[2] The court was told that Patterson was 'a very wicked and infamous Person' in that he had accused Walpole 'of having attempted to commit a detestable Crime not fit to be named amongst Christians', a crime of which he had since been acquitted, and furthermore, had planned 'to charge him with the felonious Crime of Forgery, in order to take away his Life'.[3]

The main witness for the prosecution was James Worsdale, who repeated the story he had earlier told Walpole, about Patterson's collusion with Smith over the false bond. Patterson himself called no witnesses and, 'not disproving any of the Matters aforesaid', was found guilty.[4] In passing sentence, the judge decreed that he be 'conveyed to the Place of his legal Settlement', which was Kilmacrenan, Donegal, but before deportation he was to go back to the Clerkenwell Bridewell and serve six months' hard labour there.[5] Nor was this all. Within the first month of his imprisonment he was to be 'stripped naked from the middle upwards, and publicly whipped at a Cart's Tail, until his Body be bloody, round Hanover-Square, between the Hours of Ten in the Forenoon and Twelve at Noon'.[6] Thereafter he was to be given two more floggings, at two-monthly intervals, in parts of London where he would be recognized. Accordingly, at the beginning of July, he was to be whipped down the length of Pall Mall, so that Walpole could watch the spectacle from his windows, if he so wished. Finally, at the beginning of September, the venue was to be Covent Garden, where a number of his countrymen lived.

The prospect of this painful and humiliating series of ordeals concentrated Patterson's mind. He resolved to avoid them if he could and, as he was not lacking in resourcefulness or friends, he succeeded. It was probably one of these friends who gave, or sold, the story of the escape of Cather's attorney to a journalist afterwards. The tale went as follows.

After his trial Patterson was taken back to the House of Correction, where he lived as before, away from the other prisoners, in the Keeper's apartments. Soon one of his visitors brought him a new rope. On 26 July he used this to climb down from the window of his room after he had been locked in for the night. Earlier he had noticed a ladder kept in the kitchen. So he went there, removed a pane of glass, lifted the catch, dragged the ladder out and used it to climb from the yard into a small walled garden.

The garden was inside the prison, so he tied one end of the rope to the post of a shed there and flung the other end over the main prison wall. The wall was eighteen feet high and the ladder much shorter. So he gathered some flower pots and 'made a kind of Structure or Heap of them'.[7] Resting the ladder on this improvised platform, he was able to get to the top of the wall and, using the rope, let himself down the other side.

He now found himself in the yard of the Quakers' workhouse, 'still inclosed by Houses and strong Walls, so that he could get no farther'.[8] It happened to be the night when the Quaker women, thirteen of them, were washing the clothes of the poor. One of them came out of the wash house for some reason, and seeing Patterson, called out to the others, 'Here is a Man in the Yard'.[9] Patterson begged her not to make any noise, and she asked him 'how he came there, the Gates and Doors being fast'. He told her he had been drunk and supposed the 'Person who locked the Gates did not see him, he being asleep, so he had been there all night'.[10]

He then went with her into the room where the women were at work and he sat down. Only one of the women refused to believe his story. She told him roundly that 'he had broken out of Bridewell, and threatened to call Nathan, their Porter, but he implored her not to, promising to stay where he was till morning. Then, looking at her with an air of surprise, he declared, he did not know where Bridewell was, and asked, if it was there, pointing the contrary way.'[11]

The other women, who thought he looked a nice young man, asked how he came to be so drunk that he did not know where he was. Patterson, who had now got into his stride, told them 'he was newly married, and that being out, he unexpectedly met with some Acquaintance, who had detained him, and obliged him to drink too much, that he attempted to go home to Covent Garden, and that he lost his Way, but what gave him most Concern was, the Uneasiness his Wife would be in for his Absence, which he greatly feared would frighten her. However he would stay till Daylight, and desired they would let him sit till then, which was above two Hours.'[12]

This tale turned the thoughts of the Quaker women to the plight of the mythical Mrs Patterson. One of them, contemplating 'the Trouble this newly married Wife must be in, as she supposed, advised him to go Home directly, saying that perhaps his Wife sat up for him. He said, he did not doubt she did, but that he would not give his Wife any Uneasiness for the Future, for he would never stay out again.'[13]

With this last assurance Patterson won his audience over completely. One of the women went so far as to say that if his wife doubted his explanation for being out all night, he was to send her to them, so that she could 'be informed of the Truth of this Accident'.[14] Another of them 'went to the Porter Nathan, who was then in Bed, and got the Key, under the Pretence of going for some Drink'.[15] Then she let Patterson out into the street, with directions for finding his home and wife again quickly. For this 'Piece of Civility he gave her Half a Crown'.[16] At first she did not want him to give her so much, pointing out that it would cost far less to buy a dram, 'but he insisted she should take it, saying he had no smaller Change about him'.[17]

Patterson made his way to the house of John Faulkner and his wife, who hid him while he decided what to do next. He realized he would have to get out of London when the Faulkners told him he was being hunted throughout the town.

As soon as Edward Walpole learned of the escape, he hired a thief-taker, Mr Wallbank, who 'spared no Pains in searching after' Patterson, 'both by going personally in quest of him, and offering a large Reward by Advertisement'.[18] Patterson completed his plans, finally sending Ann Faulkner to a pawnbroker's to redeem some clothes he had left there. Most of the likely pawnbrokers had had a visit from Wallbank, offering them money for information. One of these waited hopefully, because he knew he had a coat and shirts belonging to Patterson. When Mrs Faulkner came for them, he let her have them and then, after she left his shop, he followed her to see where she lived. He gave her address to Wallbank, who went with his assistants to the house that night. But, on arrival, they 'found only Faulkner and his Wife in Bed'.[19] The couple denied all knowledge of Patterson, but were arrested anyway. The next day they were taken before Justice Henry Fielding, who committed them both to the Clerkenwell Bridewell.

Patterson crossed over to Dublin, where he was put in the Irish Newgate, perhaps for debt. He was released, however, even as orders were supposedly on their way from London, asking the authorities to keep him in custody, so that he could be extradited. By the time any such instructions could arrive, he was missing again.

Walpole did not wish the other men who he claimed were conspirators to follow Patterson's example and fade from the London scene before they could be brought to trial. As soon as he realized Patterson had eluded him he went to Sir William Lee, who promptly issued a warrant for the arrest of 'John Cather and others', on the grounds that if the 'Conspirators or some of them were not secured, they would abscond, or depart out of the Kingdom'.[20]

This time Cather was found easily. Andrew White decoyed him to the Vine Tavern in Long Acre, where 'Richard Elton, one of the Judge's Tipstaffs', was waiting to apprehend him. After his arrest Cather was taken to an 'Officer's House in Chancery Lane' for a few days. From there he was brought before Sir William Lee who, on 1 August, remanded him in custody in the King's Bench prison until his case was heard.[21]

Shortly afterwards Cain was coming away from the King's Bench prison when he too was arrested. He was 'carried before Justice [Henry] Fielding who committed him to the Gatehouse'.[22] Nixon was next. He was taken as he was leaving the Mitre in Holborn, a tavern near his home where he misguidedly supposed he was safe as it was (and still is) in a sanctuary area.[23] After a few days' confinement Nixon managed to obtain bail, even though the terms were unusually high, in that he had to provide a recognizance of £400 himself, as well as finding two other persons to give sureties of £200 each. Alexander, on hearing there was a warrant out for his arrest, also obtained bail on terms similar to those stipulated for Nixon. Both men hired lawyers and, over the next few months, prepared their defence.

Cather and Cain, who could not raise the money for bail, or to hire lawyers, remained in their separate gaols awaiting trial. At this stage the date given for the trial was 'the first Day of next Michaelmas Term', that is 6 October.[24] In the event the two men would not be tried until another nine months had gone by, and they had been prisoners on remand for almost a year.

William Smith

William Smith first appeared at the Old Bailey during the July Sessions in 1750, where he was 'indicted for forging a Bill of Exchange for £45 for value received of Thomas Weekes, and also an acquittance of it'.[25] He was not charged with attempting to sell the false bond to Edward

Walpole. As this had happened at Windsor, it would have been dealt with at the Abingdon Assizes, unless Walpole had asked for another writ to transfer the case to a London court. He did not do so because there was no need. Forgery, a troublesome and burgeoning crime, was classified as a felony and if Smith was convicted on Weekes's indictment he already faced the likelihood of being hanged.[26] At the July hearing he successfully applied to have his trial postponed so that he could summon witnesses and prepare a defence.

By the time Smith came again to the Old Bailey on 12 September he had decided to plead 'Guilty'. He was taking a calculated risk that, with only one charge against him, he would be able to persuade the court to treat him leniently. Nevertheless, it was unusual for a defendant to make such a plea.[27] The judge was surprised and asked Smith if he understood 'the consequence of his pleading'. He replied that he did and added,

> My Lord, I am unhappy enough to stand here, indicted for a fact which my prosecutor can so safely prove against me, therefore from a consciousness of it, and to prevent giving the court any unnecessary trouble, I do confess my guilt, and submissively rely on the favour of the court to intercede for my life. My Lord, I have much to say in alleviation of my crime, that this is the first time I ever appear'd before a court of justice in an ignominious manner, that a case of necessity urged me to commit the fact I am charged with, and that my heart is full of sorrow and contrition for it. If therefore, your Lordship, or Mr. Recorder, will be pleased to report me in a favourable light to his Majesty or the Lords in power, it will, I hope be the happy means of inducing them to extend their clemency towards me, but if I am so unfortunate as not to be thought an object worthy of their compassion I trust the Lord of Earth and Heaven will have mercy on my soul.[28]

Smith made a good impression. The members of the court had before them a defendant out of the common run, highly articulate, with 'a good manly countenance' who, they learned, was the son of the Rector of Kilmore, Co. Meath, and educated at Trinity College, Dublin. Many of those present were reluctant to see such a man, who was still only thirty, despatched at Tyburn. They wanted him to be given a second chance which, under the existing system, meant they hoped he would be transported to the Americas.

A week later, on 19 September, sentence was pronounced and Smith was condemned to death. This was only to be expected as he was guilty of a felony but, as the defendant knew, all was not yet lost. He made another eloquent speech, again asking the judge to recommend him for a royal pardon and promising, that if it were granted, he would atone for the errors of his past and pray for his preservers. As about half the men and women in the eighteenth century who were told they were to hang had their sentences commuted, the judge might well have acceded to Smith's request, had it not been for a dramatic intervention in the court proceedings.

Smith had no sooner finished speaking than a motion was put by William Davy, asking that the defendant 'be removed by Habeas Corpus to be try'd at the Exeter Assizes for further Crimes'.[29] Davy had not come from the King's Bench to the Old Bailey before with this request because, then as now, it was not allowed to impeach the reputation of a man in the dock before the jury had reached its verdict.

Ever since Thomas Weekes had identified Smith in Reading gaol, Davy had been pursuing a series of investigations in the West Country, where he himself came from originally, and in Ireland, where Walpole's advertisement describing Smith had been circulated. Apparently Thomas Weekes was only one of several people eager to prosecute the defendant. Davy had compiled a sizeable dossier, containing five further charges of forgery. Now, in the Old Bailey, he proceeded to tell the court the previous history of the man who was pleading for his life.

After leaving Trinity College Smith had been articled to a reputable attorney in Dublin who was a friend of his father. He did not complete his articles because, after the Rector died, he had run wild and got into debt. Instead he had robbed the attorney and absconded to London. Calling himself William Dawson, he got a job as a clerk to another lawyer named William Bull, who had clients in England and Ireland. After a while, when his employer was away in the country, Smith forged a bond in Bull's name for £130, payable by a merchant in Dublin, and went over to that city to collect the money. There he received £30 in cash and two bonds payable to the bearer, issued by the Irish bankers Swift and Co., which he cashed as soon as he returned to London. In the Michaelmas term of 1746 he was indicted by the court of King's Bench in Ireland for yet another forgery perpetrated while working for Mr Bull. On that occasion he had faked the attorney's signature on a bill of exchange worth £174 19s. 3d.

Round about this time Smith absconded again. When he reappeared, he had become Captain James Webb's clerk on board a naval vessel, *The Surprize*. There he began forging seamen's tickets, the pay slips sailors took with them at the end of a voyage if they were transferring to another ship before they were due to be paid. Davy showed the court three of these tickets which Smith had sold for £100. He was also wanted for stealing £100 of the pressed seamen's wages, as well as for robbing the surgeon's mate of about £15 worth of silver plate. It was for these crimes that the naval commissioners wanted to prosecute Smith at the Exeter Assizes.

At the end of his disquisition Davy addressed the Old Bailey as follows: 'Let those Gentlemen who so strenuously solicit the Transportation of this Felon, judge, when they have read and considered the Nature of these five heavy charges of Forgery against him, whether he is that deserving Object of the Government's Clemency that they would fain represent him to be.'[30]

It is perhaps worth noting that throughout his criminal career, Smith seems always to have worked alone, which may have been one reason why he had hitherto avoided prosecution. Furthermore, there was no mention, in Davy's otherwise comprehensive catalogue, of the one occasion when Smith was supposed to have a partner, that is Walter Patterson, in the affair involving Walpole.

Back in Newgate, Smith appealed once more to the King, through the Secretary of State, for clemency. When he was refused, 'he reflected on the Honourable Edward Walpole as the author of his destruction, by an interception of the royal mercy', though they told him this was not so.[31] Indeed, there was no need for Walpole to intervene any further. Smith was doomed from the time William Davy made his journey to the Old Bailey.

As the day of his execution approached, the condemned man employed his rhetorical gifts in raising money for a Christian burial. The Ordinary at Newgate was hardly exaggerating when he said that Smith 'had a peculiar Talent in engaging people to commiserate with, and relieve the almost constant Necessities he lived in'.[32] The relatively large sums he stole never lasted long. As often as not he was destitute. But if he was in rags or ill he could always move someone to buy him new clothes, pay for him to see a doctor, or just send him on his way with a few guineas, even when the donors suspected, or knew, that he was a bad lot. In his last days he wanted to avoid the shame of falling into the hands of the anatomists after his death, so he persuaded a Mrs Browning to pay for the following advertisement to be placed in the newspapers:

> In vain has Mercy been entreated; the vengeance of Heaven has overtaken me; I bow myself unrepining to the fatal Stroke. Thanks to my all-gracious Creator, thanks to my most merciful Saviour, I go to launch into the unfathomable Gulf of Eternity! Oh my poor Soul! How strongly dost thou hope for the Completion of eternal Felicity! I am all Resignation to thy blessed Will! Immaculate Jesus! Oh, send some ministering Angel to conduct me to the bright Regions of celestial Happiness.
>
> As to my corporeal Frame, it is unworthy of material Notice; but, for the sake of that reputable Family from whom I am descended, I cannot refrain from Anxiety, when I think how easily this poor Body, in my friendless and necessitous Condition, may fall into the Possession of the Surgeons, and perpetuate my Disgrace beyond the Severity of the Law. So great an Impoverishment

11.1 In the condemned cell at Newgate

has my long Confinement brought upon me, that I have not a Shilling left for Subsistence, much less for procuring the Decency of an Interment. Therefore I do most fervently entreat the Generosity of the humane and charitably compassionate to afford me such a Contribution as may be sufficient to protect my dead Body from Indecency, and to give me the Consolation of being assured that my poor Ashes shall be decently deposited within the Limits of consecrated Ground.[33]

This appeal was successful. 'The subscriptions of the humane', sent to Mrs Browning, 'were sufficient to answer the proposed end.'[34]

William Smith was hanged at Tyburn on 3 October 1750. On that appalling day he kept his self-respect and thereby earns the respect of the rest of us. A huge mob heard him make a final eloquent plea, this time to God, whom he addressed not in prose but in blank verse:

Thee will I sing, Almighty Maker! Thee,
Father of all! Whether the rising Sun
Sheds forth his golden Beams, or when at Night
The Moon unveils her Orb, Thou art my Strength,
My Life, my Glory, and my sure Defence;
My Castle, my Deliverance, my Hope;
My better Hope, when dread Affliction's hand,
Wide wasting, me o'erwhelms.[35]

Not that the crowd had gathered at the gallows to hear Smith. He was just a side-show. Londoners were there in their hundreds to witness the end of another clergyman's son, their highwayman hero Jemmy Maclean, who was hanged on the same day, along with ten other forgotten felons.

The prosecution constructs a case

The couple who had sheltered Walter Patterson after his escape remained in the House of Correction at Clerkenwell for nearly three months until, in the Michaelmas term, they were referred again to Henry Fielding, who had to decide whether or not to give the order for their release.[36] Fielding discharged Mrs Faulkner but sent her husband back to the Bridewell. It transpired that Ann Faulkner was freed because she promised to turn King's evidence. John Faulkner did not have to stay in prison much longer either. He was already seriously ill, and for that reason was sent home, where he died shortly afterwards.

Also during the Michaelmas term Walpole's counsel drew up a formal indictment of John Cather, Patrick Cain, Walter Patterson, Daniel Alexander and Adam Nixon. Whereas the indictment of Walpole preferred at Hick's Hall had been written on a single folio sheet, the one of

Cather and the others, preferred at the King's Bench, was about two feet square and inscribed on vellum, making it a more expensive document than the common run of indictments preferred in the lower courts.[37] It was also more detailed.

In essence the five Irishmen were accused of charging Edward Walpole falsely with attempted sodomy, so as to deprive him of his good name and to procure money from him. The document went on to describe in full how Cather had preferred an indictment at Hick's Hall on 24 April 1750, which had then been removed by writ of *certiorari* into the court of King's Bench. Next came an account of Walpole's trial in which he was found 'Not Guilty', followed by the court's pronouncement confirming that the men now accused had mounted a malicious prosecution.

A Grand Jury at the King's Bench passed the indictment as a true bill, having heard evidence from a number of witnesses who included Robert Bygrave, Andrew White, James Worsdale, John Sherwood and the newly recruited Ann Faulkner.[38] Next, still in the Michaelmas term, the accused men were summoned to appear in court to answer for the 'Trespasses Contempts Conspiracies and Misdemeanours' of which they had been indicted.[39] None of them was actually called to this preliminary hearing until 23 January 1751. On that day Alexander and Nixon were represented by the attorney William Hughes and did not have to appear themselves. Cather and Cain came in person, having been brought from their separate gaols for the occasion. Having heard the indictment read out, Cain pleaded 'Not Guilty', while Hughes made the same plea on behalf of Alexander and Nixon. All, except Patterson who was still missing, submitted themselves to trial by jury.[40]

Cather's plea on 23 January is not recorded, but a week or so later he presented a petition to the court of King's Bench. It is undated, but in it Cather mentions he has been in prison for six months, which indicates that it was written by the end of January. The petitioner asks Sir William Lee and the rest of the justices on the King's Bench for a retrial of Edward Walpole, whom he still believes he can 'prosecute and convict'.[41] He also asks for money to enable him to do this as he 'has not a shilling in the world' and cannot either 'prosecute the said Edward Walpole Esq., or defend himself without private or publick assistance'.[42] The reason Cather gives for his surprising request is that on the preceding 5 July he 'was by some of the said Edward Walpole's emissaries, Patrick Farrell and other Base Artfull Persons secured away from the Court to Screen the said Edward Walpole from Justice for want of the Petitioner appearing and giving Evidence against him'.[43] Cather states that Walpole has indicted him and 'several other innocent Persons for Conspiracy' for no other purpose than to 'prevent his being further Prosecuted for his Crimes'.[44]

In conclusion Cather reminds Sir William and the other judges that 'the Publick ... is concerned in the Conviction of all Offenders notwithstanding their Titles, Riches and Interest, especially where they are made use of not only to oppress the Poor and Innocent, but also to cherish and preserve the Guilty'.[45]

The King's Bench judiciary ignored Cather's petition. This is the first and last we hear of Patrick Farrell and the other 'Base Artfull Persons' who are supposed to have decoyed the petitioner away from the court on 5 July, though the fact that he said this had happened alerted Walpole's lawyers to the need to provide another explanation for the absence of a prosecutor that day. As for the rest of the petition, a flat statement from Cather that he was 'desirous to discover on oath all the sodomitical practices' of his opponent was not enough to persuade Sir William Lee to re-open the case, when no hint was given of any evidence that could be produced in support of the charge.[46] As far as the Lord Chief Justice was concerned, Walpole's innocence had been established. Cather's petition was placed in the files and left there.

After the January hearing a further six months elapsed before Cather and the others were put on trial. Such a delay was unusual. Even a wait of six weeks was rare, most defendants being tried within a month, or even seven days of being charged.[47] The extra time was needed so that Walpole's lawyers could construct a watertight case. Whereas it was going to be easy to convict Cather because he had preferred an indictment which had already been proved false, there were problems with the other four defendants. Links between them were tenuous, while their joint involvement in a scheme to extort money from Walpole was far from obvious.

The first half of 1751 was spent by Robert Bygrave and his assistants in searching for witnesses and collecting documents to show that Cather, Cain, Alexander and Nixon, as well as the missing Patterson, were co-conspirators. Andrew White and John Brownsmith were two of the most active of Bygrave's assistants, because they had known Cather ever since the days when they had all lodged together in Maiden Lane.

By May, work on the case was sufficiently advanced to start making arrangements to strike another Special Jury. On Friday, 17 May, 'On the Motion of Mr. Davy, upon reading the affidavits of Andrew White and one other', the Coroner of the court of King's Bench, James Burrow, fixed a date of 14 June for striking the jury, whether or not Cather and Cain or their legal representatives were present.[48] Two other affidavits sworn by Mr Bygrave just before and on 6 June show that Cather and Cain were informed of this decision.[49] No record exists of whether Alexander and Nixon were told, but neither they, nor their legal representatives, seem to have come to the court on 14 June, any more than

Cather or Cain did. Nor in the event did the lawyers from either side participate in choosing the jury. As could happen, the King's Bench Coroner struck all the names of the potential jurors himself. James Burrow is quoted as saying that on the occasions when he did this, 'there was no rule by which he took the special jurors', except that 'they were expected to be persons of superior rank to common jurymen'. However, he added that he picked only those men known to him to be 'in reputable circumstances'.[50]

On 27 June Sir William Lee committed Alexander to the King's Bench prison because the two men who had entered into recognizances for him refused to continue doing so.[51] They withdrew ostensibly out of moral indignation, possibly too because they had been frightened into believing Alexander might abscond if left at liberty. Jacob Palmer and George Panthoros, who had given sureties for Nixon, remained staunch. One of them, Palmer, who had the same surname as Nixon's mother-in-law, was probably a relative.

Finally the date for the trial was fixed. It was to be held on Friday, 5 July, exactly a year after Walpole had appeared in the court of King's Bench as a defendant.

Notes

1. *Whole Proceedings*, p. 16.
2. Ibid., p. 17.
3. GLRO, Calendar for the House of Correction at Clerkenwell, 1750 (MJ/CP/P no. 169).
4. Ibid.
5. Ibid.
6. Ibid.
7. *Whole Proceedings*, p. 17.
8. Ibid.
9. Ibid.
10. Ibid., p. 18.
11. Ibid.
12. Ibid.
13. Ibid.
14. Ibid.
15. Ibid.
16. Ibid.
17. Ibid.
18. Ibid.
19. Ibid.
20. PRO, PRIS 4/2, no. 679, King's Bench Prison Commitments Book.
21. Ibid.
22. *Whole Proceedings*, p. 18.

23. Ibid. For information about sanctuary areas see David Piper, *London: An Illustrated Companion Guide* (London: Collins, 1980), p. 251.

24. PRO, KB 29/410, Controlment Roll, Trinity, 24 Geo. 2. Also KB 15/23, Process Book, Michaelmas, 24 Geo. 2.

25. *Sessions Papers*, 12–19 September 1750, case no. 501 (Guildhall), and GLRO, 11 July 1750. Indictment no. 48 (MJ/SR/2944).

26. Leon Radzinowicz, *A History of Criminal Law and its Administration*, 5 vols (London: Stevens, 1948–86), 1: 146, note 26. In the period 1749–71 81 persons convicted of forgery and coining were hanged out of a total of 678 executed throughout the country. In the first three years of this period more people were executed than in the last three years, especially in London and Middlesex, where in 1749–51 230 offenders were sentenced to death, of whom 163 were hanged, while in 1769–71 there were 107 executions for 222 death sentences. See also Frank McLynn, *Crime and Punishment in Eighteenth-Century England* (London: Routledge, 1989), p. 259, where it is suggested that 'After 1750 growing doubts about the efficacy of capital punishment tended to reduce the level of executions', with a 50 per cent pardon rate being the case by the middle of the century, though this estimate 'masks differential levels in London and the provinces'.

27. J. H. Langbein, 'Shaping the Eighteenth-Century Trial: A View of the Ryder Source', p. 116. In 171 Old Bailey cases studied by Langbein for the period 1754–56, only two pleas of 'Guilty' were entered.

28. *Sessions Papers*, 12–19 September 1750, case no. 501 (Guildhall).

29. Ibid.

30. Ibid.

31. *Newgate Calendar*, ed. A. Knapp and W. Baldwin, 6 vols, revised edn (London, 1825), 2: 74.

32. *Sessions Papers*, 12–19 September 1750, case no. 501 (British Library).

33. *Newgate Calendar*, 2: 74–5.

34. Ibid., 2: 75.

35. Ibid.

36. GLRO, Calendar for the Clerkenwell House of Correction, 19 October 1750 (MJ/CP/P, no. 175).

37. PRO, KB 10/29, London and Middlesex Indictments, Michaelmas, 24 Geo. 2, no. 26.

38. Ibid. The names of witnesses are written in the margins of this indictment.

39. PRO, KB 29/419 Controlment Roll, Michaelmas, 24 Geo. 2 and KB 15/22–29, Process Book.

40. PRO, KB 21/36, Rule Book, Hilary, 24 Geo. 2.

41. PRO, KB 1/10, Depositions etc., Hilary, 24 Geo. 2.

42. Ibid.

43. Ibid.

44. Ibid.

45. Ibid.

46. Ibid.

47. Langbein, p. 115. See also Ruth Paley, *Justice in Eighteenth-Century Hackney* (London, 1991), Introduction.

48. PRO, KB 1/10, Depositions etc., Easter, 24 Geo. 2 and KB 21/36, Rule Book .

49. PRO, KB 1/10, Depositions etc., Trinity, 24/25 Geo. 2.
50. James Oldham, *The Mansfield Manuscripts and the Growth of English Law in the Eighteenth Century*, 2 vols (Chapel Hill: University of North Carolina Press, 1992), p. 157n.
51. PRO, PRIS 4/2, King's Bench Prison Commitments Book, Trinity, 24 Geo. 2.

CHAPTER TWELVE

Blind justice

The 'evil Tendency'

On the morning of 5 July 1751 the court of King's Bench met to try John Cather, Walter Patterson, Adam Nixon, Daniel Alexander and Patrick Cain, otherwise Kane. Into the courtroom, no more than twenty-five feet square, came clerks and other officials, the six members of the counsel for the Crown, four defence attorneys and the jurors. In addition there were law students who had been told that this trial would be worthy of their attention, and sundry journalists. When everyone else had found his place, the Lord Chief Justice and the three puisne judges, resplendent in black and violet, bewigged, capped and coiffed, took their seats on the bench. Then over the day various other people came and went, including a score of witnesses, ranging from the Walpole brothers to handwriting experts, and as many bystanders as could squeeze into the remaining space. The only persons under-represented were the men who were being tried.

Patterson was still missing. Cather spent the day in the King's Bench prison, where he had been since the previous August, and Cain remained in the Gatehouse. This was possible because, although it had been established in the Middle Ages that no man could be tried in his absence, in the eighteenth century he quite often was. The law on this point had not been repealed, but a series of complex rules and expedients had turned it into a fiction.[1] Nixon's bail for the huge sum of £800 was still operative, so he voluntarily absented himself, while the two attorneys he had engaged conducted his defence. To find lawyers he had to raise yet more money, but no doubt he knew that in cases where they were employed they were often successful in getting their clients off, or at least in securing lenient treatment of them.[2]

As it was, the men Nixon had briefed could have charged high fees. They were William Whitaker and Richard Clayton, both highly respected members of the profession. In due course Whitaker would be elected Treasurer of Serjeants Inn, and Clayton would be appointed Chief Justice for Ireland. Nixon could have confidence in them. Nevertheless he was anxious and did not stray far. Throughout the trial he paced 'to and fro bareheaded, thro Westminster Hall'.[3] Before long his agitated state attracted the attention of the crowd that thronged the place, which was not only a seat of justice, but a public thoroughfare,

12.1 Interior of Westminster Hall, *c.* 1745, showing the court of King's Bench in the top left-hand corner, from an engraving by Gravelot

not to mention a shopping arcade. Booksellers, toymen and haberdashers had stalls on either side. Nixon passed and re-passed men who were conferring with their attorneys, flirting with ribbon sellers, or leafing through the pamphlets on sale, or just strolling up and down, eating roast beef and drinking beer.[4]

Until 1760 the court of King's Bench, at the far south end of the Hall, was not partitioned off. Nixon could see Sir William Lee and the other judges seated on high. Above the considerable hubbub he could hear the louder pronouncements, as well as the raised, frantic interruptions of Alexander, the only one of the five defendants who was present in court.

The proceedings began with the swearing in of the twelve members of the Special Jury, selected from the shortlist of twenty-four eligible candidates, produced earlier by the Master of the Crown Office from the freeholders' book. Freeholders in Middlesex included country gentry and men in trade in the City. Half those jurors selected by James Burrow appear in contemporary lists of prominent merchants. The foreman, Robert Vincent, was a stationer in Salisbury Court, Fleet Street.[5] Several sold their wares to the well-to-do, such as William Clarke, a Turkey-carpet merchant and Paul Whitchcott, the watchmaker. Three of them, William and Plunckett Woodroffe and George Putland, were already familiar with the case, having served on the Special Jury at Walpole's own trial the year before.[6] All had homes in affluent, still rural areas such as Hampstead, Tottenham and Chiswick.[7]

Once the jurors had taken their places, the counsel for the Crown came forward. The six members of the counsel had now to present to the court the case on which they had been working for many months. They were, or would become, eminent in one way or another. Sir Richard Lloyd, fifty-seven years old, was the eldest. He would be made Solicitor General in three years' time. Robert Henley and his friend Charles Pratt succeeded one another as Lord Chancellor. The Hon. Alexander Hume Campbell, twin brother of the Earl of Marchmont, was as active in politics as he was in the law.[8] John Ford made his mark in 1752, defending the printer, William Owen, on trial for seditious libel. It was a noteworthy defence because it led the jurors, most unusually, to disobey Sir William Lee, who had directed them to find Owen guilty.[9] Ford never rose to high office. Nor did William Davy, who, as we have already seen, played an active part in the conviction of William Smith.

Davy, nicknamed 'Bull' Davy, was an anomaly in the clubland-cum-collegiate atmosphere that prevailed among the select barristers who worked in the principal court of criminal jurisdiction in England. He had been in the King's Bench prison, where he had been incarcerated after going bankrupt as either a grocer, or possibly a druggist, in Exeter. While in gaol he began reading law and, when he was released, decided to make it his career. He soon showed a talent for his new calling. Few plausible rogues maintained their composure under his rigorous cross-examination. He also had a mordant sense of humour, which did not spare even lord chief justices. In due course he would be briefed in some of the most celebrated trials of the age, successfully prosecuting that creative liar Elizabeth Canning and, equally successfully, defending the negro Somersett against the man who claimed him as a slave.[10]

In 1751, however, Davy was still making his way. Nevertheless his name heads the list of those who acted as counsel for the Crown.[11] He had been one of the most active members of the prosecution team before the trial. He continued to play an active part during it, and so earned the lasting friendship of Edward Walpole.

The first task of the counsel for the Crown was to read aloud the indictment. This took some time, being that long and descriptive document preferred earlier by Walpole. The main charge came at the beginning, in which John Cather and the four other defendants, 'being Persons of ill Name, Fame and Reputation', were accused of

> combining, contriving, conspiring, intending, designing, and agree-
> ing, not only to deprive the Honourable Edward Walpole, Esq. of
> his good Name, Fame, and Reputation, but also wickedly, mali-
> ciously, falsely and unjustly, to charge and accuse the said Edward,
> with making an Assault on the said John, with an Intent feloni-
> ously, and against the Order of Nature, to commit that detestable
> and sodomitical Sin (not to be named amongst Christians) called
> Buggery, with the said Cather, and to subject the said Edward to
> such Punishment, as by the Law of this Kingdom, Persons guilty of
> such Misdemeanours as aforesaid, are subject and liable to, and
> with an Intent and Design, unlawfully and unjustly, to procure
> Money to themselves from the said Edward.[12]

Having gone through the indictment, the prosecution 'very copiously laid before the Court and Jury sworn, the heinous and aggravating Nature of the Crime of which the Defendants stood indicted, and took Notice of the evil Tendency that might have accrued from such an enormous, flagrant and unparallel'd Practice, if this should go unpunish'd'.[13]

Such an opening statement made it clear that the business ahead of the court had ramifications going beyond anything one might have supposed from a case that originated in a dispute between a gentleman and a boy who claimed he had been sexually assaulted. The quarrel and its aftermath were important to society as a whole. The words 'unparallel'd' and 'evil Tendency' suggest furthermore that the episode represented a novel and sinister development in the annals of crime, which prompts a question as to why so many people – perhaps the majority – regarded this trial as significant.

It is easy to see how Walpole, the victim of Cather's prosecution, might have been carried away to the point of paranoia. It is less easy to see how he gained the support of other men with keen legal minds. They knew that whereas it would be relatively simple to convict Cather, it would be no easy matter to obtain convictions of the larger and heterogeneous assortment of men Walpole said were his persecutors.

Various answers to the question of why the case was brought suggest themselves. As well as the lawyers, who were making money out of the affair, the judiciary and law-abiding citizens were grateful the trial was taking place at all. Apart from those victims of crime who could not afford to bring a prosecution, some were afraid to do so, especially if a gang was involved.[14] Walpole's resolution was welcome, therefore, all the more so because he was willing and able to pay whatever it took to win his case.

Then there was the matter of class loyalty. As we have seen, the members of the King's Bench were men who knew Walpole personally. Every effort had been made to exploit the tribal bond, down to the selection of a jury which, as well as being drawn from the rising mercantile class, included gentlemen of independent means among its members.[15]

There were also sociological factors that encouraged the authorities to bring the five men in the Cather case to trial. In the middle of the eighteenth century Londoners felt well nigh overwhelmed by one of those crime waves that engulfed the capital from time to time. On 31 January 1750 Horace Walpole began a letter to his friend Horace Mann in Florence, 'You will hear little news from England, but of robberies. Numbers of disbanded soldiers and sailors have all taken to the road, or rather the street. People are almost afraid of stirring after it is dark.'[16] Two years later the situation had not improved. Walpole wrote again, 'One is forced to travel, even at noon, as if one was going into battle.'[17] As he suggested, the crisis had been exacerbated by the large number of men disbanded after the War of Austrian Succession ended in 1748. Soon after the Peace of Aix-la-Chapelle was signed, some 30 000 English troops and 40 000 seamen were turned loose, to make their way as best they could in civilian life.[18] At the beginning of 1751 Henry Fielding had published his *Enquiry into the ... late Increase of Robbers etc. With some Proposals for Remedying this growing Evil ...* . This influential pamphlet was widely discussed and praised in various journals.[19] As Justice of the Peace for Westminster and Middlesex, Fielding wrote from his experience of dealing with miscreants of all kinds, on a daily basis, so much of what he had to say carried conviction with his many readers. On 1 February 1751, a few weeks after this topical essay appeared, a committee appointed by the House of Commons began sitting in order to consider the state of the criminal laws. Over the next four and a half months the members of the committee, who included two future prime ministers and a lord chief justice, decided to adopt several of Fielding's recommendations in the report they were writing, which was completed in June.[20]

Fielding claimed that things were even worse than the majority of Londoners supposed. The pressing, immediate problem was one of organized crime. The capital was being manipulated by a group, akin to that which 'Italians call the Banditti'. Fielding had seen 'convincing proofs' of this mafia, 'a great gang of rogues, whose number falls little short of a hundred, who are incorporated in one body, have Officers and a Treasury, and have reduced Theft and Robbery into system'. These men were not confined to the criminal underworld of St Giles or other rookeries, but were able 'to appear in all disguises, and mix in most companies'. They organized the rescue of prisoners from gaol and, if that failed, intimidated or bribed prosecutors. 'For their last resource' they had 'some rotten members of the law to forge a defence for them, and a great number of false witnesses ready to support it.'[21]

To anyone who had the *Enquiry* in mind, the defendants in the Cather trial fitted rather well into Fielding's description of an organized gang of what we would now call white-collar criminals, who could mix in any society. With the exception of Cain, classified as a labourer, they were described as gentlemen in the indictment.[22] Not only were they educated; three of them had been trained in the law, as was William Smith, who had already been disposed of. Furthermore, one of them, Patterson, had evaded justice because he had been helped to escape from gaol where, despite his supposed indigence, he had mysteriously found the money to make his brief stay quite comfortable.

Nor was it beside the point that the defendants were Irish. As we have already seen, the Irishman John Mullins failed at the Old Bailey in 1745 when he prosecuted John Twyford, because prejudice made one English witness assume he was dishonest.[23] In the 1750s Saunders Welch, who was High Constable for Holborn and Fielding's right-hand man, declared that 'most of the robberies, and the murders consequent upon them' were committed by outcasts from Ireland. He painted a lurid picture of 'fellows made desperate by their crimes' who, when Ireland became too hot for them, crossed over to England 'to perpetrate their outrages'.[24] An exasperated Welch was exaggerating, because at the time he was writing the number of Irishmen hanged in the capital never exceeded 14 per cent of the whole.[25] Nevertheless, this figure was high enough, when added to the number of convictions for lesser crimes, to ensure that Welch's view was widely shared, to the extent that one of the journalists writing about the defendants in the Cather trial could say, 'It is needless to remark that all these Gentlemen were Irish.'[26]

Members of the counsel for the Crown also had their personal reasons for supporting Walpole. It disturbed them that the defendants had been involved in making a malicious prosecution about a homosexual offence. As we have seen, the law on sodomy encouraged blackmail, yet legislation punishing that crime was difficult to frame. Indeed, the law on blackmail was still being clarified in 1968.[27] In 1751 the possibility that an organized gang, such as the one Fielding wrote about, was turning its attention to this kind of crime reinforced a growing belief that all gentlemen, with money and a reputation to lose, were vulnerable. Innocence was no safeguard. It was imperative to punish all those who, in any way, had assisted Cather to make his accusations.

The fact that Cather had chosen Walpole as his target, and had been helped by others, was seen to be heinous because of all that Walpole represented. For he was not only a well-to-do gentleman with a famous name, but a Member of Parliament who had been a friend of the Prince of Wales, until Frederick's sudden death earlier in the year. Robert Henley, the Hon. Alexander Hume Campbell and Sir Richard Lloyd, who sat in the Commons, were no doubt aware that the honour of the House was at stake in this affair, even if they did not express themselves as melodramatically as one journalist, who compared the Irish conspirators with Catiline and his followers, concluding that it was 'better for the City of Rome to be deprived of her Senate, than for the British Isles to have her Parliament composed of Members, who could be guilty of Crimes for which Fire of old showered down from Heaven, which in Time must render us a Bye Word and Proverb amongst Nations'.[28] The reference to Sergius Catilina would have reminded contemporary readers of another elected representative of the people who, thirty years before, had been involved in a sodomitical scandal. *The Conspirators, Or, The Case of Catiline*, featuring the Earl of Sunderland, had recently been reprinted, along with an even earlier work about another noble sodomite, the Earl of Castlehaven.[29]

If it was important to defend the good name of the House of Commons, it was also important to prevent any breath of scandal touching the royal family. Like Walpole, Henley, Hume Campbell and Pratt had all belonged to the Prince of Wales's circle. Frederick's behaviour in sexual matters had often been crass, but no one had ever suggested (openly at any rate) that he was other than heterosexual.[30] Walpole had to be fully vindicated, and anyone thinking of following the example of his accusers discouraged, lest such a suggestion be made about the

Prince and his friends. For although Frederick was dead, his son was the eventual George III.

Lastly, even the weather may have influenced the counsel for the Crown in speaking of 'the evil Tendency' that might accrue if the 'heinous' crime with which the defendants were charged went unpunished. The unusual experience of having had months of high temperatures, culminating in three earthquakes in the capital at the beginning of 1750, had induced one of those periodic fits of morality to which the English were prone. 'A Shower of Sermons and Exhortations' descended on the populace.[31] To the surprise of Horace Walpole, even the worldly Bishop of London, Thomas Sherlock, told his congregation that the earthquakes were divine retribution for sins 'natural or not'.[32]

Various forces, therefore, personal, judicial, social and religious, ensured that Cather and the others were tried in the court of King's Bench, and these forces helped to predetermine the result of the trial, even before the evidence was heard.

As one might expect, throughout the complex trial the name of John Cather was recurrent. He was the man whose actions had brought about the event. Otherwise it became apparent that the different prosecution witnesses had divided the labour of ensuring the conviction of the other defendants between them. Their first target was Daniel Alexander.

The case against Daniel Alexander

The trial continued conventionally enough, with the victim of the alleged crime being called as the first witness. Edward Walpole told his story in a simple yet masterly fashion. Describing his first encounter with John Cather in Dublin, he prefaced his remarks by signifying 'his Love to the Gentlemen of Ireland, in general, but in particular to the person of Lord Boyne', for whose sake he agreed to help Cather, who claimed to be the son of one of his friend's tenants.[33] Having established that he was not prejudiced against the Irish, and had not taken the initiative in getting to know the boy, Walpole went on to consolidate his credentials as a disinterested benefactor. He told the court how 'some years after' Cather came to see him in London, but that on examining him, he had 'found him incapable of undertaking any Business', and had advised him to gain experience by going into service elsewhere.[34] In the meantime, he admitted, he did not discourage the youth from calling at his house in Pall Mall from time to time, adding that he had even had thoughts of employing him as his children's attendant, if certain rearrangements he might have to make in his household staff provided a vacancy.

This situation continued for a couple of months at the beginning of 1750 until, as Walpole explained, there came an event that made him change his opinion of Cather. On 17 March Walpole's manservant William Collier was in a beerhouse, when he caught sight of the usually shabby, young Irishman quite transformed, dressed up 'in a Silver-laced Waistcoat' and 'a ruffled Shirt', looking 'very fine'.[35] Noticing the expression of astonishment on Collier's face, Cather 'seemed in some Confusion' but came over and bought him a dram.[36] Then he begged him not to tell his employer he had seen him, explaining that 'he only borrowed the cloaths in Honour of his country, it being St. Patrick's Day'.[37]

Collier lost no time, however, in describing the meeting to Walpole, who told the court that the account 'gave him a bad Opinion of Cather, imagining from thence, that he had got acquainted with some bad Company, and therefore he resolved to have nothing to do with him'.[38] So when Cather came to tell him he had found a job and asked for a letter of recommendation, he refused to give him one and forbade him ever to come to the house again.

The beerhouse story was corroborated by William Collier when he took the stand later on and repeated, word for word, everything Walpole said he had told him the year before.

In the majority of trials in which Sir William Lee was the judge, he cross-examined witnesses himself, and was quite likely to go through the testimony as it was presented, point by point. On this occasion he did not ask Walpole any questions, even though, unlike Alexander, Cather was not represented by defence attorneys whose main task would have been to take over the work of cross-examination. So the court was not told what Cather had said or done during his final interview with Walpole. Furthermore, a puzzling anomaly regarding dates went unremarked. In his indictment of Walpole Cather had claimed he was sexually assaulted on 1 March, more than a fortnight before he was supposed to have come to the house in Pall Mall as if nothing had happened.[39] However, as Walpole had already been declared innocent of the charge of attempted sodomy, anything he had to say about Cather was unlikely to be scrutinized too carefully at this stage.

Walpole went on to give the more important part of his testimony, in which he spoke of Daniel Alexander's letters and visits. He wanted to show that Alexander was culpable under the Waltham Black Act of 1723. A section of that Act covered extortion, making it a crime to send, knowingly, 'any letter demanding money, or a remission of any other valuable thing'.[40] Many extortioners sent anonymous letters threatening the recipient with murder or arson. The somewhat vague wording of the Black Act was designed to deal not only with such men, but also with those whose approach was less crude. The law was interpreted liberally by the courts, where it was decided that a 'demand need not be made in a peremptory manner, or be accompanied with a threat of bodily harm'.[41] Yet even though Walpole had a wide mandate, the case he was trying to make was not clear-cut. Alexander had not made threats of any kind, or direct demands. On the contrary, he had written saying that he had declined to take on Cather's case, offering his services to Walpole instead. This offer he repeated on the various occasions when he came to the house in Pall Mall.

All Alexander's overt actions had been well within the law, but he made his first serious mistake when he showed that he thought Walpole might have made sexual overtures to Cather. Any doubt cast on Walpole's innocence enraged him. Furthermore, Alexander offered his help in having the 'information stopped'. Walpole saw this as an attempt at blackmail.[42] In order to convince the court that Alexander had acted throughout from the worst of motives, Walpole set out to demonstrate that he was the worst of men, morally corrupt as well as being an accomplice of Walter Patterson, who had already been convicted as a rogue and a vagabond.

Walpole described how Alexander began writing him letters in April 1750, informing him that Cather intended to prosecute him for attempted sodomy, and admitting that he had initially agreed to act as Cather's lawyer but had since changed his mind, out of respect for the Walpole family. The court was then told what happened when Alexander first called to see the man he had been writing to at home. Initially the visitor stated that he did not think there was anything in Cather's charges, but it had soon become apparent that he was keeping an open mind about the matter. He launched into a defence of homosexuality, 'saying that all Men had their Passions, and that Crime that was now look'd upon in so heinous and criminal a Manner, was very much used amongst the Antients'.[43]

There was hardly anything more likely to prejudice an eighteenth-century jury against a defendant than to learn that he preached this heresy. It was barely two years since a similar argument in *Ancient and Modern Pederasty Investigated and Exemplified* had been published, whereupon its printer was arrested and the author, Thomas Cannon, had to leave the country.[44] The average citizens chosen for jury service were far more likely to sympathize with the author of *Satan's Harvest Home*, also published in 1749, which denounced sodomy as the worst kind of sexual transgression.[45]

Alexander showed himself to be most accommodating during that first visit to Walpole. He was willing to assist in 'stopping the Information' about the sodomitical attack, 'if there was any Truth in it', and equally willing to set about 'discovering the Plot' if that was what was required of him.[46] He created a very bad impression, without realizing he was doing so. Walpole was convinced he was a rogue, but carried on seeing him because he hoped that, sooner or later, he would show his hand, revealing his own part in the conspiracy which he had offered to disclose. Walpole had decided that Patterson was involved in this conspiracy – even before Worsdale began his investigations. In his capacity as Cather's lawyer, Patterson had also been to see him recently, to inform him that his client intended to prefer an indictment unless 'timely prevented'.[47] So, on another occasion when Alexander called, Walpole led the conversation round to Patterson.

Alexander, who imagined he had won Walpole's trust, had no hesitation in discussing Cather's lawyer who, he said, had helped him write some of the letters he had sent. As members of the Irish Protestant community in London, engaged in the same profession, the two men had probably known each other for some time. Nevertheless, Alexander did not have Patterson's full confidence, and knew nothing of the impending indictment until Walpole told him about it. Anxious to ingratiate himself with the man he hoped would employ him, he said nothing to contradict Walpole's suspicions of his fellow countryman. In the process he went too far for his own good. He let slip a remark which Walpole was able to use to incriminate him, not just Patterson. Walpole told the court how he had said to Alexander that he knew 'what Conversation had past between him and Patterson, when the last letter was wrote that he had received, which was that Mr. Walpole had a great deal of Money, and we must have some of it. Alexander, upon this, reply'd that they were not the express Words, but that they were much to the same Purpose.'[48]

So far, Walpole's conversations with Alexander, like the ones he had had with Cather, had taken place when no one else was there to confirm that the statements made by either of them were being reported accurately. From now on, however, there were witnesses present during some of Alexander's visits. The court was told how one day he arrived at the house in Pall Mall when Horace Walpole was there. Horace stayed in the room after Edward had said 'his Brother was no Stranger' to what he supposed Alexander was going to mention.[49]

Alexander had come with alarming news. Cather had changed his story. He no longer spoke of being the victim of an attempted sodomitical attack, but claimed 'that Sodomy was committed on him, whereby he was greatly damaged and was now under the Care of a Surgeon'.[50] This meant that if the matter came to court and Walpole was convicted, he faced the death penalty. Alexander was still sure he could help, however. He followed up his notice of this latest development by saying ' that he had learned something of the Affair that might be of great Service to Mr. Walpole, if the same came to be tried', though he also believed that Cather had reached the stage when 'it would be no hard Matter to compromise it'.[51] Walpole made it clear that he was still averse to any kind of settlement. Instead he demanded to know the name of the surgeon who was treating Cather. Alexander could not say, having been told about him by Patterson, who had not identified him.

Walpole's account of this conversation gave the impression that there were indeed various conspirators, ever more determined to frighten him into buying his way out of an ugly situation. However, we never hear any more about Cather's injuries, either from the victim himself or from Patterson, which leaves us wondering where the story originated. Perhaps Alexander was merely repeating a piece of tavern gossip, passing it off as inside information he had obtained from Patterson, in yet another effort to show Walpole he was a man worth having on his side. If so, he miscalculated. The story confirmed Walpole in his belief that Alexander and Patterson were fellow conspirators.

Walpole concluded his testimony with a description of one more visit from Alexander, who arrived at his house in an agitated state because he had heard that Walpole had come to an agreement with Cather, despite having refused his own offers to act as a mediator. Whether Alexander knew it or not, Stephen Slaughter was within earshot when he arrived, and remained, listening to all that was said. In the portrait-painter's hearing, Walpole denied that he had been in touch with Cather, and repeated yet again that he had no intention of agreeing anything with him.

Alexander, like Nixon, had found the money to hire two lawyers to defend him in court. They were a Mr Benny and a Mr Stowe, conscientious men but not particularly aggressive in making out a case for their client. When Walpole had finished speaking, one of them asked him if he had replied to any of the letters he had received from Alexander. Walpole replied that 'he did not remember that he had', whereupon the advocate produced a letter and showed it to Walpole, who then 'readily acknowledged it to be his writing, and added that he had not therein either spelt or wrote his Name as usual, not knowing what Advantage such a dangerous Set of People might take of it, if he had'.[52] Whereupon Alexander's lawyer was silenced. He did not ask for the letter to be read out in court, so we never discover what it was about, or how its existence could be reconciled with Walpole's earlier statements that he had never made any independent overtures to Alexander.

As was customary at the time, the testimony of the man bringing the case to court was followed by that of the other prosecution witnesses. In succession, therefore, Horace Walpole, Stephen Slaughter, Robert

Bygrave and William Collier came forward to corroborate most, if not all, of the story the court had been given.

The first of these witnesses to take the stand was Edward Walpole's brother. Duty and sentiment brought Horace Walpole to the King's Bench that day. Helping to convict men, even rogues, was not something he normally did. Earlier he had been celebrated in a Grub Street ballad, because he had declined to testify against the highwayman Jemmy Maclean, who had held him up in Hyde Park.[53]

Now, when he testified against Alexander, Horace Walpole was succinct and relatively non-committal, confining himself to the bare facts of the meeting he had witnessed. So he confirmed that Alexander 'strongly recommended to his Brother to stop the Proceedings', and that Edward refused 'any Compromise of so black and vile an Affair', while thanking his visitor for the 'many Protestations he made of Friendship and Willingness to serve him'.[54] Horace offered no opinion of his own except to say that Alexander 'seem'd very desirous to be employed by Mr. Walpole'.[55] He concluded his testimony by saying that, as soon as he was alone again with his brother, he made a memorandum of the substance of what had passed, lest he forget anything. He then produced these notes and read them to the court.

Horace Walpole, speaking coolly, never straying from the point, was a good witness. One journalist covering the trial voiced the majority view when he said, 'Mr. Horatio' spoke 'to the great Satisfaction of the Court'.[56] The words of both brothers carried all the more weight because of who they were. The journalist just mentioned was deeply respectful, adding that they 'behaved in a Manner suitable to the Height of their Stations and Dignity of their Birth'.[57]

The Keeper of the King's Pictures was the next witness asked to give evidence about Alexander. Stephen Slaughter added no new facts to the story that had been told so far. He was not in court for that purpose, but to reiterate a point that was clearly felt to be important, namely that Walpole had consistently refused to come to a settlement with Cather. Slaughter confirmed that on 31 May 1750 he heard Walpole tell Alexander 'that he had not, nor would not compromise any such villainous Affair'.[58]

There was a gap of at least six weeks between the conversations overheard by Horace Walpole and Stephen Slaughter. Yet in all that time Alexander remained encouraged and continued to make what he thought were acceptable offers of help. Nothing was said about this by the defence counsel, but Alexander showed himself increasingly dissatisfied with the way his relationship with Walpole was being presented, and 'frequently endeavoured to confound the evidence'.[59] The defence counsel did, however, cross-examine Slaughter about a memorandum he read out to the court. The portrait painter had, like Horace Walpole, written an account of what he had heard. Asked when he had written this, he appeared uncertain but thought it was 'three or four Days after the Conversation at Mr. Walpole's House'.[60] Slaughter was an elderly man.[61] A more ferocious cross-examiner than either of Alexander's attorneys could have suggested that perhaps the note taker's memory was not as good as it might have been, when it came to recalling all that had been said, in precise phrases, after several days' delay. As it was, this point was not pursued.

After Stephen Slaughter, Robert Bygrave came forward. Walpole's solicitor said that Alexander 'had been often with him' while the prosecution initiated by Cather 'was carrying on', and had told him that he had received money from Cather when he agreed to take on the case, but had not returned it when he decided not to go ahead after all.[62] As a result 'Cather and his Confederates' were harassing him and 'had employed one Mr. Lewis of Clifford's Inn to sue him the said Alexander, for the said Money in the Marshalsea Court'.[63]

With Bygrave's testimony financial sharp practice was added to the list of Alexander's sins. So far, however, no evidence had been produced by anyone to show that he had committed a crime. For this the prosecution relied on the letters he had written to Walpole. Several of these letters were now produced and read in court. By this time the listeners had a picture in their minds of the writer of them as morally lax and unscrupulous, and were ready to dismiss the protestations of friendship they contained as an artful strategy. So although the letters made no overt demands, it was decided that 'they were some of them soothing, and others menacing; the general Tendency of the Whole being not only to obtain Money, but also to procure a Place of considerable Profit'.[64]

Lest there be any question about who had written the letters, Walpole paid for John Grove of Hammersmith to come to the King's Bench and confirm that they were all in Alexander's handwriting. Asked by one of the defendant's lawyers how he could swear to this, 'as they were wrote in several Hands', Grove replied that he had been acquainted with Alexander's handwriting for a long time, and 'knew he could alter it when he pleased' and 'could write in many Hands'.[65]

Alexander continued to object to the construction that had been put on his actions and tried to present a paper to Walpole, but was not allowed to do so. His case was already lost. The way the letters were interpreted made it possible for him to be convicted under the all-encompassing Waltham Black Act.

The case against Walter Patterson and Patrick Cain

Trials are innately theatrical, and as the day wore on it became apparent that the trial of Cather and his confederates was a drama in which there was something for everyone. While discerning intellects followed the efforts of the best legal minds as they applied their expertise in a complex and unusual case, the imagination of the majority of bystanders was captured by the spectacle of Edward Walpole, a heroic protagonist, engaged in a struggle with the forces of darkness. For the most part the mood in the courtroom was one of high seriousness, often charged with emotion. As one of the journalists present that day wrote, 'Pity and Compassion, these natural Instincts and essential Properties of the humane Heart' filled the audience 'with Horror to think of the detestable Scheme, and the jesuitical Methods by which the same was conducted and pursued.'[66]

Then James Worsdale took the stand and provided some acceptable light relief. Using his histrionic gifts, he re-enacted the roles of recruiting sergeant and haymaker's widow, which he had played when he went in search of Cather, until, posing as Counsellor Johnson, he found Patterson playing skittles with Dennison and Faulkner in the alehouse known popularly as the Devil and Bag o' Nails. He went on to recreate conversations he had with Patterson during lengthy drinking sessions in taverns at Buckingham Gate and in Covent Garden, bringing each scene to life, often raising a laugh. Soon even more people from the body of Westminster Hall crowded into the court, drawn by a performance as accomplished as any Worsdale ever gave at the Smock Alley Theatre or Drury Lane.

Worsdale's primary task was to demonstrate to the court the guilt of Walter Patterson and Patrick Cain. He took only a passing interest in Cather, and admitted he had not met either Alexander or Nixon at the meetings he described.

When Worsdale spoke about Patterson, he confined himself to testimony relating to the charge of bringing a malicious prosecution in the hope of extorting money from Walpole. He said nothing of Patterson's supposed involvement with William Smith in the affair of the false bond, because that charge had not been included in the current indictment of the defendant. This omission weakened the case Worsdale was making. The case was weakened still further because he was unable to say that Patterson had ever admitted that he knew the proposed prosecution of Walpole was trumped up. In the end the most telling piece of evidence Worsdale produced was a remark made by the defendant at their first meeting. On that occasion Patterson said that Walpole 'was a bad Man; that he had been guilty lately of a very bad Action, no less than an

Attempt to commit Sodomy with a poor young Fellow of his Acquaintance, and had now refus'd giving him any Thing to support him; but that he believed the Person would make him pay for it'.[67] As Worsdale was speaking to the converted, the ambiguous phrase, 'make him pay for it' convinced his listeners that Patterson had been talking about extortion.

Worsdale was far less equivocal about Cain. Indeed, what he had to say about Cather's friend convinced some who heard him that the young labourer from Londonderry was the 'original Contriver' of a scheme to obtain money with menaces from the man who had wronged Cather.[68] Proof of this was supposedly contained in a conversation Worsdale had had with Cain when they were crossing the river, after the evening spent in Cuper's Gardens with Cather and White.

Worsdale and Cain were sitting at the back of the boat, while the other two were sitting at the front, out of earshot. Worsdale told the court that he had asked Cain whether he believed Walpole had 'made any attack on Cather, in order to commit Sodomy', and had received the following reply: 'No, he never made any such Attempt on him, but that he had used Cather ill in not providing for him, according to his Promises; that the poor Fellow was starving, and this Charge was calculated to get some Money from Mr. Walpole.'[69] On hearing this Worsdale, playing his part as Johnson the crooked lawyer, laughed, and saying, 'He liked the Scheme prodigiously, offered to assist in carrying it on.'[70] Much encouraged, Cain had then said 'the Scheme was laid by him; that he generally had Success in such Affairs, and that they had lately had a Sum of Money from a Gentleman, whom he then named'.[71]

Worsdale did not repeat the name of this other victim in his testimony, but the mere mention of his existence appeared to justify the prosecution's claim that the court was dealing with a ring of dangerous criminals who, according to the writer of the official report of the trial, had also informed Worsdale 'that when they had (tho' God be praised, they did not) succeeded to get Money out of Mr. Walpole, they would go upon the same Lay, as they term'd it, with the old Doctors of Physick, Surgeons, and Men Mid-wives'.[72]

No one else identified Cain as the mastermind in an extensive blackmailing scheme. To Andrew White, the witness who spoke after Worsdale, Cain remained a shadowy figure who gave Cather shelter, and was accordingly referred to as 'his particular Friend'.[73]

White concentrated on showing how Cather had been motivated by unreasonable resentment and opportunistic greed, when he accused Walpole of attempted sodomy. The picture that emerged from White's testimony was a damning, yet pathetic one, of a novice in litigation, wildly optimistic one moment, plunged in despair the next, and hopelessly out of his depth. White told the court how he had discovered

Cather at Cain's house in Princes Street, still in bed at 11 o'clock in the morning. He was lying in because he had been up half the night before, 'concerning an Affair' which he was only too willing to tell White about, because he regarded him as a compatriot and an ally.

Cather told White that he suspected he was about to be cheated by an unnamed lawyer, with whom he had been arguing the night before. This man had wanted to come to an agreement with Walpole to drop the prosecution, and Cather feared that, if such a plan went ahead, the lawyer 'would not let him know what Money he got, or give him any, if he got ever so much, when he Cather was sure there would be a Thousand or two to make it up'.[74]

It had not occurred to Cather that there could be no settlement of the affair unless he agreed to it. When White pointed this out, and offered to introduce him to Counsellor Johnson, who would not expect payment in advance, Cather was so relieved that he promised his visitor a share of whatever money Walpole paid him in the end.

According to White, Cather did not talk specifically about the alleged sodomitical attack. Instead, he had spoken angrily of how 'he came from Ireland on the Promises of Mr. Walpole providing for him in London, but that he had refused doing any Thing for him, and used him ill in forbidding him his House', so that he was resolved 'to be revenged of him, and if he would not prefer him otherwise, he should by letting him have some of his Money'.[75]

John Brownsmith was the next witness to be sworn. He said that, like Andrew White, he had once lived in the same lodging house in Maiden Lane as Cather. The only other known fact about him is that, like White and Worsdale, he had been part of Walpole's paid team of investigators for over a year. All three men gave testimony under oath, of course, but the fact that they were employed by the prosecution does raise questions about the impartiality of their testimony. Given that they had an incentive to please Walpole, a temptation to distort, if not concoct evidence, existed.

Lack of information about Brownsmith makes it difficult to assess his reliability as a witness, which is a pity because the evidence he gave was instrumental in convicting Cather, while it completely contradicted the version of events given by the young man himself in the petition he had submitted to Sir William Lee in January.

Whereas Cather had written that he was kept away from Walpole's trial on 5 July 1750 by Patrick Farrell and other of Walpole's emissaries, Brownsmith told the court he had seen Cather in Westminster Hall that day and had spoken to him, advising him 'at that Time to appear to prosecute Mr. Walpole if he had Justice on Side, but that as soon as the Tryal came on Cather left the Hall, being afraid to appear'.[76]

Brownsmith also said he had gone to see Cather on 1 August, as soon as he heard he had been arrested. Offering his services as a friend, he had accompanied him 'to an Officer's House in Chancery Lane'. There Cather asked him 'what was best for him to do in his present Circumstances', whereupon Brownsmith advised him 'to confess the Truth, which he said he would readily do, if that would relieve him'.[77] Then, after Brownsmith had assured him that 'he would be intitled to some Clemency from Mr. Walpole' if he made a confession, he had written 'an Account in which he set forth, that what he accused Mr. Walpole with, was intirely false and groundless, and that he was advised thereto by Cain and Patterson'.[78] At the same time Cather had written a letter to Walpole, 'begging Pardon for all he had done against him, and imploring Mercy'.[79]

After Brownsmith had finished giving his testimony, the confession and letter he had spoken of were produced and read to the court. As Cather was not present, or represented, the jury was not told that, six months later, he had retracted the confession he had written at Brownsmith's behest and, in his petition, again claimed that Walpole was guilty.

Eighteenth-century juries paid considerable attention to confessions, regarding them as one of the best ways of arriving at the truth – provided that certain rules and procedures were followed in obtaining them. In 1729 Giles Jacob described three kinds of confession. In the first kind 'the Criminal may confess the offence whereof he is indicted openly in Court, before the Judge, and submit himself to the Censure and Judgment of the Law, which Confession is the most certain Answer and best Satisfaction that may be given to the Judge to condemn the Offender'.[80] Such a procedure had been followed by William Smith at the Old Bailey the previous September.

However, this type of confession was far more unusual than the second kind described by Jacob, 'when the Prisoner confesses the Indictment to be true, and that he hath committed the Offence whereof he is indicted, and then becomes an Approver or Accuser of others, who have committed the same Offence whereof he is indicted, or other Offences with him, and then prays the Judge to have a Coroner assigned to him, to whom he may make relation of those Offences and the full Circumstances thereof'.[81] As, according to Brownsmith, Cather had been willing to implicate Patterson and Cain, one would have expected him to become an approver, and so have won immunity from prosecution, and it is hard to see why this did not happen.

Jacob concludes his description, though, with an account of a 'third sort of Confession, formerly made by an Offender in Felony, not in Court before a Judge, as the other two are, but before a Coroner in a

Church, or other privileged Place'.[82] This procedure, which was already old-fashioned in 1729, resembles, in one or two respects, that followed in obtaining a confession from Cather. Presumably the officer's house in Chancery Lane, where it was written, qualified as a 'privileged Place', though it is unlikely that John Brownsmith was a coroner. Furthermore, Cather was not accused of committing a felony. The charge against him, as against all the defendants in this case, was described in the indictment as a misdemeanour.[83]

Whichever procedure was followed, it was all-important that the accused confess 'freely of his own accord, without any Threats or Extremity used, for if the Confession rises from any of these Causes it ought not to be recorded'.[84] Brownsmith was at pains to point out that the confession he had obtained 'was voluntarily done by Cather in his Presence'.[85] However, all this statement means is that Brownsmith did not use physical force. We know that, despite the rules, some confessions were obtained in other dubious ways, such as getting the prisoner drunk, or by bribing him.[86] In this case Brownsmith deceived Cather with an assurance he was not in a position to give, when he told him that, if he confessed, 'he would be intitled to some Clemency from Mr. Walpole'.[87] This promise deluded the frightened Cather with false hope. Walpole had no intention of seeking clemency for any of the defendants. From all this one can only conclude that the system and methods used in persuading Cather to admit guilt were unorthodox and unscrupulous.

Brownsmith's testimony brought the first part of the trial against Cather and his confederates to an end. Although 'there were more witnesses ready to appear' and speak against Alexander, Cather and Cain, the counsel for the prosecution 'here rested their Proofs against those three' and turned their attention to demonstrating the guilt of Adam Nixon.[88]

The case against Adam Nixon

The conviction of Adam Nixon was not a foregone conclusion, for even the counsel for the prosecution was not sure that this particular defendant was guilty. However, if it could be shown that he was, Walpole and his supporters would have demonstrated clearly that the case being tried represented a new and alarming tendency in the annals of crime in the capital, just because Nixon was not an obvious criminal.

The other four defendants had been portrayed to the jury as dubious characters, living from hand to mouth on the edge of society. Nixon, on the other hand, was regarded by the men who worked with him, and knew him well, as an upright and conscientious member of the legal profession. He had been living in London for at least six years, having taken up the law after leaving the army. By 1751 he had become known as a legal clerk whose services could be relied upon. Many men employed him and he was a familiar figure in Lincoln's Inn, Hick's Hall and the Old Bailey, recognizable because he retained a military appearance and did not wear a wig.[89] He was still a young man and far from rich, but he earned enough to live on. He was also fortunate in having a loyal wife (aptly named Constance), whose people had some money which they were prepared to spend so that he could convince the court of his innocence.

In order to show that, despite appearances, Nixon was one of the conspirators, the prosecution relied on three witnesses: Robert Bygrave, William Keate and Ann Faulkner. Bygrave came forward for the second time in this trial, to say that Nixon had written him a note early in the proceedings, requesting 'that if he intended to defend the Cause of Mr. Edward Walpole, wherein Cather was Prosecutor, any Notice he had Occasion to serve in that Cause might be directed to him' at his home in Warwick Court, Holborn.[90] From this Bygrave had deduced that Nixon planned to act as Cather's solicitor, nor had Nixon denied that this was his intention when he had seen Bygrave and spoken with him at about the same time.

Asked by Nixon's counsel whether he had ever sent on notices of the case as requested, Bygrave said he had, and that Nixon 'refus'd accepting them; but that it was after Patterson was in custody'.[91] Nixon would not deny that he had sent the note referred to in this testimony, but to be on the safe side the prosecution summoned Mr Salt, Keeper of the Gatehouse, to verify the handwriting. He could do this because Nixon had been his clerk for eleven months. Questioned by the defence counsel about the defendant's character, Salt replied 'that he was honest then, and that he knew of no Dishonesty by him'.[92] Nevertheless Bygrave's testimony had sown seeds of doubt in the minds of listeners. Why, if Nixon acted in good faith in accepting Cather as a client, had he taken fright at Patterson's arrest and dropped the case forthwith?

The next witness to be sworn was William Keate, who is unidentified in any of the reports on the case, though from his testimony it is clear that he moved in legal circles. He told the court that in April 1750 he had had some business in the Clerk of Peace's Office in Lincoln's Inn. There he had seen Nixon, whom he knew well by sight, 'standing at the Desk, and giving Instructions for an Indictment against an anonymous Person, for an Assault with an Intent to commit Buggery'.[93] With Nixon was a stranger whom Keate now knew was Cather, having often seen him since.

Keate was asked by the defence counsel how he knew that the bill of indictment against an anonymous person referred to Walpole? He replied that 'Cather was mentioned in it as Prosecutor' so that, when he learned later about the impending prosecution of Walpole, 'he concluded that that was the Bill which he had seen Nixon giving Directions for, with the Blank to be left for the Name'.[94] The prosecution made much of the fact that the bill had been drawn up without the name of the indicted man being filled in, pointing out that 'it was unusual, and was never done without some bad Intention'.[95]

It is true that the indictment Keate described shows the name of Edward Walpole written in a different hand from the rest of the text, very much as if it was added later.[96] However, this same, contrasting hand has also written in John Cather's name, which appears four times in the document. It is reasonable to suppose, therefore, that if one name was left blank to start off with, so was the other. This makes it surprising for Keate to state that he knew immediately 'that Cather was mentioned ... as Prosecutor' in the bill, especially as he admitted that in April 1750 he was in no position to recognize Cather as the man he saw with a lawyer in the office of the Clerk of the Peace. Obviously the lawyer drawing up the document was making every effort to prevent idle bystanders from knowing what he was about, so one can only marvel at Keate's perspicacity, not to mention his long sight and sharp ears.

Keate's testimony, rather more than that of Bygrave, made Nixon sound a shady character. Even so, neither of these witnesses had done more than show that the young man had once agreed to act as Cather's lawyer, which was not in itself a criminal offence. If he was to be convicted of conspiracy it was necessary to demonstrate that he was colluding with at least one of the men who had supposedly set Cather on. For this purpose the prosecution called their final witness, Ann Faulkner, who, it will be remembered, was released from prison early after agreeing to act as an informer.

Mrs Faulkner freely admitted to the court that she had hidden Patterson for two or three weeks after his escape from the Clerkenwell Bridewell. Asked if anyone knew she was sheltering Patterson, she said that Nixon did and that he used to come to her room to see him. On one occasion Nixon had warned her 'not to let any Body know that Patterson was there, for if thro' her Patterson was discovered she should be very ill treated'.[97] She also said that Nixon had provided Patterson with money, giving him a guinea on one occasion and later forty guineas which he told her he had collected for the fugitive.

Mrs Faulkner's testimony was damning. In it she conjured up a picture of Nixon as a bully who issued veiled threats to ensure she did as she was told, and who was able to raise enough money, presumably from other rogues, to finance the escape of a wanted man. This last claim would have struck a chord among readers of the *Enquiry*, in which Fielding had described the existence of a treasurer among the officers in London's criminal underworld.

When Mrs Faulkner had finished speaking, Nixon's counsel tried to cast doubt on her reliability as a witness by suggesting that she was not the most respectable of women. He asked her 'if she knew a Mr. O'Roark, and if she had ever lived with him'. She replied sharply 'that she had had the misfortune to be acquainted with him, and had lived with him two or three days'.[98] That answer sufficed. No further attempt was made to discredit her, and her testimony was taken at its face value. The counsel for the defence did not think to suggest that she might not be a disinterested witness, if her willingness to testify was the price of her release from gaol. This is not surprising, because although some lawyers and justices had their reservations about the value of uncorroborated testimony given by informers, such men were in a minority in 1751. Most of the judiciary believed that without such testimony it would be impossible to bring many criminals to book. Henry Fielding, who had bargained with Mrs Faulkner when letting her out of prison, was one of those who took this pragmatic approach.[99]

The outlook was black for Nixon, who was keeping himself informed about what was being said in court, even as he paced up and down in Westminster Hall. His main hope lay now in the men who came to the King's Bench to confirm that he was of good character. Some of these witnesses, whose own good character was not called into question, were impressive. As well as Mr Salt, Keeper of the Gatehouse, who had testified earlier to Nixon's honesty, there was Gilbert Douglas, a solicitor at the House of Commons. He came forward to say he had known Nixon for nearly five years. During that time he had employed him occasionally as a clerk when he had need of an 'extraordinary Hand in his Business', and had found that he 'discharged his Duty honestly in every Respect'. In conclusion Douglas affirmed, 'I always esteemed him as a very honest young Man, nor do I believe he would be guilty of so black a Crime as laid now to his Charge'.[100]

Douglas was followed by three other lawyers who had employed Nixon and found him 'faithful', 'careful' and 'honest'.[101] One of them, Joseph Grove, who had known him for five or six years, was nervous about appearing for a defendant who was being prosecuted by a man who bore the distinguished name of Walpole. Yet he too spoke up for him, at the same time reassuring the prosecution 'that he had so great a Regard for the Walpole Family, that if he had imagined that Mr. Nixon had been concerned in so black a Cause, or was capable of being a

Conspirator, he should not have appeared for him; and that he verily believed he would not be guilty of doing a dishonest Act'.[102] Finally John Sherwood, the officer who had applied with Worsdale for an arrest warrant for Patterson, 'gave Mr. Nixon the Character of an honest Man, and said he never heard him charged with any Thing before this Affair'.[103]

As the Old Bailey trials showed, character witnesses were important. Even a convicted man might hope for a pardon if his respectable neighbours thought well of him.[104] Nixon, and also Alexander, who found four attorneys to vouch for him, might reasonably have expected the various testimonials as to their good character to influence the verdict. Much, however, depended on the judge and on what he told the jurors, who at this time nearly always followed his directions. The power of the judge was all the greater because that of the opposing lawyers was less. The main function of the counsel for the prosecution and for the defence was to cross-examine witnesses. Before 1836 they 'were forbidden to address the jury'.[105] So there were none of those eloquent closing speeches, designed to move jurors to indignation or compassion, which became a feature of major trials later on. Instead, the opposing counsels might sum up in a fairly perfunctory way why they believed the defendants should be convicted or acquitted, and this is what happened in the Cather trial. Once all the witnesses had been heard, the diverse attorneys briefly recapitulated the case they wished to make.

Mr Benny and Mr Stowe made two points on behalf of Alexander. First of all, he could not be guilty of the offence with which he was charged, 'it not appearing he was ever in Company with any of the other defendants, or knew them'.[106] In view of the evidence provided by Edward Walpole about Alexander's relationship with Patterson, this argument was hardly likely to carry much weight in the court. Secondly, Alexander's lawyers 'took Notice of a Mistake in the second Count of the Indictment, in the Name of "Cather", as it was spelt there "Ceather", and in all other Parts of the Record "Cather", therefore the Defendant ought to be acquitted of the Indictment'.[107] This purely formal objection was worth making because there were strict procedural rules enforced in all law courts, which meant it was possible for a prosecution to fail because of minor errors in an indictment, such as the incorrect description of a person's occupation or the misspelling of his name.[108] However, on this occasion the objection was overruled, and the person making it was told to raise the matter another day.

Mr Clayton and Mr Whitaker, in defence of Nixon, also made the point that it did not appear in the evidence he 'had ever been concerned with the other Defendants, or that he was ever at any of their Meetings'.[109] Nor had he approached Walpole, who admitted he did not know him. As for the testimony given by Robert Bygrave, William Keate and Ann Faulkner, they thought it was 'not sufficient to convict the Defendant in this Conspiracy'.[110]

When the opposing counsel came forward to summarize the case for the prosecution, he began by saying that there could be no doubt as to the guilt of at least three of the defendants. Cather and Cain had both confessed, the one in the officer's house in Chancery Lane, the other when he was crossing the river in the company of Worsdale. Cain had also been present when Cather had offered White a share of any money Walpole paid him, which in itself showed 'that he was concerned and assisted in the Conspiracy'.[111] As for Alexander, he had put into execution the affair planned by Cain, Patterson and others. This was shown by the letters he had written from which it was plain he 'wanted Preferment'.[112] Furthermore, his admission 'that Patterson had Conversation with him about getting some Money from Mr. Walpole, was sufficient to convict him of being one of the Chief of the Conspirators'.[113] At this point a desperate Alexander 'broke in upon the Pleading of the Council' but, as had happened throughout the trial, his objections went unheard.[114]

The counsel for the prosecution was less positive about Nixon, saying that while the transactions attributed to him by Mr Bygrave, Mr Keate and Mrs Faulkner 'were the strongest Circumstances of his being concerned in the Conspiracy', yet he would 'submit it to the Court and the Jury, if they thought these Circumstances, and what they had heard alleged against him, were not sufficient to find him guilty of the Crime'.[115]

Finally it was the turn of the Lord Chief Justice to make his representation and direct the jury. Sir William Lee's record as a judge, as well as his temperament and approach to life, were such that Edward Walpole could feel reasonably confident of a successful outcome to the case he had brought against the defendants.

Sir William Lee had been Lord Chief Justice since 1737. Sir James Burrow, who as Coroner of the King's Bench worked under him for many years, and was also his friend, described him as 'a gentleman of most unblemished and irreproachable character, both in public and in private life, amiable and gentle in his disposition, affable and courteous in his deportment, cheerful in his temper, though grave in his aspect, generous and polite in his manner of living, sincere and deservedly happy in his friendships and family connections, and to the highest degree upright and impartial in his distribution of justice'.[116] In short, he seemed an honourable, equable man, very much at ease in the world in which he lived.

No one has ever claimed that Sir William was a great chief justice, but it was generally agreed that he had a 'thorough and minute knowledge

12.2 Sir William Lee (1688–1754), Lord Chief Justice 1737–54, from a portrait by Vanderbanck

of the Common Law'.[117] If he had a failing it was that his knowledge of anything else was minimal. Even as a student he had been noticeably single-minded. He gave up the Classics as soon as he could, stopped reading the *Spectator* after the second number, and devoted himself to learning off by heart the legal set books, such as Coke's *Entries* and Saunders's *Reports*, whereupon a tutor had predicted that he might well become chief justice, 'for to plodding and perseverance nothing is impossible'.[118] When he was forty his relatives had more or less compelled him to enter parliament, so as to keep the family seat of Chipping Wycombe out of the hands of the Tories. After this he never spoke in the Commons, though he always voted with the Government. He had been born in the year of the Glorious Revolution, which led him to say, whenever he commented on his political stance, that 'as he came in with King William, he was bound to be a good Whig'.[119]

As a Member of Parliament and as a judge his guiding principle was the maintenance of political and social stability. Hence he took a hard line in any case that involved subversion. When he had presided over the treason trials in 1747 he had pressed the jury to bring in a verdict of 'Guilty' for all seventeen men accused of taking part in the Jacobite rebellion, though later half of these won a reprieve.[120] One might expect him, therefore, to see the threat to society posed by a group of sophisticated crooks engaged in dishonouring and exploiting a gentleman who had impeccable political, as well as social, credentials. Accordingly he warned the jury at the trial of Cather and his associates of 'the Danger of letting such Crimes go unpunished'.[121]

Sir William was characteristically painstaking in his summing up. He went through 'every particular that appeared in the Evidence' and read out again all the letters and other papers that had been produced by the prosecution.[122] Predictably, he told the jury that the case against Cather, Cain and Alexander had been proved beyond reasonable doubt. In making this pronouncement, Sir William interpreted the law, as it then stood, in a highly selective way. He ignored the unusual circumstances in which Cather had been persuaded to confess soon after his arrest, and took no account of the fact that this confession had been retracted by the young Irishman six months later. He also ignored the fact that, at a preliminary hearing in January, Cain had pleaded 'Not Guilty' to the charges brought against him. Similarly, he disregarded the favourable picture of Alexander and Nixon given by their character witnesses.

Another judge might have given Nixon the benefit of the doubt because, as Sir William admitted, the 'Proofs were not so plain or home against him as against the other Defendants'.[123] Added to this, the witnesses who gave evidence against Nixon, particularly Ann Faulkner, did not have the same standing as those who had spoken for him. As was mentioned earlier, it was accepted that the use of crown witnesses, such as Mrs Faulkner, was necessary, but we also know from Fielding's *Enquiry* that their evidence was not always accepted if it was uncorroborated.[124] Sir William obviously agreed with Fielding that such a proviso was unnecessary. He concluded his summing up by telling the jury that he believed that Nixon 'was concerned in the Conspiracy from the Beginning'.[125]

Alexander protested his innocence to the last. He 'even interrupted the Justice in his Representation'.[126] But it was all over. When Sir William had finished speaking, the jurors conferred briefly and, without leaving the room, brought in a verdict of 'Guilty' for all the defendants. It was decided that they would be sentenced during the next Michaelmas term. Meanwhile, Alexander was remanded in custody again in the King's Bench prison, and a tipstaff was summoned to arrest Nixon.

The sentences

As the trial drew to a close, the crowd loitering in Westminster Hall had stared at the spectacle of Adam Nixon. He was hurrying up and down like a 'Person of a vitiated Brain', seemingly 'upon the Wing, always going or sending into the Court, to know what might be the Event'.[127] Then he was gone, just as soon as the crier was heard calling for a tipstaff. He was glimpsed crossing Old Palace Yard, after which only a few people knew for some months what had become of him.

He had sailed to Ireland, where he began searching for Walter Patterson. By September he had found him, whereupon a number of Nixon's friends and relations said that, if a warrant could be obtained from London, they would pay to have Patterson apprehended and sent back to England. Their aim was to have the fugitive questioned by a justice again, so as to clear Nixon's name.

Nixon insisted that he had become involved in Cather's prosecution of Walpole almost by accident, and only very briefly. Later, on 29 April 1752, he swore an affidavit to that effect before one of the King's Bench justices, Sir Michael Foster. Nixon's story was as follows: 'Some time in the month of May 1750' Patterson had come to see him, and had informed him that he, Patterson, 'was under daily apprehension of being arrested for debt'.[128] While he kept out of the way of his creditors, he asked Nixon to arrange with Bygrave to be given any papers concerning Cather's indictment of Walpole. Nixon agreed because he had no 'knowledge or suspicion' that Patterson 'had been or was concerned in any ill practices' and therefore did 'not apprehend the least

injury could result to him', if he did as Patterson asked, though afterwards, 'to his great grief and sorrow, he experienced the Contrary'.[129]

Now that Nixon had discovered where Patterson was living, he wrote
to Bygrave from Dublin, and asked him to apply for a warrant to arrest
the man. To his bewilderment and dismay, Bygrave 'totally rejected
such a proposal'.[130] Nixon did not give up immediately. Over the next
two months, he wrote to various friends and members of his family in
London, and they, too, tried to get a warrant. One of those Nixon
wrote to was his wife. He asked her to make a personal appeal on his
behalf. Constance Nixon went to see Bygrave, as well as John Matthews,
a clerk in court at the King's Bench, but she had no more success than
anyone else. Eventually, on 1 February 1752, she swore an affidavit
before Sir Michael Foster, in which she recorded her attempt to get the
warrant for Patterson's arrest, at the same time making it clear that she
had been receiving letters about the matter from her husband since
September.[131]

While Nixon was in Dublin, Bygrave also swore various affidavits in
the court of King's Bench. These described his efforts to serve notices
that the money pledged by George Panthoros and Jacob Palmer as bail
for Nixon must soon be paid, if the missing man did not appear in time
to be sentenced. In the first affidavit, dated 14 November, Bygrave
stated that he had given one notice to Mrs Panthoros, to hand to her
husband, and had given another notice to Mrs Palmer, Nixon's mother-
in-law, who was staying in her son-in-law's house in Warwick Court,
Holborn. Bygrave also said that he had returned to that address the
next day, when Constance Nixon told him she had seen the notice. So
far, however, he had had no success in finding out where Jacob Palmer
was living.[132]

In his second affidavit, dated 18 November, Bygrave reported that he
had now been able to serve George Panthoros personally with the
notice about his recognizance. He had then gone to two addresses
where Jacob Palmer was known to have lodged formerly, but had still
not found out where he was at present.[133] In his affidavits Bygrave gave
no indication that he had received letters from Nixon, or that he knew
from Constance where her husband was. His sole comment on the
absence of both Nixon and Palmer was that he had been unable to
discover where they were, despite 'a diligent Inquiry', because they had
absconded 'on account of the said Nixon having been convicted'.[134]

Nixon was an honourable man, however. When he realized that he
was not going to get the warrant he had applied for, he made plans to
return to England, so that Panthoros and Palmer would not forfeit the
£400 they had pledged as bail for him. For a while he was delayed at
the port of Dublin by contrary winds, but set sail eventually, and

surrendered himself voluntarily to Sir Michael Foster on 21 December 1751.[135] In the meantime Nixon's co-defendants, Cather, Cain and Alexander, had already been sentenced in the court of King's Bench on 28 November.

After four months of deliberation by Sir William Lee and his fellow judges, Cather heard that he was to stand in the pillory on 17 December at Charing Cross, and on 20 December in Fleet Street, as well as a third time on Christmas Eve at the Royal Exchange. After that he was to be put to hard labour in the Clerkenwell Bridewell for four years. Finally, he was not to be released before he, and two others, found the penal sum of £80 between them, as a surety of his good behaviour for the space of three years more.[136]

This sentence was unusually harsh. As we have already seen, even the dreaded Judge Page only sent the two blackmailers convicted at the Old Bailey in 1730 to prison for one year, after making them stand in the pillory no more than twice. Nor in the intervening twenty years had heavier sentences for this type of offender become the rule. A case came up for trial in the Old Bailey in September 1754 which was similar to the one in which Walpole prosecuted Cather, except that the victim did not bear a famous name. On that occasion George Cullum Butts and Josiah Partridge were convicted, with others, of conspiring to charge Richard Mins falsely with having committed sodomy with one of them. For that crime they were sentenced to stand in the pillory twice, and to be imprisoned in Newgate for twelve months.[137] Cather's sentence was at least twice that normally meted out for the crime of which he had been found guilty. Worse still, the financial penalty imposed made it unlikely that he would be able to leave the Bridewell, even at the end of four years there. The sum of £80 was about three times the annual wage of a London labourer.[138] Yet in his petition Cather had already informed Sir William Lee that he had 'not one shilling in the world'.[139]

Daniel Alexander was sentenced next, and learned that he too faced daunting financial penalties. He was fined £50 and, when he had served a further two years in the King's Bench prison, must raise £400 to ensure his good behaviour for five years more. Like Cather, he had to find half the money himself and provide two guarantors to pledge the rest equally between them.[140] This large sum partly reflected Alexander's status as a professional man, though this proved no hindrance to his being made to stand in the pillory at Charing Cross on 17 December. Nor did the judiciary take account of whether Alexander had, or could raise, £250 on his own account. Yet, after being in gaol for several months already, where he could not earn anything, and after paying his defence lawyers (if he did), it is unlikely that Alexander was much better off than his young co-defendant. The heavy financial penalties imposed on most of the defendants in this trial were clearly meant to be an exemplary punishment. They also corresponded to the legal costs of the prosecution incurred by Walpole, who was entitled to one third of the fines paid.[141]

In comparison with the others, Cain got off lightly. He was to join them in the pillory at Charing Cross, after which he was to go to the Clerkenwell Bridewell where, like Cather, he was to be put to hard labour, but for two years, not four. Nor was he fined or asked to pay anything. Cain was probably at an advantage in being the only one of those convicted who was not described as a gentleman. Being a labourer, it was assumed that he was without financial resources. His shorter prison sentence also indicated that Sir William Lee and his assistant judges had not paid too much heed to James Worsdale's testimony that Cain was the ring-leader in an extensive extortion racket.[142]

When Nixon gave himself up in December 1751, he already knew of the sentences passed on the men who had been tried with him. He was not sentenced himself for another four and a half months, and made use of that interval to try to get his side of the story heard. Early in February 1752 Constance Nixon swore the affidavit, already referred to, in which she confirmed the reason her husband gave for going to Ireland. When Nixon swore his own affidavit on 29 April, it was just a few days before he was called to the King's Bench to be told what his sentence would be.

By the end of April Nixon probably had little hope of convincing the authorities of his innocence. Though in his statement he set out clearly how he had been beguiled by Patterson into playing a purely perfunctory role in the prosecution of Walpole, he had no way of disproving Mrs Faulkner's testimony that he had known where Patterson was after his escape and had collected money for him. It was a case of her word against his, and Sir William saw no reason to change his mind as to which one of them he believed, even though it would now appear that it was not in the defendant's interests that Patterson should leave London. Not being unduly optimistic, Nixon concentrated in his affidavit on trying to persuade the authorities that he was in no position to pay a large fine or raise hundred of pounds in sureties. The clerk who filed the document described it as being made 'to mitigate the fine' that might be imposed on the writer. Certainly, in his concluding remarks Nixon emphasized that the earlier prosecution had greatly reduced his circumstances, so that he was 'not worth five pounds in the world, his wearing apparel excepted'.[143]

Nixon was sentenced on 4 May. His punishment followed the by now familiar pattern, set by Sir William in passing judgement on Cather and Alexander. Nixon was to stand in the pillory at Charing Cross on 14

May, after which he was to be returned to the King's Bench prison for a further two years. To some extent his petition succeeded in that he escaped being fined and, with two other men of sufficient means would have to find the smaller penal sum of £200 before his release, to ensure his good behaviour for three years more.[144]

In deciding that Nixon should be punished about half as severely as Alexander, Sir William Lee and the puisne judges probably calculated that he was about half as deeply involved in the criminal conspiracy of which he had been convicted. It is unsurprising that they paid no attention to his claims that he was innocent when Sir William had already ignored not only those witessess at the trial who had expressed their incredulity that he was a dishonest man, but also the counsel for the prosecution who had hesitated to state categorically that Nixon was guilty as charged.

Notes

1. W. S. Holdsworth, *History of English Law*, 17 vols (London: Methuen, 1903–72), 9: 252–6.
2. John H. Langbein, 'Shaping the Eighteenth-Century Criminal Trial: A View of the Ryder Sources', *The University of Chicago Law Review* (Winter, 1983), pp. 1–136. Langbein records that 'in eight cases studied [1754–56] in which a defense counsel appeared, the accused was convicted as indicted in only one', p. 129.
3. *Full and genuine Narrative*, p. 25
4. *The Works of Mr. Thomas Brown*, 4 vols (London, 1707–9), 1Aa: 51.
5. *Kent's Directory for the Year 1754. Containing an Alphabetical List of the Names and Places of Abode of the Directors of Companies, Persons in Public Business, Merchants and other Eminent Traders in the Cities of London and Westminster and Borough of Southwark.*
6. PRO, KB 20/2, Posteas, Part I, Trinity, 24 Geo. 2.
7. *Whole Proceedings*, p. 3.
8. Horace Walpole, *Corr.*, and *Marchmont Papers*, ed. Sir G. Rose, 3 vols (London, 1831), *passim*.
9. *A Complete Collection of State Trials*, ed. T. B. Howell (London, 1809–26), vol. 18.
10. H. W. Woolrych, *Lives of Eminent Serjeants-at-Law*, 2 vols (London, 1869), 2: 605–33. Also J. H. Baker, *The Order of Serjeants-at-Law* (London: Selden Society, 1984).
11. *Whole Proceedings*, p. 3.
12. PRO, KB 10, London and Middlesex Indictments, Michaelmas, 24 Geo. 2, no. 26 and *Whole Proceedings*, p.4.
13. *Whole Proceedings*, p. 4.
14. *Enquiry into the Causes of the Late Increase of Robbers etc.* (London, 1751), Section 8.
15. James Oldham, *The Mansfield Manuscripts and the Growth of English*

Law in the Eighteenth Century, 2 vols (Chapel Hill: University of North Carolina Press, 1992), 1: 95.

16. Horace Walpole, *Corr.*, 20: 111.
17. Horace Walpole, *Corr.*, 20: 312. To Mann, 23 March 1752.
18. W. A. Speck, *Stability and Strife: England 1714–1760* (London: Edward Arnold, 1977), ch. 11.
19. *Gentleman's Magazine* (1751), 21: 4 and *Monthly Review* (1751), 4: 229.
20. Leon Radzinowicz, *A History of Criminal Law and its Administration*, 5 vols (London: Stevens, 1948–86), 1: 399ff.
21. *Enquiry*, Preface.
22. PRO, KB 10, London and Middlesex Indictments, Michaelmas, 24 Geo. 2, no. 26.
23. *Sessions Papers*, July 1745, case no. 316.
24. Letter to the Duke of Newcastle, 1753, quoted in M. Dorthy George, *London Life in the Eighteenth Century* (London: Kegan Paul, 1925), ch. 3.
25. Peter Linebaugh, *The London Hanged: Crime and Civil Society in Eighteenth Century London* (London: Allen Lane, 1991), p. 92.
26. *Genuine Narrative*, p. 20.
27. Theft Act, Section 21, 1968. See Mike Hepworth, *Blackmail: Publicity and Secrecy in Everyday Life* (London: Routledge, 1975). The first chapter has a summary of the history of the law covering blackmail. See also W. H. D. Winder, 'The Development of Blackmail', *Modern Law Review* , 5 (1941), 21–50.
28. Whenever celebrities were involved in sodomy cases, earlier pamplets about famous predecessors were reprinted. For example *The Tryal and Condemnation of Mervin, Lord Audley, Earl of Castle-Haven* (1699) was reissued up to 1842.
29. *Full and genuine Narrative*, p. 2.
30. However, there were unspecified 'dark insinuations' about Frederick, Prince of Wales, made by Robert Walpole. These were supposed to explain his mother's virulent dislike of her son, which was excessive even by Hanoverian standards. See P. C. Yorke, *Life and Correspondence of Philip Yorke, Earl of Hardwicke*, 3 vols (Cambridge University Press, 1913), 1: 178–9.
31. Horace Walpole, *Corr.*, 20: 133–4. To Mann, 2 April 1750.
32. Ibid., p. 134.
33. *Whole Proceedings*, pp. 4–5.
34. Ibid., p. 5.
35. Ibid.
36. Ibid.
37. Ibid.
38. Ibid.
39. PRO, KB 10/29, London and Middlesex Indictments, Easter, 24 Geo. 2, no. 4, and GLRO, Indictment no. 16 (MJ/SR/2938).
40. 9 Geo. 1, c. 22, s. 1.
41. Radzinowicz, 1: 73.
42. *Whole Proceedings*, p. 6.
43. Ibid., p. 5.
44. No extant copy of Cannon's treatise has been found. See Peter Wagner, *Eros Revived: Erotica of the Enlightenment in England and America*

(London: Secker and Warburg, 1988), p. 35 and note.

45. *Satan's Harvest Home: or the Present State of Whorecraft, Adultery, Fornication, Procuring, Pimping, Sodomy, and the Game of Flatts. Collected from the Memoirs of an intimate Comrade of the Hon. Jack S–n–r* (London, 1749).
46. *Whole Proceedings*, p. 6.
47. Ibid., p. 5.
48. Ibid., p. 6.
49. Ibid.
50. Ibid.
51. Ibid.
52. Ibid.
53. Horace Walpole, *Corr.*, 20: 188. Horace Walpole to Horace Mann, 20 September 1750.
54. *Whole Proceedings*, p. 7.
55. Ibid.
56. *Full and genuine Narrative*, p. 21.
57. Ibid., pp. 21–2.
58. *Whole Proceedings*, p. 7.
59. *Full and genuine Narrative*, p. 25.
60. *Whole Proceedings*, p. 7.
61. Stephen Slaughter's date of birth is uncertain but George Vertue listed him among the subscribers to Godfrey Kneller's Academy of Painting in 1712. See *The Vertue Notebooks*, 6 vols (Oxford: Walpole Society Publications, 1930–55), 6: 169.
62. *Whole Proceedings*, p. 7.
63. Ibid.
64. Ibid.
65. Ibid.
66. *Full and genuine Narrative*, p. 2.
67. *Whole Proceedings*, p. 8.
68. *Full and genuine Narrative*, pp. 13–14.
69. *Whole Proceedings*, p. 9.
70. Ibid.
71. Ibid.
72. Ibid., p. 18.
73. Ibid., p. 10.
74. Ibid., pp. 10–11.
75. Ibid., p. 11.
76. Ibid., p. 12.
77. Ibid.
78. Ibid.
79. Ibid.
80. Giles Jacob, *Law Dictionary* (London, 1729).
81. Ibid.
82. Ibid.
83. PRO, KB 29/410, Controlment Roll, 24 Geo. 2.
84. Giles Jacob.
85. Whole Proceedings, p. 12.
86. Ruth Paley, 'Thief-takers in London in the Age of the McDaniel Gang, *c.* 1745–1754' in *Policing and Prosecution in Britain*, eds Douglas Hay

and Francis Snyder (Oxford: Clarendon Press, 1989), pp. 311ff.
87. *Whole Proceedings*, p. 12.
88. Ibid.
89. *Whole Proceedings*, p. 13.
90. Ibid., p. 12.
91. Ibid., p. 13.
92. Ibid.
93. Ibid.
94. Ibid.
95. Ibid., p. 14.
96. PRO, KB 10/19, London and Middlesex Indictments, 24 Geo. 2, no. 4.
97. *Whole Proceedings*, p. 13.
98. Ibid.
99. *Enquiry*, Section 9. Fielding complained that some judges refused to accept the evidence of accomplices, be it 'ever so positive and explicite ... unless it be corroborated'. Langbein, pp. 98ff. uses Fielding's statement to support his argument that in the 1750s some judges had their reservations about the testimony of informers, and directed juries to acquit defendants, if an accomplice's evidence against them was not supported by others.
100. *Whole Proceedings*, p. 13.
101. Ibid.
102. Ibid., p. 14.
103. Ibid.
104. Frank McLynn, *Crime and Punishment in Eighteenth-Century England* (London: Routledge, 1989), p. 279.
105. Langbein, p. 125.
106. *Whole Proceedings*, p. 14.
107. Ibid.
108. Douglas Hay, 'Property, Authority and the Criminal Law', in *Albion's Fatal Tree*, ed. Douglas Hay (London: Peregrine Books, 1977), p. 33.
109. *Whole Proceedings*, p. 14.
110. Ibid.
111. Ibid.
112. Ibid.
113. Ibid.
114. *Full and genuine Narrative*, p. 25.
115. *Whole Proceedings*, p. 14.
116. Edward Foss, *A Biographical Dictionary of the Judges of England, 1066–1870* (London, 1870).
117. *Dictionary of National Biography*.
118. John, Lord Campbell, *Lives of the Chief Justices of England*, 3 vols, 2nd edn (London, 1858), 2: 213ff.
119. Ibid.
120. *A Complete Collection of State Trials*, ed. T. B. Howell (London, 1809–26), vol. 18.
121. *Whole Proceedings*, p. 14.
122. Ibid.
123. Ibid., p. 15.
124. *Enquiry*, Section 9.
125. *Whole Proceedings*, p. 15.

126. *Full and genuine Narrative*, p. 25.
127. Ibid., pp. 25–6.
128. PRO, KB 1/11, Depositions etc., Easter, 25 Geo. 2.
129. Ibid.
130. Ibid.
131. Ibid.
132. PRO, KB 1/10, Depositions etc., Michaelmas, 25 Geo. 2.
133. Ibid.
134. Ibid., affidavit of 18 November 1751.
135. PRO, PRIS 4/2, no. 947.
136. PRO, KB 21/36 and KB 36/139, Rule Books, Michaelmas, 25 Geo. 2.
137. GLRO, New Prison Calendar, 20 July 1754 (MJ/CP/P nos 265–7).
138. Roy Porter, *English Society in the Eighteenth Century* (London: Allen Lane, 1982), p. 57.
139. PRO, KB 1/10, Depositions etc., Hilary, 24 Geo. 2.
140. PRO, KB 21/36 and KB 36/139, Rule Books, Michaelmas, 25 Geo. 2.
141. The prosecutor was entitled to a third of the fines paid because the defendants had been indicted for 'Trespasses' as well as 'Misdemeanours' according to the Controlment Roll 24 Geo. 2 (KB 29/419) in the PRO. For this ruling see J. Chitty, *A Practical Treatise on Criminal Law*, 4 vols (1816), ch. 9, pp. 399ff.
142. *The Gentleman's Magazine*, November 1751, pp. 521–2 reports that Cain was asked to provide the same sureties as Cather, and also gives Alexander's prison sentence as three years. It is reasonable to assume, however, that these are journalistic errors, as they conflict with the official records in the King's Bench papers.
143. PRO, KB 1/11, Depositions etc., Easter, 25 Geo. 2.
144. PRO, KB 21/36 and KB 36/139, Rule Books, Easter, 25 Geo. 2.

CHAPTER THIRTEEN

The end of the story

Walpole's vanquished enemies disappeared into the shadows. Even when we are sure they survived prison, we have no idea what they did with their lives afterwards.

Daniel Alexander did not find the money he was required to pay as a condition of his release, so he stayed in the King's Bench prison, year after year, until George III came to the throne. To mark the new reign an Act of Parliament was passed in 1761 for the relief of men imprisoned for debt. From the middle of March *The London Gazette* published lists of debtors applying for release from prisons all over the country. In the *Gazette* for 28–31 March the King's Bench list contained the name of Daniel Alexander. As the purpose of printing these names was to give creditors the opportunity of objecting to the discharge of particular individuals, Alexander masked his Irish origins and occupation, describing himself as 'formerly of Glasgow in Scotland, late of St. Dunstan's-in-the-West, London, Gentleman'. No objection was raised. He was released on 9 August 1761, by which time he had spent more than eleven years in gaol.[1]

Adam Nixon was more fortunate than Alexander in that his relatives and friends enabled him to raise the £200 stipulated by the court as a guarantee of his good behaviour for a further three years after he had served his prison sentence. So he was discharged, on the order of Sir Michael Foster, on 30 May 1754.[2]

We lose sight of John Cather and Patrick Cain soon after they were sentenced. We know that Cather survived his three ordeals in the pillory without mortal injury. A highly unpopular miscreant, he could have been stoned to death. As it was, along with Cain and Alexander he was 'most severely pelted and hooted'.[3] Maybe, by his third, solitary appearance, however, the crowd took pity on him. One hopes so. It was Christmas Eve. The Calendar for the Clerkenwell House of Correction records that he and Patrick Cain reached the Bridewell on 18 January 1752, where they were to be contained 'according to the Tenor of their several Sentences, and when delivered to pay their Fees severally'.[4]

After that nothing more is said about either of them. They do not appear again in the Calendar which lists prisoners discharged, transferred to Newgate, or sent off to serve their country in the army, or at sea. The sixty or seventy men and women condemned to hard labour in the Clerkenwell Bridewell led a harsh and unhealthy existence, beating hemp by day and after dark pent up in cells nine feet long and six feet wide where they slept on bare boards, unless they could pay sixpence a night for a bed. Only one pennyworth of bread per day was provided, all other food being brought in by the prisoners' relatives and friends – if they had any. One inmate who wrote about his experiences in this particular Bridewell declared, 'It is much to be wondered at most, if not all, of the hapless offenders sent thither are not utterly debauched and starved to death.'[5] Moreover, as well as malnutrition, various epidemics killed a fair number of the prison inmates over the years. However, the names of Cather and Cain do not appear in the burial register of St James's Church, Clerkenwell, where all prisoners who died in the Bridewell were entered.[6] Cather, in one account of him, sounds mentally disturbed. He was given to sudden, violent rages which passed just as suddenly, whereupon he 'became stunned and all at once seem'd as one sunk in Melancholy and Despair', unable to hear anything said to him.[7] But if he was found to be insane, he was not sent to Bedlam, as his name does not appear on any list of inmates in that asylum.[8] There were of course other mad-houses in London, which did not keep such good records, where he could have been. Yet, even if that was his fate, it still leaves Cain unaccounted for.

It is possible both men escaped, though this would have been more difficult for them than it had been for Patterson, who succeeded in such an enterprise but was less closely supervised than they would have been. Lastly, they may have been discharged eventually but are missing from the Bridewell Calendar because of clerical error, though that means that two mistakes were made, as they were due to be released in different years.

More is known about the men who helped Edward Walpole to triumph. James Worsdale flourished yet again after his histrionic performance in the court of King's Bench. In 1752 he scored a success at Drury Lane as Lady Pentweazle in Samuel Foote's comedy *Taste*.[9] Meanwhile he gained financial security at last, when Walpole used his influence to have him made Master Painter to the Board of Ordinance.[10] As well as a regular stipend, this post brought Worsdale welcome commissions, including one to paint George II, which resulted in a portrait promptly presented to Walpole's Great Yarmouth constituency.[11]

William Davy hardly needed anyone's influence to secure the briefs which his growing reputation as an advocate brought him. Walpole remained grateful, though, and sought to promote Davy's career whenever possible. On 23 January 1757 he wrote to the Duke of Devonshire with a request that the man he now called his 'particular friend' be made a King's Serjeant.[12] Apparently other grandees stood in the way of this appointment, but on 3 December 1758 Walpole wrote to the Duke again, repeating his request.[13] Again the plea failed. Davy was finally made a King's Serjeant four years later.[14]

Horace Walpole, perhaps because he was embarrassed, did not discuss his brother's predicament. Although he had always written freely about 'Ned's' conduct in letters to friends, on this occasion he gave no hint of the trouble with John Cather. In 1750, when Edward had successfully defended himself in court against the charge of attempted sodomy, his brother wrote a letter two weeks after that event to Horace Mann, apologizing for not writing before, adding, 'for anything I have to tell you, I might have kept [this letter] a month longer'.[15] Then in the following year, writing eleven days after his own appearance as a witness in the Cather trial, he told Mann 'there is no kind of news'.[16]

Horace Walpole's reluctance to write that his brother had been suspected of sodomy would be all too understandable if, as has been suggested, he was himself a covert homosexual.[17] But in any case he did not have the temperament to relish the battle with the so-called conspirators. Nor did he have any illusions about some of the witnesses who followed him in giving evidence. His comments on James Worsdale in the *Anecdotes of Painting in England* (1762–71) are less corrosive than those of George Vertue, whose *Notebooks* he was using as his source, but the difference between the two entries is one of tone rather than substance. Vertue's lying mountebank who, with 'many artful wayes, pushed himself into a numerous acquaintance', becomes in the *Anecdotes* an artist destined to have been 'little known' had he been distinguished by no talents but his pencil and who, by trading on his connection with Sir Godfrey Kneller, and by his 'excellent mimicry and facetious spirit, gained many patrons and much business'.[18]

Family loyalty led Horace Walpole to help Edward when the latter was in trouble, and the support he gave ended the quarrel between the brothers. From then on the two of them 'lived on fair terms', though they were 'never affectionate'.[19] These terms were not close enough for Horace to contemplate asking Edward for a favour over the matter of the Customs House patent which they shared, even though this solution to a money problem he had was one proposed by the minister Henry Pelham in 1752.[20]

The success of Edward Walpole's long and expensive campaign to clear his name was publicly recognized when he was made a Knight of the Bath in 1753.[21] Horace Walpole was 'astonished' that his brother accepted the 'red riband', as he felt it 'had fallen much below par' in recent years.[22] He might have been even more surprised if he had known Edward had requested a knighthood, writing to the Duke of Newcastle to do so. The reason he gave for wanting a title was a 'wish to be employed abroad in His Majesty's service, to which purpose this kind of trapping has its subservience'.[23] The Duke could not see Walpole as a diplomat, so he did not give him the appointment he asked for, but saw no reason to deny him a K.B.

Walpole did not leave England, but was never fully at ease there from the day Alexander's first letter had arrived, telling him of Cather's intentions. Even though he put the men who had in any way supported Cather in gaol, there was always fear that others would make him their target again. As indeed they did.

Six years after the Cather trial, Walpole's Irish enemies had not given up. In 1757 two of them, Ann Vaughan and John Cameron, were trying to get Sir Edward to pay them for papers which compromised him in some way. Mrs Vaughan went to see Lord Mountney, one of the Barons of the Exchequer in Ireland, about the matter. Richard Mountney, who had been at Eton and King's College, Cambridge with Sir Edward, wrote to him about this and received a furious and agitated answer, dated 16 July. A copy of this letter, possibly a draft, has survived. It reads as follows:

> Dear Sir,
> I send you the inclosed from Mrs. Vaughan, by which you will see that Mrs. Ann Vaughan Widow is a most execrable Bitch. Whether John Cameron is a Bull or not I can only guess. But it is very plain that there are a set of Villains who would do some villainous thing or other by me, and most likely in requital of my overthrowing that Knot of Irish rascals who attacked me a few years since.
>
> Therefore I desire you will not give this Woman one farthing more than you have already bestowed upon her, which I hope is no more than the Half Guinea you wrote me Word of.
>
> What papers they have or can have that relate to me I can't conceive. I fancy, none but what they forge, for the papers which her husband once sent me were forgeries and imitations of my hand.
>
> You see plainly that if they had papers they would allways keep some behind in order to get farther gratifications. And you never could be certain that she had delivered all, which indeed if they are forgeries, could have no end.
>
> I must beg the favour of you therefore to tell Mrs. Vaughan, that if she has any Demand upon me, she will proceed as her Advisers shall advise, as I shall not take any farther notice of her letters.
>
> I shall be obliged to you for an early Answer to this.
> P.S. I hope you have not   I am your
> given the Bull and Bitch   faithfull & Obedient
> any more money.   humble Servt.[24]

With this letter we walk into a drama that has been going on for a while, ever since Mr Vaughan, who was dead by 1757, sent Walpole the papers which Mountney is told were forged. Whether all the papers Mrs Vaughan now has are forged is unclear. Sir Edward seems to be admitting that some of them might be genuine when he uses the phrase 'if they are forgeries'. We do not know what was in the papers, though as Sir Edward makes the connection between the Vaughans and John Cameron and those he calls 'the Knot of Irish rascals' who had attacked him before, it is conceivable that, like Cather's indictment and petition, the subject was his supposed sodomitical practices.

At all events Sir Edward was less dismissive of Ann Vaughan and John Cameron than his letter to Mountney suggests. He probably solicited the help of William Davy in dealing with his new enemies, which is why, at the beginning of 1757, he first tried to have Davy made a King's Serjeant. In writing to the Duke of Devonshire about this, he added an enigmatic postscript to his letter of 23 January, which said, 'It may prove of singular advantage to me to obtain this favour for Mr. Davy, as I will explain to your Grace.'[25] With or without Davy's help, Mrs Vaughan was silenced. At least we hear no more of her.

After this episode Sir Edward's tendency to avoid mixing in the world became more pronounced. He remained a Member of Parliament until 1768, but rarely went to the Commons. In 1759 he explained to the Duke of Bedford that his 'retired and very private life' prevented him from being actively concerned in politics.[26] Instead, he continued his habit of keeping in touch with those in power by writing letters to ministers requesting favours, often for others.

His three daughters, helped by their good looks and generous dowries from their father, made fine marriages. His favourite, Maria, was introduced by her uncle Horace to her first husband, James, the second Earl Waldegrave, a descendant of the Stuarts and the most eligible bachelor in England.[27] Then, when the Earl died of smallpox after four years of marriage, Maria was courted by George III's brother, the Duke of Gloucester, and married him.[28]

Sir Edward's son was given his heart's desire when he obtained a commission in the Dragoons in 1755. Before that he had spent an unhappy few years apprenticed to a leading merchant in Austin Friars, John Peter Blaquière, because his father had hoped to make a sober business man of him, whereas the youth himself pined for a career in which he could cut a dash.[29] There was usually tension between the son and his father, not least because Sir Edward kept the boy short of money. As a soldier young Walpole had a brilliant but short military career. He was mentioned in despatches and became the youngest commander in the English army.[30] With the end of the Seven Years' War, however, he could not think what to do with himself, apart from drinking too much and gambling heavily. No doubt Sir Edward was proud of his son when people spoke of him as a hero, but before and after that interlude, his relationship with his heir was punctuated by outbursts of paternal exasperation and rage. The girls adored their brother but when he died of tuberculosis at the age of thirty-four, Horace Walpole considered his loss 'no misfortune', as his debts were well on the way to ruining his father.[31]

There was never any question about Sir Edward's devotion to his daughters. After they were all married he continued to help them financially whenever this was necessary. So he made generous provision for the eldest, Laura, when her husband, the Bishop of Exeter, died suddenly in 1777, leaving her with four children and very little to live on. Seeing to the well-being of Laura, Maria and Charlotte occupied a good deal of his time. Otherwise he filled in the hours as he had always done. When he entertained, his friends were, as often as not, men his brother referred to as 'Ned's inferior companions'.[32] When alone he continued to compose melancholy music and write the occasional essay and poem. Hardly any of these works have survived although among his miscellaneous papers there is the manuscript of some verses he called 'Delusive Hope', which he derides as the 'False Promiser – Mock Herald of the ever distant Hour'.[33]

He never went into society. Instead, every so often, he bought a new house to provide himself with a change of scene. He acquired the last one, on the banks of the Thames near Richmond, when he was seventy-seven, telling his brother he would call it 'Raspberry Plain', adding ruefully that he did not expect it to become as famous as Strawberry Hill.[34] There he could sit in the bow window of the great room, watching barges going up and down the river and folk crowding on to the Isleworth ferry that left from the landing stage below his terrace. By now he refused to meet strangers and rarely stirred outdoors, save 'with the lilies and bees and the insects'.[35]

People imagined he was happy and he had much to make him so – a good income, affectionate children and grandchildren. For years his health had been excellent, while in appearance he was a precursor of Dorian Gray. Horace Walpole wrote often and enviously of his brother's eternal youth, because Edward in his seventies had 'a charming colour and not a wrinkle'.[36] Then, at the age of seventy-eight, he developed problems with his digestion. His doctors did not know what was wrong, so he decided to cure himself by not eating. By the time he discovered that this did not help, he was unable to eat. His condition deteriorated rapidly. He returned to London in November 1783 and shut himself up in his house in Pall Mall, where he died in the new year on 12 January, having seemingly 'starved himself to death'.[37] The medical men who had attended him remained mystified and decided to perform an autopsy. The doctors, Henry Watson, Charles Nevinson and George Aveline, wrote a detailed report of their findings, but were still unable to name the disease that had killed him.[38] Reading what they had to say two and a half centuries later, it would appear that Sir Edward Walpole died miserably of cancer of the pancreas.[39]

His young granddaughter Horatia was taken to the house the night her grandfather died, and made her way to the room where the body lay. Finding the door open, she went in to take a final look at the 'very handsome old man' she remembered. She fled in horror, having seen 'there was not the smallest Idea of his Face, as it was nothing but a Skeleton'.[40]

Notes

1. PRO, PRIS 4/2, King's Bench Prison Commitment Book.
2. Ibid.
3. *The Newgate Calendar*, eds A. Knapp and W. Baldwin, 4 vols (London, n.d.), 2: 376–8 [published *c.* 1773].
4. GLRO, MJ/CP/P203, Calendar of Prisoners, House of Correction, Clerkenwell.
5. 'Reasons offered for the Reformation of the House of Correction in Clerkenwell', quoted by William J. Pinks, *A History of Clerkenwell* (London, 1865), p. 182.
6. GLRO, *Burial Register, St James's Church, Clerkenwell.*
7. *Full and genuine Narrative*, pp. 2–3.
8. Bethlehem Royal Hospital Archives and Museum, Beckenham, Kent.
9. *Dictionary of National Biography.*
10. *Dictionary of Irish Artists*, ed. W. G. Strickland, 2 vols (Dublin and London, 1913).
11. Ibid.
12. Letters from Edward Walpole, Devonshire MSS, Chatsworth, 1st series, 245: 13.
13. Ibid., 245: 14.
14. H. W. Woolrych, *Lives of the Eminent Serjeants-at-Law*, 2 vols (London, 1869).
15. Horace Walpole, *Corr.*, 20: 162. Letter, 25 July 1750.
16. Ibid., 20: 264. Letter, 16 July 1751.
17. Timothy Mowl, *Horace Walpole: The Great Outsider* (London: John Murray, 1996).
18. *The Vertue Notebooks*, 6 vols (Oxford: Walpole Society Publications), vol. 3, and Horace Walpole, *Anecdotes of Painting in England*, 5 vols (Strawberry Hill, 1760–71).
19. *The Last Journals of Horace Walpole during the Reign of George III*, ed. G. F. R. Barker, 4 vols (London, 1894), 2: 102–3.
20. Horace Walpole, *Corr.*, 40: 73–5. Letter, 25 November 1752.
21. Imperial Society of Knights Bachelor. Edward Walpole was made a K.B. on 27 August 1753 and was installed on 27 December.
22. Horace Walpole, *Corr.*, 22: 381. Letter to Horace Mann, 5 January 1766.
23. BL, Add. MS 32732, f. 516.
24. Lewis Walpole Library. Edward Walpole to Baron Mountney.

25. Devonshire MSS, Chatsworth, 1st series, 245: 13.
26. *History of Parliament: The Commons, 1754–1790*, eds Lewis Namier and John Brooks, 3 vols (London: HMSO, 1985).
27. Horace Walpole, *Corr.*, 21: 284–5. Letter to Horace Mann, 11 April 1759.
28. Ibid., *passim*. Also Violet Biddulph, *The Three Ladies Waldegrave* (London: Peter Davies, 1938), pp. 48ff.
29. Lewis Walpole Library. Letters from Edward Walpole to his son, 1737–71.
30. Biddulph, p. 41.
31. Horace Walpole, *Corr.*, 23: 300. Letter to Horace Mann, 26 April 1771.
32. *Last Journals*, 2: 102–3.
33. Lewis Walpole Library. Miscellaneous items.
34. Horace Walpole, *Corr.*, 36: 200. Letter from Edward Walpole, 4 July 1781.
35. The Clements Library, University of Michigan. Letter from Edward Walpole to Lord George Germain, 1 June 1777, no. 151.
36. Horace Walpole, *Corr.*, 24: 529. Letter to Horace Mann, 12 November 1779.
37. Ibid., 25: 463. Letter to Horace Mann, 8 January 1784.
38. *An Account of the Appearances observed upon opening the body of the Rt. Hon. Sir Edward Walpole on the 13th January 1784, being the day after his decease.* University of Chicago Library, Walpole MS 274.
39. Dr David Brown, Consultant Histopathologist, Whittington Hospital, London.
40. Quoted by Biddulph, p. 172.

PART VI

Last questions

CHAPTER FOURTEEN

Who was to blame?

Did Edward Walpole assault John Cather?

Nearly two and a half centuries later there are a number of things we do not know in this story of Edward Walpole and the conspirators. We cannot even be sure whether our hero was the heterosexual he claimed to be. As was pointed out earlier, he was never the subject of scandal until John Cather made his accusations. Nevertheless, it is possible to draw up a list of pros and cons regarding his sexual orientation just as it is possible to do so for Samuel Foote who, twenty-five years later, was also acquitted in the court of King's Bench of an attempt to sodomize a servant.[1]

For instance, we might point out that although Walpole condemned Daniel Alexander's liberal views about sodomy, he himself showed no disapproval of Lord George Sackville-Germain who was well known to be homosexual. Instead, he wrote amiable letters to him to the end of his days.[2] Furthermore, Walpole's sexual leanings, like those of Foote, can be queried for the same reasons. On the one hand, while both kept a mistress for a time and fathered children, they chose not to marry and preferred the society of men to that of women. Both had one dear male friend. Just as Foote had a constant companion in Sir Francis Blake Delaval, so Walpole formed a close friendship with Lord Boyne which lasted more than fifteen years until that young man died prematurely in 1746. After the pair met while on the Grand Tour, they were often seen together in London as well as Dublin because the Irish peer became the Member of Parliament for Newport, Isle of Wight, in 1736 and attended parliamentary sessions in the capital. Round about that date Lord Boyne, who was a connoisseur of art, commissioned Hogarth to paint *A Night Encounter* as a 'modern moral conversation' piece recording an adventure he shared with Walpole. It shows them on the way home from a tavern. Walpole is resisting arrest by a watchman and Lord Boyne has come to his assistance. Neither of them has noticed that they are about to be run down by Lord Peterborough's coach.[3] In this picture of them together we see two averagely rowdy gentlemen who are out on the town and have drunk more than is good for them. So it provides us with a stereotype of conventional masculine behaviour. But, even supposing we had evidence to prove that they were lovers, we still would not know if Walpole made a sodomitical assault on John Cather without yet more evidence coming to light. However, the ease with which alternative scenarios can be devised for almost any man's sex life indicates how difficult it is to give decisive answers to questions once these have been raised.

Was there a conspiracy?

In the trial in the court of King's Bench on 5 July 1751 John Cather's associates were all members of the relatively small group of Irish Protestants who had come to London looking for work. They might be expected to know something of each other. Yet this does not appear to be the case. The convivial Walter Patterson is the only one who knew all the others. The charge that he connived with William Smith to present the forged bond was never fully investigated and it is conceivable that Smith was acting alone, as he usually did. Adam Nixon insisted he knew Patterson, but no one else, and, as far as we can tell, Daniel Alexander had only met Cather, apart from Patterson.

Alexander admitted that he had been asked by Cather to act for him but had decided to offer his services to Walpole instead. Both he and Patterson were prepared to believe that Walpole had sexually assaulted Cather and fully expected him to pay the boy something to keep quiet about it. Such a proposition was normal practice. As we have seen from the Old Bailey trials, supposedly innocent men threatened with accusations of sodomy declared in open court that they had paid, or were willing to pay, sizeable sums in order to avoid the publicity of a prosecution.

Alexander may have known Patterson, but he did not know very much about what he was doing, and James Worsdale never saw them together. Throughout Alexander gave every indication that he was acting independently in offering to mediate with Cather. In return he hoped the influential Walpole would help him to become something better than a hackney clerk. This was a reasonable wish in an age of patronage. It was never claimed that he demanded money for his services. However, he made the mistake of letting Walpole see that he thought him capable of sodomy. So when he came up for trial, much was made of the fact that he was desirous of employment and the Waltham Black Act was used to show that this meant he was an extortioner, whereas it is more likely he was a lone opportunist who, unlike James Worsdale or Andrew White, played his hand badly.

Patrick Cain is the most enigmatic of the defendants. The unquestioned facts about him are that he was a labourer and gave Cather shelter. According to one pamphleteer, he was also a Presbyterian Elder and took Cather with him to the Meeting House in Crown Court.[4] James Worsdale claimed that Cain was the leader of a ring of blackmailers but that uncorroborated assertion was not taken up by anyone else at the King's Bench where Cain was treated with relative leniency when the sentences were pronounced.

It is worth mentioning that none of the defendants in the 1751 trial had a criminal record. If any of them had been in trouble with the law earlier, one can be sure that the indefatigable William Davy would have uncovered their misdeeds just as he did those of William Smith.

Despite the best efforts of the prosecution to show that Cather's associates were in league, they showed few signs of co-operating together. The evidence shows that they were not conspirators so much as divers persons who were arraigned in the court of King's Bench because they had dared to countenance an angry youth whom Walpole cast off. The notion of a conspiracy on their part was a chimera. If a conspiracy existed, the members of it were Walpole's supporters who, motivated by self-interest and fear, were determined to obtain convictions even when this meant bending the law.

Was there a miscarriage of justice?

A reading of the available records for the Cather case reveals a tale of evidence suppressed and confessions obtained by dubious means. Accounts of the two King's Bench trials show that jurors heard only Walpole's version of events, much of this given by witnesses who were on his payroll.[5] This is alarming because although some prosecutors might well pay the expenses of those who came to court to testify on their behalf, it was unusual to hire future witnesses for months on end to build up a case against the defendants. The impartiality of such men when they gave testimony is called into question. We do not know if James Worsdale, Andrew White and John Brownsmith invented or distorted the evidence they provided in order to please their employer, but the temptation to do so existed. Added to which, the reputation of one of them for telling the whole truth and nothing but the truth was not high. Instead, Worsdale was known among his contemporaries for satisfying the needs of all would-be benefactors.

Money is a key factor in this story. Cather was poor; Walpole was rich. If that situation had been reversed, who can doubt that there might have been a different ending? Although usually careful with money, Walpole spent without stint on this occasion. As well as the expenses of his investigators, he paid several sets of court fees which, though small, mounted up because there were so many of them.[6] Other payments included those to the thief-taker Mr Wallbank, to Smith's prosecutor Mr Weekes, to various constables and to the unusally large number of witnesses who had their expenses covered. Nor should we forget the cost of sundry advertisements and reward notices. No doubt Walpole paid the largest sum of all to his legal advisers. Eight of them are named, including the six prestigious members of the prosecution team retained in the two King's Bench trials. Among these, William Davy worked especially hard. He not only helped to prosecute Cather and the supposed conspirators; he also traced the criminal career of William Smith in two countries and ensured his conviction. His services cannot have come cheap.

It is impossible to estimate the precise cost of Walpole's campaign but it could be that by the time it ended he had spent more than a thousand pounds. Such a sum was not unheard of in less complex cases. For instance, in 1743 the Chetwynd v. Ricketts trial was held in the court of King's Bench with Sir William Lee as judge. Chetwynd was a fifteen-year-old boy who stabbed and killed a school fellow in a quarrel over a piece of cake. His well-to-do relatives were determined to get him off a charge of murder. By the time they succeeded the fees they had paid to counsel at the trial in the King's Bench, at the Lord Chancellor's, at the Attorney General's and at the Lord Privy Seal's amounted to £1300.[7] The Chetwynd case lasted four months. Cather lodged his indictment at the end of April 1750 and was convicted at the beginning of July 1751 in a case that had encompassed four trials and lasted over fourteen months.

Walpole won his case and received a knighthood which set the seal on his social acceptability. Yet his victory was incomplete. This was inevitable because, like others before and after him, he could not win indemnity. It was predictable that John Cameron and the Vaughans, if not Walter Patterson (who was still at large) would continue the Irish vendetta against him. He had also to contend with the sceptics among his own countrymen. Always sensitive to slights, the knowing look, the ironical innuendo would be quite enough to drive him in upon himself and make him increasingly reluctant to go anywhere and meet anyone. As the years went on, his reclusiveness became excessive. He was highly gratified when his favourite daughter's marriage to the Duke of Gloucester was officially recognized yet, as Horace Walpole lamented to his friend in Florence in 1773, 'my bother has so long shut himself up in his own house, that no consideration could draw him out of it. I need but tell you that his daughter the Duchess, even in summer, could not prevail on him to wait on the Duke.'[8]

Conclusion

Walpole has our pity as well as blame. The prime cause of the travesty of justice he initiated was the law which made sodomy a criminal offence. When this law found its way into the statute books during the Tudor period its impact on society was minimal because there were few prosecutions. In the eighteenth century homosexuality became an issue and accusations of sodomy proliferated. The law proscribing sodomy ratified the homophobia of the zealous, who predicted dire consequences for society if homosexuality were tolerated. In the first three decades of the century public hysteria, whipped up by the Societies for the Reformation of Manners, ensured that pogroms were organized against the newly discovered mollies, several of whom were put to death.

It was impossible to eliminate homosexuality by means of legislation because England, at all levels of society, was homoerotic. Inevitably there was a reaction against the minority of reforming zealots. From the 1730s until the nineteenth century, judges and jurors showed themselves reluctant to see the law enforced in its full rigour. They employed specious stratagems to avoid convicting men of sodomy and so sending them to the gallows. This did credit to them as human beings but made a mockery of the judicial system. Increasingly, practising homosexuals who found themselves in court were found guilty of 'attempted sodomy' – a term that was often no more than a polite fiction. Such men were punished, but in a haphazard and inconsistent fashion, depending on the subjective reactions of those involved in trying them.

The zealots had retreated but they left behind them a legacy of hypocrisy and fear. A homosexual met with varying degrees of tacit acceptance by the rest of society as long as he did not become the subject of public scandal. In that event, whatever his sexual orientation, he had to establish himself as a heterosexual if he was to avoid becoming a criminal and a pariah. The fate of most of the men who lacked influential friends and were convicted of sodomitical practices was the pillory, subjection to the derision of the mob, as well as prison, followed by life as a social outcast.

A gentleman who was indicted for sodomy or attempted sodomy might well receive the support of his social equals and senior members of the legal profession in clearing his name because it was in all those persons' interests that he should do so, lest they too find themselves the targets of blackmailers looking for easy money, or of enemies who bore them a grudge. That being so, the rights and wrongs of a particular case did not enter into it. The ultimately abortive campaign waged by Edward Walpole is merely an extreme example of the paranoia and injustice created by a law erratically implemented for over three hundred years.

Notes

1. *Annual Register*, 1776, p. 199. See also Chapter 8 in this volume.
2. Historical Manuscripts Commission, Stopford-Sackville, 1: 349 and the Germaine Papers, University of Michigan, William L. Clements Library.
3. Ronald Paulson, *Hogarth*, 3 vols (Cambridge: Lutterworth Press, 1991–93), 3: 270–71.
4. *Full and genuine Narrative*, p. 7.
5. *Whole Proceedings*, pp. 6–7.
6. For costs of King's Bench cases see Richard Gude, *The Practice of the Crown Side of the Court of King's Bench*, 2 vols (London, 1828), reprinted 1991, list at end of vol. 2.
7. *Complete Collection of State Trials*, ed. T. B. Howell (London, 1809–26), vol. 18.
8. Horace Walpole, *Corr.*, 23: 461. To Mann, 17 February 1773.

Bibliography

Manuscript sources

British Library, Manuscript Collections. Additional MSS. Edward Walpole's letters. To: 1st Duke of Newcastle, 32704, 32708, 32711, 32713–14, 32716, 32718, 32720, 32726, 32857, 32867–8, 32874, 32894. To: 1st Lord Hardwicke, 35586, 35589, 35591. Sundry papers, 21555, 5832, 42711.

Devonshire MSS, Chatsworth, 1st series. Fifteen letters from Edward Walpole to the 3rd and 4th Dukes of Devonshire.

Greater London Record Office. Indictments, Middlesex, 1750, MJ/SR/2938, and MJ/SR/2944. Calendar of Prisoners, House of Correction, Clerkenwell, 1751–65, MJ/CP/P. Book of Freeholders, Middlesex, 1747–53, MR/FB/8.

The Lewis Walpole Library, Farmington, Connecticut. Fifty letters from Edward Walpole to his children and other correspondents, together with miscellaneous documents, including his will and a poem.

Public Record Office, King's Bench Papers. KB 29 (Controlment Roll), KB 1 (Depositions), KB 36 (Draft Rule Book), IND 1/6669–77 (Index of London and Middlesex Defendants 1673–1843), PRIS 4/2 (King's Bench Commitments Book), KB 28 (Plea Roll), KB 20 (Posteas), KB 15 (Process Book), KB 21 (Rule Book).

University of Cambridge, Chomondeley (Houghton) MS 2576. Two letters from Edward Walpole to his father in 1730 and 1736.

University of Chicago Library. MS 274. Autopsy performed on Sir Edward Walpole, 13 January 1784.

University of Michigan, William L. Clements Library. Sidney Papers and Germaine Papers. Correspondence between Sir Edward Walpole and Lord George Sackville-Germain, 1777.

Printed sources

Newspapers, journals, pamphlets and broadsheets

The Bon Ton Magazine, or Microscope of Fashion and Folly

Britannicus (Thomas Gordon?), *The Conspirators, Or, The Case of Catiline*. London, 1721.

The Craftsman

Dunton, J., *The He-Strumpets, a Satyr on the Sodomite Club*. London, 1710.

The Female Tatler

Gentleman's Magazine

Jackson, J., *Sodom and Onan, a satire inscribed to [————] Esq. alias the Devil upon two Sticks*. London, *c.* 1776.

Lloyds Evening Post

London Chronicle

London Daily Advertiser

London Evening-Post

London Gazette

The Monthly Review

Parker's Penny Post

Satan's Harvest Home: or the Present State of Whorecraft, Adultery, Fornication, Procuring, Pimping, Sodomy, And the Game of Flatts. Collected from the Memoirs of an intimate Comrade of the Hon. Jack S–n–r: London, 1749.

This is not the Thing: or, Molly Exalted. London, 1763.

The True Life of Betty Ireland with her Birth, Education and Adventures. Together with some Account of her elder Sister, Blanch of Britain, 6th edn. Dublin and London, 1750.

Ward, E. (Ned), *The London-Spy Compleat in Eighteen Parts*. London, 1701.

Weekly Journal

Whitehall Evening-Post, or The London Intelligencer

The Women-Hater's Lamentation. London, 1707.

Trial reports and related writings

1.   General

An Account of the Proceedings against Captain Edward Rigby. London, 1698.

An Answer to a Late Insolent Libel ... Anon., but probably by Jonathan Wild. London (1718?).

A Complete Collection of State Trials, ed. T. B. Howell. London, 1809–26.

A Complete Narrative of all the prisoners who were try'd ... *at the Sessions-House in the Old Bailey*. London, *c.* 1740.

Dalton, J., *A Genuine Narrative of all the Street Robberies Committed since October last by James Dalton and his Accomplices*. London, 1728.

Douglas, S., *Reports of Cases* ... *in the Court of King's Bench* ... 2nd edn. London, 1786.

A Full and True Account of the Discovery and Apprehending A Notorious Gang of Sodomites in St. James's. London, 1709.

Jackson, W., *The New and Complete Newgate Calendar*, 8 vols. London, 1818.

Knapp A. and W. Baldwin, *The Newgate Calendar*, 4 vols. London, n.d. [published *c.* 1773].

A Narrative of the Remarkable Affair between Mr. Simonds, the Polish Jew Merchant and Mr. James Ashley, Merchant of Bread Street. London, 1752.

Select Trials for Murders, Robberies, Rape, Sodomy ... To which are added Genuine Accounts of the Lives ... of the most Eminent Convicts. From the year 1720 to 1724, 2 vols. London, 1734–35.

The Trial of Richard Branson for an Attempt to commit Sodomy on the Body of James Fossett, one of the Scholars belonging to God's Gift College, in Dulwich. Tried at the General Quarter Session of the Peace, held at St. Margaret's Hall in the Borough of Southwark, January 18, 1760. London, 1760.

A True State of the Case of Bosavern Penlez. London, 1749.

The Tryal and Conviction of Mervin, Lord Audley, Earl of Castle-Haven. London, 1699.

The Tryal and Conviction of several Reputed Sodomites. London, 1707.

The Tyburn Chronicle, 4 vols. London, *c.* 1769.

The Whole Proceedings upon the King's Commission of Oyer and Terminer and Gaol Delivery for the City of London, and also the Gaol Delivery for the County of Middlesex, 1714–1830 ... in the Old Bailey. Known as the *Sessions Papers*.

2.   The prosecution of John Cather and others in 1751

A Genuine Narrative of the Conspiracy by Kather, Kane, Alexander, Nickson, etc. against The Hon. Edward Walpole Esq. With an Account of their Trial before the Right Hon. Lord Chief Justice Lee, In the Court of King's-Bench, Westminster-Hall, July 5th. 1751. London, 1751.

(This version, with many misspelt names and other minor errors, was in Tom's Coffee House by 12th July).

A Full and genuine Narrative of the Confederacy carried on by Cather, Cane, Alexander, Nixon, Paterson, Falconer, and Smith, which last was executed at Tyburn with McLeane, against The Hon. Edward Walpole, Esq. Charging him with the detestable Crime of Sodomy, in Order to extort a large Sum of Money from him; together with an Account of their remarkable Trial and Conviction before the Rt. Hon. the Lord Chief Justice Lee, in the Court of King's-Bench, Westminster, July 5th. 1751. The Second Edition with Additions. London, 1751.

(This edition corrected the errors of the first and added biographical information about John Cather and Patrick Cain.)

The Tryal of John Cather, Adam Nixon, David [sic] *Alexander, and Patrick Cain, otherwise Kane, at the King's-Bench in Westminster-Hall by a Special Jury of Gentlemen on Friday the 5th. of July 1751, for a Conspiracy against the Hon. Edward Walpole, Esq. In endeavouring to extort Money from him, under Pretence of an Assault with an Intent to commit Buggery on the Body of John Cather, with Copies of the several Records, and original Papers relating thereto: And at the End of which Trial is inserted a full and impartial Narrative of the Whole of that wicked Conspiracy, particularly That of the Attempt to charge Mr. Walpole with Forgery. To which is Annexed, for the Use of Gentlemen of the Law, an Examined Copy of the remarkable Record on which the Defendants were tried for the said Conspiracy, well worthy of Perusal, the same having been settled by the greatest Men of the Profession.* London, 1751.

(This new version of the trial appeared several weeks after the first two because time was needed to collect the records and original papers referred to. The pamphlet was reprinted soon afterwards in Dublin by G. Faulkner.)

The Whole Proceedings on the wicked Conspiracy carried on against the Hon. Edward Walpole, Esq. by John Cather, Adam Nixon, Daniel Alexander, Patrick Cane alias Kane, and others. In Order to extort a large Sum of Money, under Pretence of an Assault, with an Intent to commit Buggery on the Body of the said John Cather. In which are inserted, the Tryal at large of the said Cather, Nixon, Alexander and Cane: and a full Account of the Attempt of Smith (who was executed at Tyburn for Forgery) and Patterson, to charge Mr. Walpole with Forgery, etc. London, 1751.

(This pamphlet appeared at the end of the year and is a reprint of *The Tryal* with two more pages giving the sentences passed on Cather, Cain and Alexander. As well as being published on its own, *The Whole Proceedings* ... was included in the *Sessions Papers* for 1751).

The law and related writings

Baker, J. H., *The Order of Serjeants-at-Law.* London: Selden Society, 1984.

Beattie, J. M., *Crime and the Courts of England 1660–1800.* Oxford: Clarendon Press, 1986.

Bentham, J., 'Jeremy Bentham's Essay on "Paederasty" introduced and edited by Louis Crompton', *Journal of Homosexuality* (1978), 3: 383–405 and 4: 91–107.

Blackstone, W., Sir, *Commentaries on the Laws of England*, 4 vols. London, 1765–69.

Blanc, J. B. le, *Letters on the English and French Nations*, 2 vols. London, 1747. Written *c*. 1737.

Campbell, A. H., 'The Anomalies of Blackmail', *Law Quarterly Review*, 55 (1939), 382–99.

Campbell, J., Baron, *Lives of the Chief Justices of England*, 3 vols. 2nd edn. London, 1858.

Chitty, J. *A Practical Treatise on the Criminal Law*, 4 vols. London, 1816.

Cowell, Dr, *A Law Dictionary, or the Interpreter of Words and Terms*. London, 1727.

De Veil, T., Sir, *Memoirs of the Life and Times of Sir Thomas Deveil, Knight, One of His Majesty's Justices of the Peace for the Counties of Middlesex, Essex, Surrey and Hertfordshire, The City and Liberty of Westminster, The Tower of London and the Liberties thereof, etc.* London, 1748.

Dobson, M., *The Life of Sir Michael Foster*. London, 1811.

Eden, W., *Principles of Penal Law*. London, 1771.

Fielding, H., *An Enquiry into the Causes of the Late Increase of Robbers etc. With some Proposals for Remedying this growing Evil in which the present reigning Vices are impartially exposed; and the Laws that relate to the Provision for the Poor, and to the Punishment of Felons are largely and freely examined.* London, 1751.

Foss, E., *A Biographical Dictionary of the Judges of England, 1066–1870.* London, 1870.

Gilbert, G., Baron, *The Law of Evidence*, 2nd edn. London, 1760.

Gude, R., *The Practice of the Crown Side of the Court of King's Bench*, 2 vols. London, 1828, reprinted Colorado: Rothman, 1991.

Hay, D., E. P. Thompson and P. Linebaugh, eds, *Albion's Fatal Tree*. London: Peregrine Books, 1977.

Hay, D. and F. Snyder, eds, *Policing and Prosecution in Britain 1750–1850*. Oxford: Clarendon Press, 1989.

Hepworth, M., *Blackmail: Publicity and Secrecy in Everyday Life*. London: Routledge, 1975.

Holdsworth, W. S., *History of English Law*, 17 vols. London, 1903–72, vol. 9.

Jacob, G., *Law Dictionary*. London, 1729.

———, *A New Law Dictionary, 9th Edition with great Additions and Improvements*. London, 1772.

Keane, E., P. B. Phaik and U. Sadler, eds, *King's Inn Admission Papers 1607–1867*. Dublin: Irish Manuscripts Commissions, 1982.

Langbein, J.H., 'Shaping the Eighteenth-Century Trial: A View of the Ryder Sources', *University of Chicago Law Review* (Winter, 1983), 1–136.

Lévis, P. M. G., Duc de, *L'Angleterre au commencement du dix-neuvième siècle*. Paris, 1814.

Linebaugh, P., *The London Hanged: Crime and Civil Society in the Eighteenth Century*. London: Allen Lane, 1991.

McLynn, F., *Crime and Punishment in Eighteenth-Century England*. London: Routledge, 1989.

Montesquieu, C., Baron, *De l'esprit des lois* (1748), trans. T. Nugent, revised J. V. Pritchard. University of Chicago, 1952.

Muralt, B. L. de, *Letters describing the Character and Customs of the English and French Nations*, trans. from French. London, 1726. Written in 1694.

Oldham, J., *The Mansfield Manuscripts and the Growth of English Law in the Eighteenth Century*, 2 vols. Chapel Hill: University of North Carolina Press, 1992.

———, 'The Origins of the Special Jury', *University of Chicago Law Review* (Winter, 1983), 137–221.

Paley, R., ed., *Justice in Hackney: The Justicing Notebook of Henry Norris and the Hackney Petty Sessions Book*. London Record Society, 1991.

Peake, T. A., *Compendium of the Law of Evidence*. London, 1801.

Prévost, Abbé, *Adventures of a Man of Quality* (1728), trans. and ed. M. E. I. Robertson. London, 1930.

Radzinowicz, L., *A History of Criminal Law and its Administration*, 5 vols. London: Stevens, 1948–86.

Rumbelow, D., *I Spy Blue: The Police and Crime in the City of London from Elizabeth I to Victoria*. London: Macmillan, 1971.

Sainty, J., Sir, *The Judges of England 1272–1990*. London: Selden Society, 1991.

Saussure, C., de, *A Foreign View of England in the Reigns of George I and George II (1725–35)*, trans. Madame Van Muyden. London: John Murray, 1902.

Welch, S., *Observations on the Office of a Constable, with Cautions for a more safe Execution of that Duty*. London, 1754.

Winder, W. H. D., 'The Development of Blackmail', *Modern Law Review*, 5 (1941): 21–50.

Woolrych, H. W., *Lives of Eminent Serjeants-at-Law*, 2 vols. London, 1869.

Society, philosophy and the arts

Annual Register, 1758–59.

Ashbee, H.S. (pseudonym: Pisanus Fraxi), *Catena Librorum Tacendorum: Being Notes bio-biblio-iconographical and critical on curious and erotic Books*. London, 1885, reprinted 1960.

Barrin, J., *Venus in the Cloister*, 1724. No copies extant. Extracts were, however, quoted in the indictment of Edmund Curll in 1725. See D. Thomas, *A Long Time Burning*. London: Routledge, 1969, pp. 343–8.

Bee, J., *The Works of Samuel Foote, Esq. with ... An Essay on the Life, Genius and Writings of the Author*, 3 vols. London, 1830.

Biddulph, V., *The Three Ladies Waldegrave and their Mother*. London: Peter Davies, 1938.

Brown, T., 'A Comical View of ... London and Westminster' in *The Works of Mr. Thomas Brown*, 4 vols. London, 1707–09, 1Aa.51.

Charnock, J., *Biographia Navalis*. London, 1795.

Cibber, C., *The Plays of Colley Cibber*, ed. R. L. Hayley, 2 vols. New York: Garland Publishing, 1980.

Cibber, T., *The Lover: a Comedy*. London, 1730.

Clark, J. C. D., *English Society 1688–1832*. Cambridge University Press, 1985.

———, *Revolution and Rebellion: State and society in England in the seventeenth and eighteenth centuries*. Cambridge University Press, 1986.

Cleland, J., *Memoirs of a Woman of Pleasure*, ed. P. Wagner. Harmondsworth: Penguin Books, 1985.

Cooke, W., *Memoirs of Samuel Foote*, 3 vols. London, 1805.

Egmont, *Diary of the First Earl of Egmont*, ed. R. A. Roberts, 3 vols. London: Historical Manuscripts Commission, 1920–23.

Endelman, T., *The Jews of Georgian England: tradition and change in a liberal society*. Philadelphia: Jewish Publications Society of America, 1979.

Felsenstein, F., *Anti-Semitic Stereotypes: A Paradigm of Otherness in English Popular Culture 1660–1830*. Baltimore: Johns Hopkins University Press, 1995.

Foxon, D., *Libertine Literature in England 1660–1745*. New York: New Hyde Park, 1965.

George, D. M., *London Life in the Eighteenth Century*. London: Kegan Paul, 1925.

History of Parliament: The House of Commons 1715–1754, ed. R. Sedgwick. London: Her Majesty's Stationery Office, 1970.

History of Parliament: The House of Commons 1755–1790, eds L. Namier and J. Brooks, 3 vols. London: Her Majesty's Stationery Office, 1985.

Howson, G., *Thief-Taker General: The Rise and Fall of Jonathan Wild*. London: Hutchinson, 1970.

Johnson, S., *The Lives of the English Poets*, ed. G. B. Hill, 3 vols. Oxford: Clarendon Press, 1905.

Kent's Directory for the Year 1754. Containing an Alphabetical List of the Names and Places of Abode of the Directors of Companies, Persons in Public Business, Merchants and other Eminent Traders in the Cities of London and Westminster and the Borough of Southwark. London, 1754.

Killanin, Lord, *Sir Godfrey Kneller and his Times, 1646–1723*. London: Batsford, 1948.

Knight, R. P., *Discourse on the Worship of Priapus, and its Connexion with the Mystic Theology of the Ancients* (1786–87), reprinted in A. Montagu, *Sexual Symbolism: A History of Phallic Worship*. New York: Julian Press, 1957.

Lawson, J. and H. Silver, *A Social History of Education in England*. London: Methuen, 1973.

A Letter from a Lady to her Husband. London, 1728.

Lewis, W. S., *Horace Walpole: The A. W. Mellon Lectures in the Fine Arts 1960*. London, 1961.

London: A Complete Guide to all Persons who have any Trade or Concern with the City of London and Parts Adjacent. London, 1749.

Love Letters between a Certain Late Nobleman and the Famous Mr. Wilson (1723), ed. M. S. Kimmel. New York and London: Harrington Park Press, 1990.

Marchmont, *The Papers of the Earls of Marchmont, 1688–1750*, ed. Sir G. Rose, 3 vols. London, 1831.

Memoirs of the Extraordinary Life, Works and Discoveries of Martinus Scriblerus (1741), ed. C. Kerby-Miller. Oxford University Press, 1950.

Montagu, M. Wortley, Lady, *Complete Letters of Lady Mary Wortley Montagu*, ed. R. Halsband, 3 vols. Oxford: Clarendon Press, 1965–67.

Montaigne, M. de, *Essays of Michel de Montaigne*, trans. C. Cotten, 3 vols. London, 1685–86.

Mowl, T., *Horace Walpole: The Great Outsider*. London: John Murray, 1996.

Robb, N. A., *William of Orange: A Personal Portrait*, 2 vols. London: Heinemann, 1962–66.

A New History of Ireland, Volume 4: Eighteenth-Century Ireland 1691–1880, eds T. W. Moody and W. E. Vaughan. Oxford: Clarendon Press, 1986.

Nichols, J., *Literary Anecdotes of the Eighteenth-Century*, 9 vols. London, 1812–15.

Northcote, J., *Life of Sir Joshua Reynolds*, 2 vols. London, 1818.

Paulson, R., *Hogarth: Art and Politics 1750–1764*. Cambridge: Lutterworth Press, 1993.

Phillips, H., *Mid-Georgian London: A Topographical and Social Survey of Central and Western London about 1750*. London: Collins, 1964.

Pilkington, L., *Memoirs of Laetitia Pilkington*, ed. A. C. Elias, Jr, 2 vols. Athens and London: University of Georgia Press, 1997.

Pinks, W. J., *A History of Clerkenwell*. London, 1865.

Piper, D., *London: An Illustrated Companion Guide*. London: Collins, 1980.

Pope, A., *Correspondence of Alexander Pope*, ed. George Sherburn, 5 vols. Oxford: Clarendon Press, 1956.

Porter, R. *English Society in the Eighteenth Century*. London: Allen Lane, 1982.

Radicati, A., Count of Passerano, *A Philosophical Dissertation upon Death. Composed for the Consolation of the Unhappy. By a Friend to Truth*, trans. Joseph Morgan. London, 1731.

Riquetti, H. G., Comte de Mirabeau, *Secret History of the Court of Berlin*, trans. S. Bladon. London, 1789.

Smollett, T., *The Adventures of Peregrine Pickle* (1751). Oxford University Press, 1969.

———, *The Adventures of Roderick Random* (1748). Oxford University Press, 1981.

Speck, W. A., *Stability and Strife: England 1714–1760*. London: Edward Arnold, 1977.

Spence, J., *Observations, Anecdotes and Characters of Books and Men*, ed. J. M. Osborn, 2 vols. Oxford: Clarendon Press, 1966.

Stone, G. W. and G. M. Kahrl, *David Garrick: A Critical Biography*. Carbondale: Southern Illinois University Press, 1979.

Stone, L., *Broken Lives: Separation and Divorce in England 1660–1857*. Oxford University Press, 1993.

Strickland, W. G., *Dictionary of Irish Artists*, 2 vols. London: Maunsel, 1913.

Swift, J., *Gulliver's Travels and Other Writings*, ed. L. A. Landa. Boston: Riverside Press, 1960.

Survey of London, gen. ed. F. H. W. Sheppard. University of London, 1960, vol. 29.

Thomas, D., *A Long Time Burning: The History of Literary Censorship in England*. London: Routledge, 1969.

Thornbury, W., *Old and New London: A Narrative of its History, its People and its Places*, 6 vols. London: Cassell, Petter, Galpin, n.d.

Uglow, J., *Hogarth: A Life and a World.* London: Faber, 1997.

Vanbrugh, J., Sir, *The Relapse, or Virtue in Danger.* London, 1696.

Vertue, G., *The Vertue Notebooks*, 6 vols. Oxford: Walpole Society Publications, 1930–55, vols 3 and 6.

Victoria History of the Counties of England, Middlesex, vol. 2. Oxford University Press, 1970.

Voltaire (Arouet, F.-M.), *Philosophical Dictionary* (1764), trans. and ed. T. Besterman. Harmondsworth: Penguin Books, 1971.

Walpole, H., *Anecdotes of Painting in England*, 5 vols. Strawberry Hill, 1760–71.

————, *The Complete Correspondence of Horace Walpole, ed. W. S. Lewis and others*, 48 vols. Yale University Press, 1937–83.

————, *The Last Journals of Horace Walpole during the Reign of George III*, ed. G. F. R. Barker, 4 vols. London, 1894.

————, *Memoirs of the Reign of King George II*, ed. Lord Holland, 3 vols. London, 1846.

Ward, E. (Ned), *A Compleat and Humorous Account of all the Remarkable Clubs in the Cities of London and Westminster.* London, 1709.

————, *The Second Part of the History of London Clubs.* London, 1720(?).

Watson, J. S., *The Reign of George III 1760–1815.* Oxford: Clarendon Press, 1960.

Weldon, A., Sir, *The Secret History of the Court of King James.* London, 1650, reprinted 1817.

Williams, B., *The Whig Supremacy 1714–1760*, revised edn. Oxford: Clarendon Press, 1962.

Wodrow, R., *Analecta*, 4 vols. London: Maitland Club, 1842–43.

Wilmot, J., Earl of Rochester, *Sodom, or the Quintessence of Debauchery* (1684), introduced by A. Ellis. North Hollywood, California: Brandon House, 1966.

Yorke, P. C., *Life and Correspondence of Philip Yorke, Earl of Hardwicke*, 3 vols. Cambridge University Press, 1913.

Sexology: some modern studies

Barker-Benfield, G. T., *The Culture of Sensibility: Sex and Society in Eighteenth-Century Britain.* University of Chicago Press, 1992.

Bray, A., *Homosexuality in Renaissance England.* London: Gay Men's Press, 1982.

Davenport-Hines, R., *Sex, Death and Punishment: Attitudes to Sex and Sexuality in Britain since the Renaissance.* London: Collins, 1990.

Dollimore, J., *Sexual Dissidence: Augustine to Wilde, Freud to Foucault*. Oxford: Clarendon Press, 1991.

Epstein, J. and K. Straub, eds, *Body Guards: The Cultural Politics of Gender Ambiguity*. London: Routledge, 1991.

Foucault, M., *The History of Sexuality: An Introduction*, trans. R. Hurley. New York: Pantheon Books, 1978.

Gerard, K. and G. Hekma, eds, *The Pursuit of Sodomy: Male Homosexuality in Renaissance and Enlightenment Europe*. New York and London: Harrington Park Press, 1989.

Gilbert, Arthur N., 'Buggery and the British Navy 1700–1861', *Journal of Social History*, 10.1 (1976), 72–98.

Goldberg, J., ed., *Reclaiming Sodom*. London: Routledge, 1994.

Harvey, A. D., 'Prosecutions for Sodomy in England at the Beginning of the Nineteenth Century', *Historical Journal*, 21.4 (1978), 939–48.

———, *Sex in Georgian England: Attitudes and Prejudices from the 1720s to the 1820s*. London: Duckworth, 1994.

Hitchcock, T., 'Redefining Sex in Eighteenth-Century England', *History Workshop Journal*, 141 (1996), 73–90.

Laqueur, T., *Making Sex: Body and Gender from the Greeks to Freud*. Harvard University Press, 1990.

Maccubbin, R. P., '"'Tis Nature's Fault": Unauthorized Sexuality during the Enlightenment', *Eighteenth-Century Life*, 9 (1985), 109–79.

McCormick, I., *Secret Sexualities 1600–1800*. London: Routledge, 1996.

McKean, M., 'Historicizing: The Emergence of Gender in England 1660–1760', *Eighteenth-Century Studies*, 28.3 (1995), 295–322.

Messenger, A., *His and Hers: Essays in Restoration and Eighteenth-Century Literature*. Lexington: University Press of Kentucky, 1986.

Norton, R., *Mother Clap's Molly House: The Gay Subculture in England 1700–1830*. London: Gay Men's Press, 1992.

Porter, R. and L. Hall, *The Facts of Life: The Creation of Sexual Knowledge in Britain 1650–1950*. New Haven and London: Yale University Press, 1995.

Rousseau, G. S. and Roy Porter, eds, *The Ferment of Knowledge*. Cambridge University Press, 1980.

———, *Sexual Underworlds of the Enlightenment*. Manchester University Press, 1987.

Sedgwick, E. K., *Between Men: English Literature and Male Homosexual Desire*. New York: Columbia University Press, 1985.

———, *Epistemology of the Closet*. Berkeley and Los Angeles: University of California Press, 1990.

Senelick, L., 'Mollies or Men of Mode? Sodomy and the Eighteenth-Century London Stage', *Journal of the History of Sexuality*, 1 (1990), 33–67.

Shapiro, S., '"Yon Plumed Dandeprat": Male Effeminacy in English Satire and Criticism', *Review of English Studies*, 39 (1988): 400–412.

Staves, S., 'A Few Kind Words for the Fop', *Studies in English Literature*, 22 (1982), 413–28.

Straub, K., *Sexual Suspects: Eighteenth-Century Players and Sexual Ideology*. Princeton University Press, 1992.

Trumbach, R., 'Gender and the Homosexual Role in Modern Western Culture: The Eighteenth and Nineteenth Centuries Compared', in *Homosexuality, Which Homosexuality? Proceedings, International Conference on Gay and Lesbian Studies*. London: Gay Men's Press, 1989, pp. 149–70.

——, 'London's Sodomites: Homosexual Behaviour and Western Culture in the Eighteenth Century', *Journal of Social History*, 2 (1977), 1–33.

——, 'Sodomitical Subcultures, Sodomitical Roles and the Gender Revolution of the Eighteenth Century: The Recent Historiography', *Eighteenth-Century Life*, 9 (1985), 109–21.

——, 'Sodomy Transformed: Aristocratic Libertinage, Public Reputation and the Gender Revolution of the Eighteenth-Century', *Journal of Homosexuality*, 19 (1990), 105–24.

——, 'The Birth of the Queen: Sodomy and the Emergence of Gender Equality in Modern Culture, 1660–1750', in *Hidden from History: Reclaiming the Gay and Lesbian Past*, eds M. B. Duberman, M. Vicinus and G. Chauncey, Jr. New York: New American Library, 1989, pp. 129–40.

Vicinus, M., M. B. Duberman and G. Chauncey Jr, eds, *Hidden from History: Reclaiming the Gay and Lesbian Past*. New York: New American Library, 1989.

Wagner, P., *Eros Revived: Erotica of the Enlightenment in England and America*. London: Martin Secker and Warburg, 1988.

Woods, G., *A History of Gay Literature: The Male Tradition*. New Haven: Yale University Press, 1998.

Index